UNDERSTANDING Y

EDITED BY

charlie caruso

WILEY

First published in 2014 by John Wiley & Sons Australia, Ltd
42 McDougall St, Milton Qld 4064

Office also in Melbourne

Typeset in 11.5/14 pt Rotis Serif Std

© Puggle Media (Holdings) Pty Ltd 2014

The moral rights of the author have been asserted

National Library of Australia Cataloguing-in-Publication data:

Title:	Understanding Y / Charlotte Caruso, editor.
ISBN:	9780730312215 (pbk)
	9780730313816 (ebook)
Subjects:	Generation Y—Australia
	Generation Y—Australia—Attitudes
	Intergenerational relations—Australia
Other authors/	
contributors:	Caruso, Charlotte, editor.
Dewey Number:	305.20994

Cover design and illustration by Wiley

Amanda Lenhart, Kristen Purcell, Aaron Smith and Kathryn Zickuhr. 'Social Media & Mobile Internet Use Among Teens and Young Adults'. Pew Research Center, Washington, DC (February 3, 2010) www.pewinternet.org/files/old-media//Files/Reports/2010/PIP_Social_Media_and_Young_Adults_Report_Final_with_toplines.pdf accessed on March 7 2013.

Printed in Singapore by C.O.S. Printers Pte Ltd

10 9 8 7 6 5 4 3 2 1

Disclaimer
The material in this publication is of the nature of general comment only, and neither purports nor intends to be advice. Readers should not act on the basis of any matter in this publication without considering (and if appropriate, taking) professional advice with due regard to their own particular circumstances. The author and publisher expressly disclaim all and any liability to any person, whether a purchaser of this publication or not, in respect of anything and of the consequences of anything done or omitted to be done by any such person in reliance, whether whole or partial, upon the whole or any part of the contents of this publication.

Each generation goes further than the generation preceding it because it stands on the shoulders of that generation. You will have opportunities beyond anything we've ever known.

Ronald Reagan

CONTENTS

ACKNOWLEDGEMENTS

I've always found acknowledgement pages pretty boring. I usually flick past them and, quite honestly, I wasn't going to include one. Then I realised it wasn't all about me. Yes, many people will skip this page, but for those who have contributed to this book – for them – this page is a big deal! And so it should be. There are more people that I want to thank than can conceivably fit on this page. For those I miss, check the website – I haven't forgotten you!

To my brilliant co-authors, thank you for your efforts, your support, your time, your patience, your understanding and your awesomeness! I am honoured to have had the opportunity to work with you all on this project! Bernard, you were the original inspiration for this book – thank you for your support and your time over the past few years. It was your wise words about Gen Y and their future potential that inspired my light-bulb moment, which very quickly transformed into *Understanding Y*. To Rob Kaldor – without your efforts and support, this book might have remained one of my many pipedreams. Thank you for being brilliant and helping turn my dream into a reality.

My amazing editors, Sarah Crisp, Christine Moore, Keira de Hoog, Allison Hiew, Lucy Raymond and Alice Berry – you have collectively made this journey one of the best experiences of my life. Sarah – I will forever cherish our long chats, your guidance and support! Christine, you did such an amazing job at whipping this book into shape, and were so fun to work with – thank you for your patience and for dealing with all the email bombing like a trooper! Keira – thank you for being my training bra and supporting me through this transition period! Allison, thanks for letting me be cheeky where I wanted to be, but reining me in when I needed to be. Also for forgiving me for making a hundred changes last minute. Never a complaint and always the professional. And to Alice and Lucy, thank you for guiding me through the final stage of the book's development – it came off like a dream! Thank you all!

Big thanks to Wiley for being a great believer in the future. I was thrilled to work with such an outstanding publishing house that has a reputation like no other for producing cutting-edge, informative and sometimes boundary-pushing content. If only there were more organisations like Wiley, which looks for opportunities to push the limits rather than continually de-risking and 'playing it safe'.

So many people contributed to the formation of *Understanding Y*. Sure, we have 15 co-authors, but there were literally hundreds of contributors to this book. I sought many permissions to include the brilliance from other thought leaders in this space, and was blown away by the encouragement and support I received from basically everyone I approached. There was never any, 'Who are you and what do you want?', only, 'How can I help?' Thank you to all who did, for your contribution not only to this book, but to this topic in general.

My beautiful girls, Annabelle and Bianca – thank you for your patience, love and your continual reality checks. There might be some science behind the value of breaking up writing sessions with playing Lego, plaiting hair, sculpting play dough and playing hide-and-seek. I hope that when you both grow up, you will read *Understanding Y* with pride, as this book, in many ways, is emblematic of the biggest lesson I wish to bestow on you. Never doubt yourself, your capabilities or your worth. The only thing that will ever limit your potential to achieve your dreams is you. Not your age, not your gender, not your income – only your doubts. Be empowered by the knowledge that you're in the driver's seat – and you can turn the wheel any which way you want. Never let go of the wheel – who knows where you might go? Be your dreams and live your potential.

To my loving husband Matthew. You are my home, my other half. You have supported me and my ambitions since I was 17. Ten years on, I might have finally finished one! The biggest sacrifice made for this book has been our time together, which you selflessly gave up for the past year to allow me to spend many nights typing away. Thank you for your patience, your love, thank you for...everything.

My amazing parents, Carol and Terry – thank you for providing me with the opportunities you have. You're the ultimate representation of the Boomers – and I am so proud to be your daughter. What would I have done without the best babysitters in the world on call? Louise, thank you for being my sister. No matter what – I can always count on you. Your house was like my writing retreat when I needed some quiet time – and your help in Bali during my writing retreat was a big part of the success of this book – thank you, I'll never forget it.

Mark, my mentor, father-in-law and friend. You have supported me, my ideas and my dreams in a way no-one else ever could. Your generosity will never be forgotten and I am so grateful to have had your support over the last ten years, not only in my career, but in my life.

And a big thank you to my precious Laura – my sounding-board and life support over the past few years. What would I have done without you? Not this book more than likely! Thanks for everything.

Finally – Elisa. My best friend of 14 years and the most understanding person in the world. You have never doubted me. You know me better than anyone else ever could. BFF (love you too Nic). x

PREFACE

On the morning of the 12th of August, I woke up with the words 'Understanding Y' imprinted on my mind. It was almost like my subconscious brain had been working at this all night – on the idea to create a book that brought about a better understanding of Generation Y. It seems my sleeping mind had devised a plan that would bring together an eclectic mix of inspirational writing on Gen Y, and a collection of thought leaders and career professionals who have dedicated a large proportion of their adult life trying to better understand Y.

I would later discover that the 12th of August was International Youth Day. The coincidence of the two events has not been lost on me.

I'd like to point out that I acknowledge the mere concept of grouping 900 million individuals together simply due to the fact that they were born during a set period of time is entirely flawed – and, essentially, nothing more than a potentially damaging stereotype. And it's a stereotype that, in my experience, has been largely misunderstood.

Yet despite my usual aversion to any form of stereotyping, I do concede that there *are* differences in the way that those within the Gen Y age bracket behave and think. As such, these identifiable and consistent traits are useful for discussing and appreciating this new breed of adults.

A further clarification to make: while this book's contributors will constantly refer to 'Gen Y', it is clear to me that we are essentially talking about a 'Western' or affluent group of people born between the late 1970s and late 1990s. The 'Gen Y' that has grown up with continued famines in Africa, or the bitter and persistent wars in the Middle East, has faced quite a different set of circumstances. For the Gen Ys in India who have been and are still confronted by the serious threat of rape for themselves, their sisters, mothers and daughters, growing up Y has been tragically different. It would be neglectful of me not to acknowledge the significantly divergent realities that many individuals of Gen Y have faced. They have been raised in a world different from the one described in this book.

I would have loved to compile a book that gave an in-depth analysis of Gen Y throughout the world; but of course, there is only so much one can include in a single publication.

It was my intention to produce a book that provided a better insight into the minds and behaviour patterns of one of the most misunderstood generations of our time. It has always been my intention to provide Baby Boomers and Gen Xers with significant insight to the enigmatic Millennial generation. I wanted to produce a book that provided valuable information on how to engage, work with, encourage and lead us. I have had the great honour of meeting and collaborating with some inspirational people on this book, and I thank them all for their contribution to *Understanding Y.*

I hope this book might also provide Ys with relatable content. It's meant to sooth inquisitive minds and alleviate that niggling question, reassuring that, 'Yes – what you think/do/believe is a common experience for many your age.'

Sometimes this world we live in disappoints me, saddens me and frustrates the hell out of me. Sometimes I fear for the world my children will soon be inheriting. Yet I see glimmers of hope shining through the tragedy, loss and despair that engulf our world. I feel the simmering of great change – change on a revolutionary scale, unlike any we have seen before. It is positive change that comes from a collection of people dedicated to peace and parity. There's a new breed of social warriors who aren't afraid of breaking rules in the name of equality and justice. Some people ask me what that hope might be.

My answer is always, 'Y.'
Charlie Caruso

CHAPTER 1

The Enigma that is Gen Y

Bernard Salt

Our fathers had their dreams; we have ours; the generation that follows will have its own. Without dreams and phantoms man cannot exist.

Olive Schreiner

Whenever a new star or planet is discovered, its name, coordinates and other vital statistics are registered with the International Astronomical Union located in Boulevard Arago in the 14th Arrondissement in Paris. It is unfortunate that a similar system isn't in place to determine the parameters of the names of newly discovered human generations.

The Baby Boomers were easy to identify and made themselves known from about 1946 onwards. It's less clear when exactly this generation ended and the next began. Those who followed the Boomers were named Generation X by Canadian author Douglas Coupland, who published a book on this very subject in 1992. The logic that followed was, well, if there is an X then there must be a Y. And if there's a Y, then there must be a Z. But hang on — since Generation Z straddles the millennium, perhaps a better tag is the Millennium Generation.

And wait—maybe Generation Y ended before the end of the millennium, in which case perhaps something along the lines of iGen would be more appropriate.

I wonder whether the International Astronomical Union's Paris headquarters might have a spare room where social scientists and demographers could deliberate and make serious pronouncements about all the generations, their starting years and ending years, and the traits commonly associated with their behaviour and preferences. But in the absence of such a command centre, I suggest a compromise.

How about we focus less on the totality, and more on the core of the generation? Using this logic, the core of the Baby Boomer Generation was aged 50 to 59 in 2013, and so was born between 1954 and 1963. Generation X sprawled across the 35 to 44 decade in 2013, which places their birth years between 1969 and 1978. Generation Y covers the twenties between 20 and 29 in 2013—which means that they were born between 1984 and 1993.

This classification system allows for gaps—disputed territories, if you like—that lie, rather like mortar, as filler between the main demographic bricks. I don't know when Boomers end and Xers start or when Xers end and Ys start—but neither does anyone else. And without some sort of classification system, the whole debate would never move beyond bickering over each generation's coordinates.

For the record, each of these generations has a worldwide population around the 800 to 900 million mark. In Australia, there are roughly 2.9 million Boomers, 3.2 million Xers and 3.3 million Ys. But what this classification system *doesn't* say is that the generation that preceded the Boomers and that straddled the War and the Great Depression years peaked at barely 1.5 million. So, whatever infrastructure—housing, schools, shops, roads—required during the 1950s and 1960s to accommodate War and Depression babies at maturity had to be *doubled* to accommodate the Boomers. Then, whatever infrastructure that had to be developed for the Boomers had to be upped by 10 per cent to accommodate the Xers. And whatever infrastructure that had to be developed to accommodate the Xers had to be upped by less than 10 per cent to accommodate the Ys.

And that is why it has always been about the Boomers. They are like a generational tsunami washing from youth to middle age over half a century and now careening towards retirement. In fact, you could argue that it has always been about the Boomers – whether they're labelled as hippies, dinks, yuppies or sea-changers. Perhaps the reason Generation Y has garnered such interest in popular culture is because Ys are the Boomers' children. No wonder Generation X tends to feel like the Overlooked Generation.

There are those who say that generational theory is like demographic astrology: that it is flawed logic to ascribe singular characteristics and behaviours to entire generations. However, I disagree. There's little doubt that the Depression Generation was both frugal and distrustful of debt as a community. As such, members of this generation were in many ways the first to pursue sustainability – not because they wanted to save the planet, but because it was wonderfully efficient and cost effective to re-use and recycle. If a community that experiences depression and/or war can be unified by a particular way of thinking, then why wouldn't this logic also apply to succeeding generations?

Some argue that there are material differences between the generations. The Baby Boomer Generation was reared by the Depression Generation, and the Boomers came from large families. They therefore learned early on that families and society were deeply hierarchical. There wore hand-me-down clothes and there was a pecking order within the family home. Times were tough. There was only one income earner; kids waited their turn. They viewed self-sacrifice positively: 'Ask not what your country can do for you, ask what you can do for your country.' Authoritative and imposing and sometimes even scary institutions like the Church, unions, schools and the government shaped society.

Work was plentiful and did not require excessive education. It was possible in postwar years for a working man in metropolitan Australia to buy a house and to raise a family without having completed secondary schooling. And because of the Boomers' tsunami effect, their movement into the workforce was always preceded by a surge in demand for houses, for schools, for shops, for nurses, for teachers, for everything.

Now fast-forward from the 1950s and the 1960s to the first decade of the twenty-first century. Generation Xers are pushing into their late thirties and early forties. The children of the baby Boomers, so-called Generation Y, is entering the workforce – and igniting some resentment. The Australian economy is booming; job growth is soaking up labour and skills. Generation Y graduates entering the job market in the decade prior to the 2008 global financial crisis are immediately feted by Boomer management desperate to reduce churn and to capture the boom. 'Are we paying you enough, Generation Y?' 'Is anyone being mean to you, Generation Y?' 'Can I get you a pillow, Generation Y?'

All the while, an increasingly older and more resentful Generation X is thinking, 'What about me?' Generation X sees Y as the children of rich, guilty and indulgent Boomer parents who felt guilty because both parents worked – so they indulged their kids as a consequence. Generation Xers, on the other hand, are much more comfortable with the concept of both parents working: 'Look, kid, I work. Get over it. It's what puts food on the table and a roof over your head. You're not special; that's the way it is.' Members of Generation Y are more likely than any preceding generation to have come from small, if not one-child, families, where both parents work. The combination of two working parents and one, perhaps two, kids at home during the 1990s resulted in an indulged – and, indeed, 'special' – generation.

Perhaps in response to the rigour and the harshness of parenting by the Depression Generation, Boomers as parents were – as they see it – kinder, more giving and more understanding with their own children. And because they only had one or two kids, their offspring were especially precious. Generation Y children received validation and positive feedback from an early age. The idea of competition vanished from schools in the 1980s. School reports no longer admonished students, but cajoled them and their parents with softer, kinder words like 'establishing' and 'developing' instead of 'not making the grade' or, something even more shocking, the dreadful f-word. Report cards in the 1960s had 'fail' written on them for the child to see. Can you imagine that? A child being told that they failed? That they weren't up with the rest of the class? That they had to work harder? How primitive, mean and archaic is *that*?

Not only were parents and schooling changing from the early 1990s onwards – the economy was booming as well. Imagine being raised to adulthood in an era of unfettered prosperity. If every year during childhood and the teens is better than the previous year, then it's no wonder an entire generation of Ys might get to thinking, 'Why save for a rainy day or invest in the future? The universe has always provided in the past; why won't it be the same in the future?'

As a result of this outlook, Generation Y quickly developed a reputation as people who love to live in the moment. Ys even developed their own acronym to extol the philosophy: YOLO, which stands for 'you only live once'. Generation Y largely ignored or, at the very least, postponed various traditional institutions and practices. They postponed marriage to the late twenties, along with commitments like taking out a mortgage or settling on a career. Children now come in the early thirties rather than in the mid-twenties.

Generation Y has also exhibited a rising predisposition to atheism. Why believe in a hereafter if the here-and-now is so damned good? In came fashionable new belief systems like hedonism, materialism, nowism – viewpoints that differ vastly from Boomers' and older generations' thinking and behaviour. Whatever the reason, Generation Y began to shift behaviours and beliefs to such an extent that they quickly drew older Xers' and even Boomers' ire and then judgement. Perhaps it's time to take stock of who the Ys are and where they're headed.

Gen Y is the most educated generation in history. Many have lived at home with their mum and dad well into their twenties. Very few have embraced marriage or mortgage or children, or indeed careers, in their twenties. Speak to Generation Y in corporate Australia in the years since the global financial crisis and you certainly get a sense that they appreciate their jobs, understand that they have to work hard and that work isn't always about them. But press the conversation and you'll often hear them admit that what they *really* want to do is to build a business.

Generation Y very likely is, or has the capacity to be, the most entrepreneurial generation in history. Due to their reluctance to tie themselves down at a young age, they have the capacity as well as the predisposition to be their own bosses and follow their own dreams. The Boomer Generation was always too cautious to yield a culture of entrepreneurialism; it's really rather hard to be adventurous with kids, a spouse and a mortgage. It's likely that the next decade in Australia and perhaps elsewhere in the developed world will see a Generation Y Entrepreneurial Dividend – a payoff for all the time, love, feedback, validation, education and money that Boomers have invested in Generation Y over 20 years.

Surely it cannot be that Generation Y's immediate future is the sad transition from parental home to barely affordable house-and-land package on the urban fringe. Or is their future path an opportunistic and chaotic connection that only a bold and footloose mind could see? If this nation and others are to see an entrepreneurial dividend emerge from Generation Y, then there must be a concurrent culture that supports failure. Not all entrepreneurial spirit is well placed; some is misguided and misdirected. Perhaps the real legacy of Generation Y isn't so much that they have been 'special', or spoilt, or even simply lucky. Perhaps it is that they are the social innovators and the entrepreneurs that will take society and prosperity to places where the Boomers and the Xers are unable to survive – that is, deep into the twenty-first century.

The impact of Y has only just begun. The sky is not the limit. This generation sees no limit. Millennials and whatever lies beyond will create their own history.

But it's virtually impossible to predict their potential without first truly understanding Y. We'll spend the next chapter removing misconceptions and commencing conversations that delve deeper into the misunderstood Millennial psyche – a process that will hopefully inspire the world at large to better appreciate and embrace the changes this new force will bring.

CHAPTER 2

Y the Misunderstanding?

Charlie Caruso

> We're all islands shouting lies to each other across seas of misunderstanding.
>
> *Rudyard Kipling*

It seems like everyone's got a label for Y, and if you believe any of the recent media portrayals, Millennials are an unreliable, spoilt, directionless, narcissistic, self-entitled (epidemically so), leeching cohort. The media laps up the various authors and academics who seem to be hell-bent on framing such characteristics as quintessentially 'Millennial'.

However, it appears that most accusations lack substance and struggle to be anything more than a blanket lament that proposes today's 20-somethings are quintessentially naive. Young people – naive? What a shocking revelation!

Finding a theory that accurately encapsulates the quintessential archetype of Y is a contentious proposition. Yet many have attempted it and dedicated a significant amount of research to better understand the 'echo Boomers' and their so-called divergent qualities. Somewhere between the academic studies, media reports, blogs and various books, certain Millennial traits have fashioned the popular belief about who Ys are and what they stand for. But how much is true – and how much has been contrived in order to sell magazines and newspapers? The truth is difficult to distinguish, and hidden behind a cloud of chaotic contradictions and clichés. Because of this confusion, there has been a growing divergence between the reality and perception of the Millennial generation.

This chapter will explore the most common Millennial myths, and analyse the data that has contributed to the labels that have personified the Y cohort up until this point.

Generation 'Me' narcissists

Despite what you may have heard about our generation, I have never come across a fellow Millennial falling in love with his or her reflection in the water at the local swimming pool.

The term 'narcissism' is derived from the tale in Greek mythology of a hunter who was renowned for his beauty. Exceptionally proud, he disdained those who loved him. As the legend goes, by divine punishment, he fell in love with his own reflection in a pool, not realising it was merely an image. He wasted away to death, not being able to leave the beauty of his own reflection.

Yet today's interpretation of narcissism is commonly used in reference to those who pursue gratification from vanity, or egotistical admiration of their own physical or mental attributes.

So does that explain the proliferation of 'selfies'?

David Thomas, author of *Narcissism: Behind the Mask* suggests that narcissists typically display most, and sometimes all, of the following traits:

- an obvious self-focus in interpersonal exchanges

- problems sustaining satisfying relationships

- a lack of psychological awareness

- difficulty with empathy

- problems distinguishing the self from others

- hypersensitivity to any insults or imagined insults

- vulnerability to shame rather than guilt

- haughty body language

- a tendency to flatter people who admire and affirm them (narcissistic supply)

- detesting those who do not admire them (narcissistic abuse)

- using other people without considering the cost of doing so

- pretending to be more important than they really are

- bragging (subtly but persistently) and exaggerating their achievements

- claiming to be an 'expert' at many things

- inability to view the world from the perspective of other people

- denial of remorse and gratitude.

So as you can see, narcissism isn't a label to take lightly. If it is indeed true that Ys are plagued by narcissistic tendencies, this might just be what prevents Ys from creating the change the world is depending on them to make.

Dr Jean Twenge is the predominant authority on this topic and the author of *Generation Me: Why Today's Young Americans are More Confident, Assertive, Entitled and More Miserable than Ever*. Twenge describes narcissists as those who lack empathy, overreact to criticism and favour themselves over others. They're incapable of cheering anyone else's success and ultimately lead miserable lives because they cannot form and maintain healthy relationships.

Twenge presents data that displays generational increases in self-esteem, assertiveness, self-importance, narcissism and high expectations based on surveys of 1.2 million young people, some dating back to the 1920s. These analyses indicated a clear cultural shift toward individualism and focusing on the self.

Twenge's research drew on the reciprocal nature of the relationship between personality and culture, and proposed that societal changes have driven increases in narcissism and vice versa. According to Twenge, such a proposition is supported by the growth of narcissistic lyrics in popular songs, and the unfathomable popularity of TV shows that glamorise wealthy, neurotic plastic-surgery junkies who display overtly narcissistic tendencies. All of these factors have advanced a popular culture that celebrates these individuals, their behaviours and conceited tendencies, as though they are to be admired and aspired to. In his book *Fame Junkies*, Jake Halpern reported the following finding:

> Three times as many middle school girls want to grow up to be a personal assistant to a famous person as want to be a senator, as well as, four times as many would pick the assistant job over the CEO of a major corporation.

Dr Keith Ablow, American psychiatrist and member of the Fox News Medical A-Team, wrote in his article 'We Are Raising a Generation of Deluded Narcissists':

> On MTV and other networks, young people can see lives just like theirs portrayed on reality TV shows fueled by such incredible self-involvement and self-love that any of the 'real-life' characters should really be in psychotherapy to have any chance at anything like a normal life. These are the psychological drugs of the twenty-first century and they are getting our sons and daughters very sick, indeed.

In a Pew Research Center 2007 survey of 18-to-25 year olds that asked what they felt their generation's most important goals were:

- 81 per cent stated it was to get rich (64 per cent named it as the most important goal of all)

- 51 per cent said it was to become famous

- 30 per cent said it was helping others who need help

- 10 per cent named becoming more spiritual.

Seriously? At what point did our aspirations get so messed up? And *how* did they get so messed up? Was it something our parents did wrong?

Sure, the Baby Boomers changed up the parenting formula by adding the 'you can achieve anything you want' flavour to the parenting recipe (which is great, providing a sufficient amount of competence is added for balance), but at what point did the aspirations for 'anything' turn from senator to Kardashian?

The parental blame game is a perennial favourite. It's not like the Boomers were the first generation accused of taking a 'new' approach to raising their kids. Yet finger-pointing in the Boomers' direction seems quite popular in the Gen Y and narcissism debate, with the likes of Twenge and many others believing that perhaps the increase in narcissism is the result of 'soft' child-rearing practices.

And I can assure you, Twenge is not alone here. There are literally hundreds of research papers and studies about this very topic. In a 2011 thesis submitted to the University of Birmingham titled 'The Role of Parenting in the Development of Narcissism and Parental Illness Perceptions of ADHD', the authors explored the relationship between parenting and the development of narcissism, taking a special interest in the role of overindulgence. What I found interesting was the distinction they made between 'healthy' and 'unhealthy' narcissism.

> The relative term 'healthy narcissism' shall be taken as meaning it is associated with positive mental health indicators, such as normal levels of self-esteem for the individual. Conversely, 'unhealthy narcissism', shall be understood as that which is associated with low self-esteem, depression and anxiety.

Yet, they concluded that both types of narcissism were found to be associated with low levels of parental monitoring and higher levels of overvaluation.

Furthermore, the thesis explored the commonly held proposition that parental overindulgence and the excessive or instant gratification of a child's needs might be a factor that encourages a child to develop narcissistic traits as an adult. As the theory goes, those who are taught that they can have whatever they want at a young age might just go on to expect as much throughout the rest of their lives.

Lorna Otway and Vivian Vignoles of the University of Sussex published an article titled 'Narcissism and Childhood Recollections: A Quantitative Test of Psychoanalytic Predictions', which found that adult narcissists report childhood recollections of their parents putting them on a pedestal, believing they had exceptional talents, often praising and rarely criticising them.

Hrm.

These results are alarming. Are Millennials really *that* bad? Could the Boomers' well-intended 'tweak' to the parenting formula really have backfired so badly?

Dr Twenge bases her sentiments largely on research she and her team conducted at San Diego State University, which was published in her book *The Narcissism Epidemic* that she co-wrote with W. Keith Campbell. The book cites research carried out on some 50 000 college students, and reports that in 2006, 10 per cent of Americans in their twenties met the criteria for narcissistic personality disorder – and another 15 per cent in that cohort had pronounced narcissistic traits. The vast majority of research that alludes to the fact that Gen Y is plagued by narcissism is based on the premise that the Narcissistic Personality Inventory (NPI) test does indeed accurately reflect such a sweeping proposition. The test, developed by Raskin and Hall in 1979 for the measurement of narcissism as a personality trait, has dominated the field of study on narcissism since the 1980s, as acknowledged by Nicole Cain, Aaron Pincusa, and Emily Ansell in their article 'Narcissism at the Crossroads'. But just because it's been used a lot in research, does that mean it's an accurate reflection?

I had to find out for myself, and decided to take the test online. I'm not suggesting that, by taking the test, I now have a better understanding of its place in this field of study (I am Gen Y, but I am completely at peace with the limitations of my knowledge), but I felt I couldn't fully appreciate what the NPI might be able to offer unless I myself took the test and compared my results to 'the average Y'.

FYI—I scored 8. According to Psyche Central, between 12 and 15 is average; 'celebrities' often score closer to 18. Narcissists score over 20. *Over 20!*

As a display of transparency on this topic, my results are as follows.

Figure 2.1: Charlie's NPI test score results

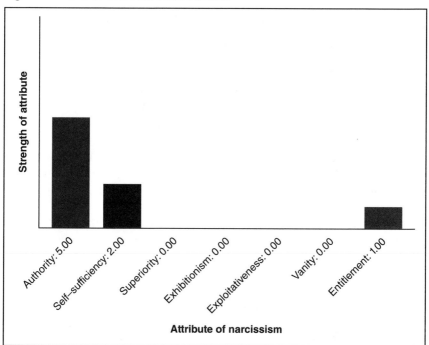

The components are defined as follows:

- The **Authority** aspect of the NPI refers to a person's individual leadership skills and power. People who score higher on authority prefer to be in charge, often for power's sake alone.

- The **Self-sufficiency** component of the NPI score relates to how much a person relies on others versus on their own abilities to meet their needs in life. Having a high score in this area and low scores in others does not necessarily indicate narcissism, and it could just mean that a person rarely relies on others.

- The **Superiority** score refers to whether a person feels they are better than those around them.

- The **Exhibitionism** trait of the NPI indicates an individual's need (and willingness) to ensure that they are the centre of attention (even at the expense of others' needs).

- The **Exploitativeness** component of the NPI refers to how willing individuals are to exploit others in order to meet their own needs or goals.

- The **Vanity** score relates to a person's belief in their own superior abilities and attractiveness compared to others.

- Finally, the **Entitlement** trait refers to the expectation and amount of entitlement a person has in their lives; that is, irrational expectations of especially favourable treatment or of automatic compliance with one's expectations.

Twenge's research indicates that in 2009, 30 per cent of students scored over 20, compared to only 17 per cent in 1982. Thirty per cent! With a score over 20! In the test I took!

I found this statistic shocking. Surely there can't be *that* many self-absorbed Ys? Surely there are others who share my scepticism with respect to the proliferation of narcissism among members of this generation?

As it turns out, I am not the only one to find the results hard to believe. (Although I will admit that 'hard to believe' doesn't always mean 'inaccurate'.) There are a number of academics and researchers alike who question these findings, and the tactics used to develop and defend them. Some take issue with Twenge's research methods, while others feel the NPI is a better metric for positive traits like confidence or assertiveness than for pathological egomania.

Michigan State University psychologist Brent Donnellan was quoted in the infamous *Time* magazine article 'Millennials: The Me Me Me Generation' as stating, 'We calculated self-esteem scores from 1976 all the way up to 2006 and we didn't see much difference at all.'

Yet it is also worth noting that Donnellan's study is the *only one* that does not show an increase in self-esteem. Twenge reminds us that increases in self-esteem have been an individual-level manifestation of the cultural shift towards focusing on the individual.

But self-confidence and narcissism are two *very* different things. When asked her thoughts about whether Gen Y displayed more narcissistic tendencies than previous generations, Twenge made her views very clear in an interview with Joseph Cotto of *The Washington Times*:

> This isn't a matter of agreeing or disagreeing ... Eleven studies show a generational increase in narcissism. They include respondents from high school age to adults, four different ways of measuring narcissism, three different research methods, four different ways of recruiting respondents, three different countries, and eight sets of authors. Five [of them] compare Gen Y with their predecessors at the same age. This includes one data set that originally claimed to show no change that demonstrates significant change when analysed correctly. Nine additional studies show increases in positive self-views.

Confused about the truth? Me too.

My commitment to logical reasoning and academic rationale has forced me to realise that my desire to believe that narcissism was somehow being confused with Ys' self-confidence was irrational. But again, self-confidence is a *long* way from narcissism and, as Twenge points out, 'narcissism's technical definition describes something more complex than overblown self-esteem'.

Technical definition ... hmm. Shall we go there?

Because so far we have 'healthy' and 'unhealthy' narcissism – are there any more distinctions on the ever-complex narcissism spectrum?

Well ... research conducted by Shaun Davenport and his team at Appalachian State University has emphasised that there is an important distinction between clinically diagnosed narcissism and subclinical narcissism. Apparently, subclinical narcissism is 'a personality trait that normal, healthy individuals possess to varying degrees'.

So if there is a distinction between 'clinical narcissism' and 'subclinical narcissism' – which category does Generation Y fall into?

It would certainly be a very serious issue if 57 per cent of Y were considered *clinical narcissists*. Davenport and his colleagues seem to agree that 'to extrapolate Twenge's results as proof that 57 per cent of Millennials are clinical narcissists – a classification that applies to just one per cent of the world's population – is a stretch'.

However, Dr Twenge has clarified that narcissistic personality, as measured by the NPI, is not the same as clinical narcissism (NPD).

> Our studies do not examine NPD at all, nor have we ever claimed that they do. Another study (Stinson et al) does, and finds that NPD is more prevalent among the young generation, but that's a different question, using very different measures. (And Stinson concludes that 9.4 per cent of those in their twenties have already experienced NPD, so the 1 per cent estimate doesn't hold anymore.) Overall, it's important to understand that narcissistic personality is not the same as clinical narcissism.

There is *so* much content on this matter that trying to see the truth through all the clutter has proven challenging. It seems the Y who have been studied are indeed showing signs of narcissistic personalities. We're not exactly sure if this is healthy or unhealthy narcissism – but we do know that we are not referring to clinical narcissism.

I'll admit that I don't like the thought of belonging to a generation demonstrating epidemic proportions of narcissistic traits – certainly not if they are as described earlier in this chapter by David Thomas. But while I'm comforted by those who disagree with Twenge, I recognise we cannot discount her research and underlying propositions. The nagging reality – that I am regularly witness to demonstrations of behaviour one could only describe as self-absorbed – is testament that there is, in many cases, a lack of psychological awareness in the self-centred, unquestionably 'odd' behaviour that many Gen Ys are currently displaying, most commonly via social media platforms.

Example – what is up with those who post birthday messages or picture collages to Facebook for their parents or young children who clearly don't have Facebook accounts? Why not write it on a card? What is the thought process behind posting such a message – and who is that post actually *for*? To answer these questions, one is forced to further examine the evidence that we are living in an age of narcissism. Posts such as these are manifestations of the poster's inclination for shameless self-promotion via the internet.

Y *are* we behaving in this manner? And are Gen Ys the only ones doing it?

Nope. There's a social shift emerging – and it's a shift towards the mirror.

Mirror, mirror on the wall...

Which generation is the worst of all?

The 'selfie'

Christine Rosen, senior editor of *The New Atlantis*, published a thought-provoking contribution to this conversation titled 'Virtual Friendship and the New Narcissism' that assists in answering this question. Rosen makes the point that, for centuries, the rich and the powerful documented their existence and their status through the portraits they commissioned – because they had the means to do so. Many years ago, these paintings were considered a marker of wealth and a bid for immortality, offering admirers then and now intriguing insinuations about those immortalised on the canvas – their professions, ambitions, attitudes, and, most importantly, social standing.

She makes reference to historical selfies:

> Self-portraits can be especially instructive. By showing the artist both as he sees his true self and as he wishes to be seen, self-portraits can at once expose and obscure, clarify and distort. They offer opportunities for both self-expression and self-seeking. They can display egotism and modesty, self-aggrandisement and self-mockery.

Let's compare this with the self-portraits of today. Our digital selfies are crafted from pixels rather than paints and, like the painters that continually retouch their work, we too alter, update and tweak our virtual representations of ourselves. These future artefacts might one day be a history lesson presented to future generations. What impression will we leave them of the society that exists today? It's impossible to know and futile to predict, but it's safe to say that right now we are witnessing a significant cultural shift in the portrayal of the 'self-Y'.

The role of social media

Four professors from Appalachian State University and High Point University in High Point, North Carolina, conducted a study titled, 'Millennials, Narcissism, and Social Networking: What Narcissists Do on Social Networking Sites and Why', and came to some interesting conclusions. While they admit social networking may appeal to narcissists, they emphasise that it does not *create* narcissists. Instead, the experts agree that Generation Y's narcissistic reputation results from older generations' misperceptions – something Ys themselves have claimed. What looks like self-centredness to many is actually a vital means of communication, self-expression and professional advancement for members of this generation.

Such a thought reminded me of what is possibly my favourite paragraph from Joel Stein's article 'Millennials: The Me Me Me Generation' for *Time* magazine. Stein noted that, while it's easy for other generations to view Gen Ys as oversharing Kardashian types, he questioned whether posting photos on Facebook is more or less obnoxious than Baby Boomer couples trapping friends in their lounge rooms to watch their holiday slides. The article goes on to cite Scott Hess, senior vice president of human intelligence for SparkSMG, whose Tedx speech, 'Millennials: Who They Are and Why We Hate Them', advised companies on marketing to youth.

> Can you imagine how many frickin' Instagrams of people playing in the mud during Woodstock we would've seen? I think in many ways you're blaming Millennials for the technology that happens to exist right now. Yes, they check their phones during class, but think about how long you can stand in line without looking at your phone. Now imagine being used to that technology your whole life and having to sit through algebra.

Bazinga!

It's clear that this Millennial 'myth' is contentious, complex and controversial. There is no denying the damning data out there. The question is whether or not the data is emblematic of the zealous ignorance of a highly intelligent, confident (and disenchanted) youth, or whether the results paint a bleaker picture of a cohort uniquely afflicted with widespread delusion. This is a matter of interpretation that can only be substantiated by the sands of time. If it does turn out to be the latter, then there is a real threat that the selfie generation is at great risk of being smothered by self-obsession and tunnel vision – making it likely to face an unprecedented economic and psychological cost in the future.

Perhaps the best thing Y (and frankly, everyone else) could do as a cohort is reflect a little on our own behaviour. Sit and review our Facebook posts and analyse how much is about ourselves, versus everything else important to us. Is this filtered image of us something others want to see on their timelines? Should we continue posting pictures of every meal we eat?

It's truly food for thought.

Entitled Millennials

The concept of Millennial 'entitlement' is thrown around as often as the narcissism label. But is it closer to the truth? Do Ys feel entitled – and, if so, to *what* exactly? What does 'entitled' even mean in this context?

According to Urban Dictionary, this is an attitude, demeanour, or air of rudeness, ungraciousness or combativeness, especially when making excessive demands for service.

Ken Coates, professor of history at the University of Waterloo, and author of 'Gen Y Can't I Have Everything I Want...and Now!' which was posted on theconversation.com, repeatedly labels Y as 'The Entitlement Generation':

> Entitlement Generation expects the world to respond to their demand for a simple and unchallenging route to adulthood and financial well-being. The mix is an unhappy one.

Personal opinions aside, what evidence is there that supports such a proposition?

In a survey of 2546 employers, conducted by CareerBuilder.com in 2007, *87 per cent* said that some or most of Gen Y workers feel more entitled – in regard to compensation, benefits and career advancement – when compared with older colleagues.

Specifically, the study cites that

- 74 per cent of the employers surveyed said Gen Y workers expect to be paid more

- 61 per cent of the employers said Gen Ys expect to have flexible schedules

- 56 per cent of the employers said Gen Ys want to be promoted within a year

- 50 per cent of the employers said Gen Ys want more vacation or personal time

- 37 per cent of the employers said Gen Ys demanded access to state-of-the-art technology.

The consulting arm of Ernst & Young conducted an online generations study in June 2013 that collected data from over 1200 respondents evenly spread across the three generational groups. Ninety-eight per cent of the respondents worked full-time; 95 per cent had some higher education; and 57 per cent reported household income greater than $75 000 a year.

The study validated the proposition that respondents believed Millennials appeared more entitled than the other two generations. Although the study did confirm that 60 per cent of Millennials had identified with a sense of entitlement, it also revealed that 40 per cent of Gen X and 27 per cent of Baby Boomers did too.

So – do Millennials truly feel more *entitled* to position, pay and particular working conditions? Or are they more *comfortable* expressing their expectations and more willing to take steps to pursue what is truly important in the workplace?

Sean Lyons, co-editor of *Managing the New Workforce: International Perspectives on the Millennial Generation*, was quoted in *Time* magazine's infamous Y article:

> This generation has the highest likelihood of having unmet expectations with respect to their careers and the lowest level of satisfaction with their careers at the stage that they're at. It is sort of a crisis of unmet expectations.

Yet Jerry Stilson, a Baby Boomer and partner with business consulting and HR firm Cenera, believes that Gen Ys are simply ambitious and bold. He also happens to believe that they're overwhelmingly good for the workplace. As digital natives and born problem-solvers, Stilson feels Millennials are dedicated employees:

> [Millennials will] work flexibly, anywhere, as long as you give them complete access to information and the 'why'. Their values are different. They will not…marry the company [like Boomers did when they were young]. They're much more aware than we were when we got into the [job] market.

Stilson declares that he has witnessed a demonstration of entitlement by all kinds of people – not just Ys. In fact, he claims that he's seen it especially from those nearing retirement – people who feel at liberty to 'coast' after a long career.

> I see Gen Y as saying, 'I'm in a hurry, I'm very aware, and I want it now.' [They're not necessarily] entitled; they're just impatient. If Gen Ys have to learn anything, it's patience.

I admit that I am impatient, and I know many Ys who would openly admit to the same. But *entitled*? I am still not convinced that we are any more or less so than other generations.

Drew Foster, doctoral candidate in sociology at the University of Michigan, recently posted an article on Salon.com in which he noted that many of the conclusions have been based on misunderstood research. As many of the articles cite the work of Paul Harvey, a professor of management at the University of New Hampshire, Foster took it upon himself to locate the specific study that connected feelings of self-entitlement among young people being raised in the

1980s and 1990s – and was unable to pinpoint it. He then took it upon himself to ask Professor Harvey as to the whereabouts of the article in question, and discovered, via correspondence with Harvey, that the article he had been searching for had never existed. As it turns out, Harvey had never looked at generational differences in entitlement; it appears that this assumption has been something created by the media, then continually re-hashed until it was generally accepted that there was indeed a study that had evidence for such conclusions.

It is clear to me that substantiating the theory that Gen Y exhibits unique levels of entitlement would require a longitudinal study that effectively produces evidence that 'feeling entitled' is specific to the Millennial generation and not simply a function of age. After all, how can we draw any real distinction between the inconsistencies of youth and the faults of an entire generation when every member of the generation is *currently young*?

In order to conclude that Generation Y is more entitled than others, we would have to have studied every generation in the last 100 years in the exact same manner during their youth. And we haven't – or at least I have not come across it.

Ryan Gibson, creator of the Generation Y blog and co-author of this book, believes that Ys' sense of entitlement is often simply misinterpreted ambition.

> Generation Y was told that anything was possible from a young age, and so have high hopes for what their careers and lives in general will involve. They are not afraid to aim a little bit higher than previous generations may have done, but often aim in different directions – for instance, a high salary is less important to Millennials than quality family experiences. They are ambitious in what they want to achieve, and make no apologies for going after those goals, making them driven and focused, rather than self-centred and disrespectful. It is important that older generations acknowledge the benefits of Millennial attitudes, and utilise that drive and ambition in the work place.

I happen to agree wholeheartedly with Ryan's sentiments. Gen Y entitled? Entitled to what exactly? Mind-blowing levels of student debt? Inheriting an economy that is teetering on collapse? Taking responsibility for the environment that previous generations have mercilessly exploited to generate *their* wealth — leaving us with the mess and the cheque?

cough

Regardless of its validity, I feel this 'myth' will continue to dominate the banter vis-a-vis Y until Millennials are the largest cohort in the workforce. As the older generations retire, so, it is my belief, will this myth. If Gen Y does indeed exhibit a significantly greater sense of 'entitlement' than our predecessors had at our age, I am reasonably sure that the cold, hard concrete of reality will quickly erode any disparity between what Y expect, and what Y get.

Unreliable young'uns

A survey from Sensis in 2007 found that small- to medium-sized businesses were less likely to take on Generation Y employees than Baby Boomers. As author Christena Singh reported:

> Australian small and medium business owners told us Generation Y lacked reliability to a certain extent.

> When we look at the other side of the scale we're seeing that Generation Y is valued for their enthusiasm but then reliability was a key issue.

Nearly half of recruiters surveyed (46 per cent) think the greatest challenge in hiring a Millennial is their unknown long-term commitment to a company, according to Adecco's Staffing Mature Worker Survey conducted in 2012.

Australian social researcher Michael McQueen believes that members of other generations have deemed Ys 'unreliable' because of the difference in their approach to planning for their future:

> They don't think about and plan for the future in a linear way. They are far more responsive and reactive and don't want to commit. It comes down to a different way of looking at the world rather than an inherent character flaw.

But again, is this not just a commonality for young people in general, rather than specifically Y?

Jule Gamache, author of article 'What Employers say Millennials Are Lacking and How to Fix It', seems to think so.

> It is definitely a challenge to demonstrate loyalty when you're young. You've probably had multiple internships with different companies and are still trying to figure out where you belong in the professional world. If your resume has a lot of short-term jobs, [you want] to explain your reasons for making so many jumps. If you support these explanations by letting employers know why you would love to work for their company, they'll have more faith in your commitment.

Loyalty to a career path or organisation is one thing (and the next on my agenda of generational myth busting). But the accusations that I have heard about Gen Y seem to relate more specifically to the regular issue of texting (not even calling!) in sick, standing people up for interviews, and the proliferation of excuse-making and the general lack of accountability that Gen Ys have in their responsibility to others.

I am a proud member of Y, and I can admit that, at times, I can be unreliable. So can many of the Ys I know. And so can many of the *people* I know.

To propose that Y is an unreliable generation would insinuate that we as a cohort cannot be relied upon. But the truth is that it's not easy to find and retain a truly reliable employee in this day and age, regardless of the generation. You may think you are a reliable employee, but the moment you gossip, take too much time for lunch, start creating ways to take advantage of your job situation, or make a habit of reading and sending personal emails at work, you might be perceived as 'unreliable' yourself. So why are Ys seen to be less reliable than other generations?

I did a bit of research online and drew up a list of the most commonly whinged-about issues that are raised with respect to Gen Y and our so-called 'unreliability issue'. I discovered that the following are the most commonly believed reasons as to why Ys are considered so unreliable:

- They operate according to their own agenda.
- They care mostly about their own self importance.

- They lack accountability.

- They display immaturity.

- They don't realise the impact their actions or lack thereof might have on people.

But aren't these simply common traits of the young and naive? The 'real world' usually straightens young'uns out. The 'young' have always been forced to grow up at some stage. Or, has the age of smart phones and the convenient lack of face-to-face or verbal accountability generated a uniquely unreliable cohort?

Canadian author and freelance writer Mike Wicks recently produced a piece for *Douglas* magazine about this very issue.

> Unreturned phone calls, missed appointments, over-promising and under-delivering ... Unreliability is endemic in today's business world. It's time to [reverse this trend].

> Being reliable used to be a virtue, but these days it's accepted that few people will actually deliver what they say they will. You're no longer guaranteed a reply from an email you send; leaving a message on someone's voice-mail is often like speaking into a black hole. Everybody is so busy that many no longer [exhibit] the basic good manners and business etiquette that underlie being reliable — and demonstrate integrity ...

> When delivering on time and doing what was agreed upon becomes 'a breath of fresh air,' then something's seriously wrong. We've become accustomed to, and even accepted, unreliability as a normative business practice. That's because we're all guilty of it to some degree.

> We need to start improving our own reliability and expect it of those we work with. If we don't, this spiraling inefficiency will affect all our bottom lines.

In the article, Mike lists common issues people have with Gen Ys: not responding to emails and phone calls, being late for or not showing up to appointments, not delivering agreed-upon results and not following instructions. I agree with many of Mike's sentiments and am ashamed to admit I have been guilty of some of the conduct he has described. I could blame it on the fact that I currently have 2703 unanswered emails sitting in my inbox; but the honest truth is that it's a reflection of my tendency to take on way more than I can chew at any one time, and my tendency to be reasonably unreliable about responding to email correspondence.

And I'm not sure how much of this behaviour is specific to Y. I happen to believe that a lot of the social crimes that Mike describes point to a broader change in society – in pace and the *priority* for politeness. I think members of Y are a product of this evolution; as such, their conduct positions them as the worst perpetrators for the behaviour they were merely conditioned to display.

The truth is we will only ever habitually do what we are allowed to get away with. This is a simple rule that applies for young children, Gen Y – and Gen everyone else. If businesses and individuals alike don't challenge this behaviour and draw firm lines in the sand regarding the reliability they demand, members of Generation Y will continue to text instead of call in sick.

Ys have emerged as adults in a time where we are demonised for having our eyes constantly connected to a screen, and told to 'put the phone down for a while'. Yet at the same time, we are accused of being unreliable for not responding to the constant email procession – one that is no longer restricted to office hours and has instead expanded to 24/7.

We can't win. It seems no-one is happy to be in your company if you're responding to the emails, texts and phone calls placed by others; but those same people will be the first to criticise you when you're not picking up the phone, responding to the text or email, because you're with someone else!

Is the frantic pace of our constantly connected lifestyles making it harder than ever to be reliable? Or are we getting flakier in the information age, where personal accountability can be obscured by digital communications?

I'm not sure. What I do know is that being unreliable is not something anyone wants on their resume or character reference. Being labelled as unreliable will negatively affect your relationships at work, as well as with your friends and family.

And we all have that friend or family member that will make plans, only to break or change them at the last minute. You might even *be* 'that' friend – the one that everyone soon learns they need to make 'alphabet plans' (Plan A, B, C, D, even plans E to Z) around, so that you're not left at a table for one or eating popcorn by yourself at the movies.

The fact is that we're all guilty of the occasional flake. But is this a uniquely Y trait? Or has everyone, in every generation, got one of these people in their close network?

Whatever the answer, the solution is fairly simple: if you have flaky friends, employees or colleagues, you should reprimand these unreliable individuals – Ys or otherwise. You work hard on setting the new, desired level of reliability, using your own actions, and point out when someone lets you down. Don't sit back, suffer in silence and complain to others about those you alphabet-plan around; tell them you expect more and fix the issue at hand. That, or accept it and stop complaining. There are more serious issues facing this world.

DisloyaltY

Y stick around if you're not happy at work – right? Do Millennials really think this way? Does loyalty to one's workplace or employer exist anymore?

The Future Workplace's 2012 study 'Multiple Generations @ Work' found that 91 per cent of the Millennials surveyed expected to stay in a job for less than three years. That significant statistic certainly identifies Y with the stereotype that exists in the minds of many.

Ben Weiss, digital marketing strategist for Infusive Solutions and regular contributor to the website usnews.com, discusses the consequences of this statistic, and the pejorative associations that have arisen about Millennial employees, in a recent article. According to popular belief, Ys are loyal only to themselves and will jump ship for another opportunity the moment a job has become anything less than ideal. But Ben contends that we need to think *inside* the box, and has pointed out plenty of compelling reasons that might lead a professional Y to seek a new employer.

Ben's article 'How Gen-Y Employees Can Handle Negative Stereotypes' told the story of Teddy Dziuba, a 29-year-old new business/underwriting manager who has stayed at his post at a Massachusetts-based wealth management firm for a half decade. Teddy pointed out that many of his peers are compelled to seek new opportunities, not because they're in a bad environment, but simply due to their hyperactive wiring.

> '[Millennials don't want] to be sitting at a computer completing a spread sheet,' he says. 'They have to be checking Facebook, listening to iTunes, sending a text message and Snapchatting a photo of their cluttered desk WHILE working on that spreadsheet. This is not a slight on my peer group; it is just an unfortunate compulsion to have constant and varied stimuli, which also causes Millennials to get tired of the status quo very easily and seek new challenges via new employment opportunities.

This certainly sounds familiar to me. I am not a fan of monotony, at least not for an extended period of time. I have always been drawn to vocations that provide me with constant challenges and a wide variety of work. Yet I have stuck it out for years in office jobs, staying for the simple fact that I was continually promoted until I reached a point that I could progress no further or the positions no longer challenged or interested me.

I have seen evidence that Millennials are perhaps less patient than previous generations when it comes to job dissatisfaction. Yet is it not feasible that we might just be the first generation who will not settle for a job we hate? Ys are willing to fight for a happy life – happy to participate in the vocation we choose, because we simply do what we love.

I know that I'm fortunate to live in a country that provides Ys with far more opportunities than elsewhere. One reason for our 'wandering eyes' might be that many members of Y are still young enough to not have children or dependants – so the absolute need to provide isn't necessarily there. We can afford to wander around looking for greener pastures.

Jennifer J. Deal, senior research scientist at the Center for Creative Leadership in San Diego, California, and the author of 'Retiring the Generation Gap', has undertaken research that shows that Millennial employees have about the same level of organisational commitment as Boomers and Gen Xers:

> [One reason] this myth might be so prevalent is that young people of every generation change jobs more frequently than older people. Boomers changed jobs when they were in their twenties more frequently than they did when they were in their thirties and forties (or fifties and sixties), and we saw the same pattern with Gen Xers. And there is no evidence to show that the pattern is changing with Millennials.
>
> A second possibility is that people at lower levels in organisations — who tend to be younger—are slightly less committed to their organisation than people at higher levels. Those in the latter group are paid more and are responsible for organisational strategy, and are therefore likely to be more invested. It is therefore difficult for any organisation to retain younger people. When young people change jobs and look for new opportunities to learn and grow, it does not represent a lack of loyalty; it's simply the time in their lives when they are seeking these experiences.

Additionally, Lauren Schaefer, US blogger for the Lancaster Chamber of Commerce and Industry, agrees that the lack of loyalty Gen Ys are accused of is not specific to their generation:

> We tend to take new jobs for many reasons: a better offer, lack of appreciation at our current job, more opportunity for growth, [or the feeling that our current] employer is unable [or unwilling] to invest in our future. Our generation values a meaningful workplace culture, one that includes mentor programs, continuing education and giving back to the community.
>
> However, it turns out this is not only a Gen Y issue either. A recent study found 66 to 75 per cent of people are actively looking for a new job, which could mean that it is a cultural change instead of generational.
>
> [Gen Ys] aren't the only generation that values appreciation, work–life balance or a positive workplace culture; we are just the generation that is *most vocal* about wanting it all. If companies can develop

relationships with employees that foster these beliefs, we would be able to create a stable, engaged workforce. Maybe Gen Ys aren't the spoiled, needy, entitled individuals we tend to be stereotyped as; maybe we are actually just outspoken, determined idealists.

The conclusion we come to is that we must question employers here also. Perhaps if employers showed some loyalty to Y and all other employees, then the people they employed might do the same.

Countless Gen Ys have witnessed their Baby Boomer parents being made redundant or simply fired for being too old or too expensive, or because of a change in management – sometimes after 30-plus years of loyal service. In the days of multinational corporate mergers, where the bottom line counts and the employees that make that bottom line exist don't – what exactly motivates Ys to devote themselves to a company that could drop them tomorrow without a word of notice? Why would Ys feel compelled to exhibit *any* loyalty to the 'business world' when it's clear there is no guarantee of loyalty offered in return?

If you're a decent employer who encourages leadership over mediocre management, and provides individual growth and development opportunities and a comfortable working environment, then you will retain good employees that stay because they enjoy their work and the company they work for. Loyalty will not be an issue for you – from Gen Ys or otherwise. If you're not an employer who offers this, then you might find loyalty difficult – from Gen Ys or otherwise.

Similarly, if you're a hardworking, reliable, polite and diligent Y who seeks out challenges instead of expecting them to land on your lap, you're less likely to be thrown out on the pavement. If you can't be described as having these traits, you will struggle finding a regular job you enjoy – whether you're Gen Y or otherwise.

Spoilt rotten

Spoilt: an individual who exhibits behavioural problems from overindulgence by his or her parents

I'm going to address this myth by divulging the fact that I am a mother of two young daughters. I am very conscious of the fact that my daughters are well cared for, have many toys, and will live an early life far more privileged than many their age around the world. I'm always mindful of their attitudes regarding what they receive, be it others' time or gifts. I do this because, as parents, it is my and my husband's job to not raise spoilt children. If we did, whose fault would it be – theirs or ours?

The earlier definition clearly states overindulgence from one's *parents*. If Ys are spoilt, then our parents, the Baby Boomers, spoilt us. That's not to say we can point our fingers and engage in the blame game to rid us of any accountability for how spoilt we might be as adults. We are more than capable of adjusting our attitudes according to the norms and expected levels of our society and environment.

Millennials' pathways to independence have been varied – but we are working hard for our money, despite not really having real-world expenditures. Some of our parents have allowed, perhaps encouraged, us to bring home our dirty clothes on the weekend and visit once a week for a home-cooked meal.

We have also been raised in a world of instant gratification. Expecting everything now and 'on demand' has inevitably encouraged a tendency towards being self-absorbed and 'me' centric. The internet has allowed us to essentially buy whatever we want, and put it on our credit cards to pay off later. And while that's been the reality for the emerging Y, it's only half of the story. It's the 'ying' that everyone likes to harp on about, while ignoring the equally significant 'yang'.

Hillary Rettig, author of *Say Sayonara to Perfectionism*, decided to explore a little more about the 'yang'. In her blog she answers a Y who asks her if their generation is spoilt:

> Everyone my age [fifties] and older should show a little of the vaunted wisdom and perspective that's supposed to come with age, not to mention common decency, and shut the hell up about the supposed flaws of young people, if for no other reason than that things are so much tougher now than they were for us. Back in the eighties (when I was in my twenties), the economy was so strong; we could flit in and out of jobs almost at will; and many

of us worked for a few months and then casually—almost without a second thought!—quit to pursue art or travel or activism, fully secure in the knowledge we'd find a new gig when we needed to. That kind of freedom and security is currently unimaginable.

It is true that we have access to so many time-saving awesome gadgets that previous generations never had—and we are so far removed from world wars or rations that many Ys are complacent about many aspects of their lives. But we are also facing serious financial hardship: financial recessions and a less-than-ideal entry into the housing market and job market. We have it easier in some aspects, and face hardship in others. But spoilt brats? I'm going to say that Y is more likely misunderstood.

Disrespectful Ys

Leonardo da Vinci once said, 'Nothing strengthens authority so much as silence'. But then again—Gen Y isn't exactly the silent type.

So does Gen Y oppose hierarchy?

You might have noticed respect is a persistent theme in the age-old game of 'Let's Dump on Young People!', a perennial favourite of the more senior generations. But is there any truth to the myth that Ys are disrespectful and show no deference to authority?

Jennifer Deal conducted research that sought to de-bunk this Y myth, and found that, in a sample of more than 5000 respondents, Millennials were *more* likely than Baby Boomers and Gen Xers to agree that employees should obey management without questioning them. As Deal says:

> Our research shows (unexpectedly, I must admit) that Millennials currently in the workforce are more willing to defer to authority than either Baby Boomers or Gen Xers. One possible explanation for this behaviour has to do with the coaching Millennials received from their parents and teachers growing up: they learned at a young age that doing what an authority figure tells them is more likely to result in success. Therefore, they believe that doing what their managers tell them will have the same effect.

Deal concludes her article 'Five Millennial Myths' by saying that Millennials are more likely to thrive if they know what is expected of them. As self-sufficient as many Gen Ys seem to be, they are actually yearning for leadership and mentoring. 'It's such a key driver for this group, wanting to connect with adult figures, particularly leaders,' Michael McQueen, Australian Gen Y commentator, says.

According to the Center for Creative Leadership's World Leadership Survey, Millennials are the most inclined to be submissive to authority. The Centre reports that 41 per cent of Gen Ys believe that employees should do what their manager tells them, even when they can't see the reason for it. Only 30 per cent of Baby Boomers and 30 per cent of Gen Xers would do this.

Such findings are in stark contrast to the popular belief that's perpetuated by individuals like Susan M. Heathfield, a self-proclaimed human resources expert who wrote an article for about.com titled 'The Downside of Hiring Gen Y'. Heathfield believes that Gen Ys have no respect for leaders and no loyalty to employers:

> They want praise, praise, praise and thank you. Yes it is difficult to critique Gen Y employees. They do not respond well to authority and the leaders and managers must prove that they are worth following—or the Gen Ys you most want to keep will network their way right out of your organisation.

Unfortunately, Heathfield isn't alone in her thoughts.

Millennials aren't afraid to tell their side of the story – right or wrong. That doesn't mean we have authority issues; rather, authority comforts us. We crave mentorship and those who can guide us with energetic leadership and wisdom.

Noam Chomsky, an American linguist, philosopher and cognitive scientist once said:

> I think it only makes sense to seek out and identify structures of authority, hierarchy and domination in every aspect of life, and to challenge them; unless a justification for them can be given, they are illegitimate, and should be dismantled, to increase the scope of human freedom.

Timothy Leary was quoted saying:

> To think for yourself you must question authority and learn how to put yourself in a state of vulnerable open-mindedness; chaotic, confused vulnerability to inform yourself.

And, if I hadn't already made my point clear, it was Albert Einstein who said:

> To punish me for my contempt for authority, fate made me an authority myself.

You might have noticed a theme. None of these quotes has anything to do with Gen Y. Y? Because Gen Y isn't 'special' in this regard – in fact, we're very average. The idea that Gen Ys are especially anti-authoritarian is ludicrous. Myth busted – Gen Ys are no more rebellious than our hippie parents.

Lazy leeches

Apparently, Ys don't know the meaning of true 'stress' or how to work hard. Michael McQueen, Australian social researcher and Gen Y commentator, was quoted by Caitlin Fitzsimmons in her *BRW* article 'Eight Myths about Gen Y that Leaders Must Understand' stating:

> There's a myth that Gen Y are lazy and don't have any work ethic and that's a view sometimes held by the Baby Boomers who wear their lack of work–life balance sometimes as a badge of honour. [But] the fact that Gen Y have grown up seeing the heart attacks, strokes, broken marriages in their parents, often because of a lack of balance, means they are starting their careers wanting that flexibility and balance.

A desire for flexibility and balance is a far cry from being flat-out *lazy*. So we don't want to live to work, instead work to live. Surely that is a far more healthy approach to work–life balance, is it not?

While it hasn't been part of the game plan for all of us, many Ys have been accused of staying at home, leeching and living off their parents who continually pay them out while they gallivant around the planet on adventures and ignore real responsibilities, like a long-term, stable career and a mortgage.

It's true that, as a group, Generation Y is living with their folks longer and delaying such rites of adulthood as marriage and children. A study by Statistics Canada found that 51 per cent of Generation Ys between the ages of 20 and 29 lived with their parents in 2010. Just 31 per cent of Generation Xers and 28 per cent of late Boomers lived at home during that same age period. There is even a neologism to describe this! The term 'Twixter' describes the new generation of Ys who are trapped, in a sense, betwixt (between) adolescence and adulthood. Twixters live with their parents or are otherwise not independent financially. If they are employed, they often have unsteady and low-paying jobs. They may have recently left university or high school, or recently embarked on a career, and stereotypically marry later than usual and gain more college or career training.

Time published an article called 'Twixter Generation: Young Adults Who Won't Grow Up' about Twixters in January 2005, putting this relatively ambiguous term in the spotlight. (I don't think it caught on.) The article focused on upper- and middle-class Twixters who were being financially supported by their parents. The article made no distinction between people who lived on their own with their parents' help and people who lived with their parents, nor did it mention lower-class Twixters similar to NEETs and freeters in other societies. NEETs? Freeters? More names!

Since the 1980s and 1990s, Japan has seen the growth of a parasite-single or 'freeter' segment of the youth population that lives at home and works at undemanding jobs. They are employees who avoid promotion in order to minimise stress and maximise free time. Likewise, in Europe since the 1990s, there has been a growing number of NEETs, those 'Not engaged in Education, Employment, or Training'.

In October 2007, Italy's former minister of economy and finance Tommaso Padoa-Schioppa called people in their twenties and still living with their families *bamboccioni* ('big, dummy boys'), stirring controversy within the Italian media. Newspapers received numerous letters from readers taking personal offence and pointing out that he knew little about the situation of a considerable part of twenty-something Italians, who live on approximately €1000 per month and cannot afford to leave their parents' house. A similar case is also seen in Spain, with the term *mileurista* to describe the youth who live on a monthly salary of €1000 (*mil euros*). In Greece, the minimum monthly salary is €700 and the Greek media popularised the term the '€700 generation'. This generation evolved in the circumstances leading to the Greek debt crisis and participated in the protests of 2011 to 2012.

But again – how is this necessarily *bad*? There would need to be a good reason for our Baby Boomer parents being content with the extension of our 'incubation' period – wouldn't there?

It's clear that getting into the property market is incredibly tough for many members of Y – a lot tougher, some might argue, than it was for our parents. Our parents' generation is also working longer and not letting Y into the labour market in the way that we might have expected them to (perhaps *because* Ys are still living with them).

Benjamin Tal, deputy chief economist of CIBC World Markets, says Generation Y is more financially savvy than past generations, and that's part of the reason why they're living longer with parents – to save money. Tal also explains that they have the luxury of being the children of the affluent Boomer generation, which has the financial resources to support their children well into adulthood. And given that this group will be in the prime of their careers at a time in the near future when Boomers are retiring in droves, they may well stand to be the most prosperous generation in history.

Final rebuttal – if parents are enabling their adult children to leech, then perhaps parents need to cease the facilitation of this conduct. Or they can continue supporting their children, as long as they quit whining about it. Simple really.

Totally addicted to tech

Many studies have been conducted in an effort to examine Y's use of technology and its potential for related health issues. Researcher Angela Blackadder reviewed this trend in a paper titled 'Gen Y – Addicted to Technology', which analysed the existing research and literature about this Millennial myth.

Blackadder's exposé cited data from the International Center for Media and the Public Agenda, which conducted research on 1000 students, asking them to unplug from all technological devices.

They found that four in five students experienced significant mental and physical distress, panic, confusion and extreme isolation when forced to unplug from technology for an entire day. They also found university students across the globe admitted to being 'addicted' to modern technology such as mobile phones, laptops, television and of course social networking such as Facebook.

Throughout this short study, students suffered psychological effects including feeling lonely, panicked and anxious, and literally had heart palpitations. They experienced many emotions – confusion, anxiety, irritability, insecurity, nervousness, loneliness, depression and paranoia, to name a few. Because they experienced these results and emotions within 24 hours of unplugging from technology. Yikes!

The 2012 'Cisco Connected World Technology Report' on Gen Y reported that 29 per cent of Gen Ys admit they check their smart phones so constantly that they lose count, and 60 per cent of Gen Ys compulsively check their smart phones for emails, texts or social media updates. Around 83 per cent of 18-to-29 year olds sleep with their mobile phones within reach. Over a third of users surveyed admitted that they had used their smart phone in the toilet, and one in five admitted to texting while driving. Forty per cent of respondents would go through a 'withdrawal' effect and 'would feel anxious, like part of me was missing' if they couldn't check their smart phones constantly.

This addiction to technology has effects on social behaviour as well. Generation Y repeatedly turns to technology as an escape from boredom – but it eventually turns into something more. Technology offers an escape from their private lives, personal feelings and problems. In turn, this tendency damages the social structure of the home and community environment, as well as the potential for intimacy. Countless individuals neglect family members and other personal relationships as a result of this excessive behaviour.

We are living in times when improvements and updates in technology will continue exponentially and never end. It is changing the way we live, communicate and socialise forever. Millennials rely so heavily on digital media to manage their daily life activities, to keep up to date, and as a habitual knee-jerk reaction to fleeting moments of boredom.

Many believe that digital media has such a significant role in their lives, and they are so dependent on it, that Ys cannot imagine living without it. This dependency can quickly transform into addiction – a serious problem that can cause many health and psychological problems. And as reported in *Seventeen* magazine's May 2010 issue, a survey by the magazine and the AAA found that a significant danger from smart-phone addiction is rapidly emerging: 86 per cent of drivers admit to driving while texting – even though 84 per cent admit that they know it is dangerous.

Angela Blackadder explains that nothing is currently being done to reduce the use of technology among both Generation Y and previous generations. In fact, it's quite the opposite. As students, we are being encouraged to complete all assessments and contact teachers via the internet.

The Second International Congress of Technology Addiction was held in Istanbul on 26 and 27 October 2013. The congress's aim is to raise awareness about 'technology addiction' – a phenomenon the organisers feel is the 'disease of our age'. The congress planned to discuss preventative measures for the many forms of addiction, including internet, online porn, game, shopping, chat, mobile phone, television and computer game.

I commend the organisers of this congress for their efforts in raising awareness of such issues, and at least attempting to incite some positive change.

High maintenance

In *Time* magazine's May 2013 issue, Gen Y was dubbed the 'trophy generation' – a reference to the perception they were the recipients of 'participation trophies' as children. *Time*'s cover story 'Millennials: The Me Me Me Generation' states that Ys have a sense of entitlement far beyond that of their older peers. It's easy to see where this perception comes from. *Time* cites a study that exposed the finding that 40 per cent of Gen Y believes they should be promoted every two years, regardless of performance.

Social commentator Michael McQueen believes there is truth to the notion that Generation Y is high-maintenance, needing constant affirmation. He cites a study in the US where Gen Y employees were surveyed about how often they want praise from their boss. The results? Sixty per cent of Ys said they would want praise from their boss at least once a day, and 35 per cent said two to three times a day would be preferable.

'This generation can often be high-maintenance', McQueen says:

> There is a constant need for external validation and feedback and often a lack of ability to deal with negative feedback or constructive criticism that can be seen as a personal attack.

McQueen agrees that Y's Baby Boomer parents might be to blame. 'Having grown up in the self-esteem era, being told their whole lives that they're special, magnificent and wonderful, all the positive praise means that they crave that constantly', he says.

Many believe that this has a lot to do with Y's delay in entering the traditional roles of 'adulthood' despite being in their twenties.

In 2000, psychologist Jeffrey Arnett coined the term 'emerging adulthood' to describe extended adolescence that delays adulthood. He proposed the theory that twenty-somethings today no longer view themselves as adults. There are many theories on why this might have occurred (if indeed it has), including, but not limited to, longer life spans, helicopter parenting, high student debt, and a passion for travel and adventure. If Arnett's theory stands true, it seems that this limbo state that Y is facing is negatively affecting their mental wellbeing. According to a 2012 study by the American College Counselling Association, 44 per cent of college students admit to experiencing symptoms of depression.

Supporting this position is a 2013 study in the *Journal of Child and Family Studies* that found that students who experienced helicopter parenting reported higher levels of depression and use of antidepressant medications. Intrusive parenting interferes with an individual's ability to develop autonomy and competence, which leads to increased dependence and decreased ability to complete tasks without parental (or authoritative) supervision.

Brooke Donatone suggests that there are many contributing factors that have led to Y being high maintenance. In her piece for *Slate* magazine titled 'Why Millennials Can't Grow Up', she proposes that this era of instant gratification has led to a decrease in what therapists term 'frustration tolerance', which describes the way we handle emotional situations. When we lack frustration tolerance, moderate sadness may lead to suicide in the self-soothingly challenged.

But I must pose the same question I've already asked several times throughout this chapter: is the need for feedback and affirmation really *all that bad*?

Peter James is a Baby Boomer and chairman at Ninefold, a provider of cloud-based virtual servers, who employs 35 full-time staff in his Sydney office, 90 per cent of whom are Generation Y. Although James describes his role managing Generation Ys as sometimes being like herding cats, he says he enjoys the vibrant attitude of this generation of employees: 'They're very honest people—they will speak their mind…without fear or favour. That is refreshing as an employer. You have to be able to be prepared for that.'

James lists a few other Generation Y attributes—resistance to layers of hierarchy, a need to contribute value, to be challenged and to have fun:

> [It's crucial to give] them an agile, innovative environment in which they can be individuals and participate in making a difference… They don't just want to turn up and get paid.

Perhaps Ys *are* high maintenance—but only when compared to a vintage servicing model.

Think of Y as a new model of car (solar powered, if you will). They're different and require a whole new approach to their servicing needs. So, sure, they might *seem* high maintenance when we look at them through an old, dusty lens. But change the system to suit the new model, and this new breed of cars' benefits and potential efficiencies might just blow your mind.

Don't be scared of the new; embrace the change I say.

So…are all the myths busted?

Perhaps not.

Y?

Because every individual member of Gen Y is different.

And while some of the 'myths' surrounding Gen Y might be validated by science and statistics, many are just baloney. A lot of the cluttered chaos of labels and misunderstandings that currently surround the Millennials is simply a reflection of our youthful ignorance, something that Y will soon grow out of. Ys aren't the first generation of 'know-it-alls', and they're not the first cohort with an inclination towards optimism and naivety. Gen Ys are nothing more than the collective embodiment of youthfulness. Having had our Baby Boomer parents bring us up, reminding us that we were special, hasn't actually made our generation any more or less special than any other. If nothing else, it might have just given the Y a more pleasant, hopeful childhood.

And that's something to celebrate, not condemn.

CHAPTER 3

PsycheY

Leanne Hall

The more you know yourself, the more patience you have for what you see in others.

Erik Erikson

The Gen Y brain

The human brain is a complex organ. Weighing less than 2 kg, it contains over 11 *billion* intricately organised and interconnected neurons. Until recent years, it was thought that the brain reached its maturity during adolescence. We now know that in fact the brain continues to develop throughout early adulthood, *at least* into our mid-twenties. The implications of this for Gen Y are extremely significant. After all, if their brains are still developing, do Gen Ys even have the *capacity* to think and behave in certain ways?

Our brain overproduces networks when we are children. Throughout adolescence, these networks are *pruned* as a way of consolidating neural pathways and increasing brain efficiency. Think of a garden. Before spring, we pull out weeds and dead growth to make way for the new plants. These new plants then grow even stronger, forming a more mature and robust garden. Of course the plants that grow are the ones that are fertilised and nurtured in much the same way as our neural pathways. Environmental factors play a significant role in helping to determine which networks we fertilise – and which we prune.

Generational changes within the environment have direct effects on neural pruning. Nowadays, developing brains are multitasking more than ever. As a result, these neural pathways are consolidated and 'fertilised', perhaps at the expense of other redundant functions, such as those used in long division.

The last part of the human brain to develop is the prefrontal cortex, or the frontal lobes – the part that sits right at the front of our skull, behind our forehead. According to Bryan Kolb and Ian Whishaw, authors of one of the very first textbooks about contemporary human neuropsychology, the prefrontal cortex is involved in higher functions, such as planning, reasoning, problem-solving, judgement and impulse control. It is thought that the final process of neural pruning occurring in our twenties contributes to the prefrontal cortex's final development. Therefore, until this development occurs, Gen Ys respond to their environment a little differently.

For example, when faced with a relationship difficulty, they are much *more* likely to make emotional decisions that are perhaps interpreted as a little egocentric, and much *less* likely to use empathy and rational problem-solving. In other words, they tend to rely more on their emotional brain (the limbic system), which results in greater impulsivity and reactivity. This is partly why Gen Y has been unflatteringly characterised as 'self-absorbed', 'emotionally reactive' and even 'narcissistic'. A more rational and accurate interpretation is that these young people are still negotiating a number of developmental milestones.

This is also partly why a twenty-three year old who has just finished university cannot really create a detailed map of where they feel they are headed in life. They are still trying to figure out who they are. And trying to answer such a hefty question shouldn't take priority over achieving such critical developmental milestones. Just because it was common practice in the past to put such responsibilities on young people doesn't mean it was the developmentally right thing to do.

In fact it can have negative consequences. Many Gen Ys succumb to social and family pressure to map out their lives in minute detail. Anxiety can then begin to creep in when these young people realise that the path they had set for themselves is not really the path that *they* want to follow. This can then turn into resentment, anger, depression and helplessness if they don't confront and work through it.

As the brain develops into the mid and late twenties, our cognitive functioning in some aspects improves. For example, according to developmental psychologist John Santrock, the dualistic thinking typical of adolescence gives way to multiple thinking, as we begin to understand perspectives other than our own. In other words, we start to realise that the truth is quite subjective. We also begin to think things through, playing out the consequences of our actions and the actions of others in our heads, at times a little too much. This is also the time when we typically switch from acquiring to *applying* knowledge. A perfect example of this is a young person beginning their career after many years of learning and studying.

Professor Timothy Salthouse, director of the Cognitive Aging Laboratory at the University of Virginia, has suggested that, while some aspects of cognitive functioning are developing, others actually begin to decline between our twenties and thirties – specifically, cognitive tasks requiring novel and complex problem-solving (think mathematics!). However, I would suggest that this is possibly due to the fact that once we hit our late twenties, we have modified our environment to reduce cognitive demands and adapted the nature and pattern of our activities to a point where certain cognitive functions (such as those used in solving complex math problems) are no longer necessary.

Think of the ever-increasing number of mobile phone apps, as well as predictive text, spell check and even Google. Advances in technology continue to make a number of cognitive functions completely redundant. These functions are 'pruned' to make way for other functions, such as those used in multitasking and collaboration. Perhaps this is not really about cognitive decline, but rather a sign of cognitive *evolution*.

But what, you might wonder, happens to intelligence as we age, independent of the neural pruning that takes place?

According to John Santrock, at the age of 30, Thomas Edison invented the phonograph, Hans Christian Anderson wrote his first volume of fairy tales and Mozart composed *The Marriage of Figaro*. While the brain is continuing to develop during this time, it can clearly still manage to achieve some extraordinary things. Some believe that this is in part a product of intelligence, or IQ. While that may seem like an obvious conclusion, the waters are little muddier than that. Firstly, as indicated by Kolb and Whishaw, IQ can change over time. This is in part due to normal testing error, brain development and environmental factors. It's also important to remember that conventional IQ tests are very limited in the type of intelligence that they measure; they do not account for creativity or intuition. In fact, IQ tests are really only a measure of *developed skills* rather than native intelligence.

So if it's not about IQ, how can we make sense of these achievements? Well, rather than focus on intelligence, many researchers – including psychologist Dean Simonton at the University of California, Davis – have looked at the point in adult development at which creative production peaks. Although having a high IQ is certainly related to being a creative genius, it is not really *necessary*. In fact, Simonton has indicated that it's more about the structure of IQ: highly creative people are able to spontaneously make large numbers of remote associations between separate ideas. The 'structure' of IQ refers to the structure of the brain mechanisms underlying IQ (general ability), or the way certain parts of the brain communicate with each other.

If we think about what is happening in the brain at this time, the garden is still quite full, with a wide variety of plants and weeds – which means more networks are available. This would certainly provide support to Simonton's theory about highly creative people being able to make multiple associations between ideas, especially if the environment both supports and encourages these ideas. This suggests that now is the time for some Gen Ys to start exploring those creative outlets – before the brain enters its final pruning phase.

Gen Y and relationships

In addition to the changes occurring in their brains, Gen Ys are also maturing and developing both emotionally *and* socially. Once again, this has implications for how they respond to their environment, especially within the context of relationships both with the self and others.

Developmental psychologist Erik Erikson believed that psychosocial development is a lifelong process, and that personality develops in a series of stages. Erikson's theory describes the impact of social experience across the whole lifespan. Each stage is about achieving competence in an area of life. If the individual handles the stage well, he or she will feel a sense of mastery, which is sometimes referred to as ego strength or ego quality. As stated by John Santrock, Erickson proposed that if the stage is managed poorly, the person will emerge with a sense of inadequacy that they then carry through to following stages.

According to Erikson, Gen Ys are currently in the middle of Stage 6 (19 to 40 years old) — intimacy versus isolation. This is when the young adult strives to form intimate, loving relationships with other people. Eventual success leads to strong relationships, while failure results in loneliness and isolation when it occurs in the absence of self-awareness and reflection.

Success at any stage does depend on whether the person has 'mastered' previous stages. Developing a healthy relationship with the self is something Erickson identified as critical before one can move on to developing meaningful relationships with others. If a person does not achieve this, they often base relationships on *idealised* perceptions of what a fulfilling relationship is. The self then becomes something that morphs and changes according to perceptions about what the other person finds desirable.

For example, imagine an 'insecure' 25-year-old female who develops a crush on a much older man. She may begin dressing and talking in a certain way to appear more 'mature' and desirable. She may win her man; however, maintaining this facade will become exhausting after a while. She'll miss her friends, and eventually begin to resent her partner for keeping her away from her former life. The relationship will deteriorate. With a lack of self-awareness and insight, she may place blame on her partner for the demise of the relationship, only to continue to make the same mistakes in her subsequent relationships. The only way she can resolve this inner conflict is to take time out to develop a more secure sense of self.

Erikson believed that, in each stage, people experience conflict that serves as a turning point in development. These conflicts are centred on either developing or failing to develop a psychological quality. The potential for both personal growth and failure is high during these times. The outcome will be determined by whether the person has the insight to be able to reflect on their behaviour and the environment. Self-reflection allows individuals to develop the skills to identify the thoughts and behaviours they may need to change. Without self-reflection, they're more likely to blame external sources – and personal growth is unlikely to occur.

It's easy to see the application of this theory if we think about a typical teenager. Most, if not all, teenagers experience some degree of developmental conflict during their teen years. Some *externalise* this conflict and play it out in their family or school environment. Others *internalise* it, which often contributes to mood or anxiety difficulties. Given that the brain is still developing at this stage, many teenagers need encouragement and support for self-reflection. Furthermore, asking for help can be extremely confronting at a time when identity is developing. For many, it's just not an option. Instead, these young people progress through their teens with ongoing and unresolved conflicts. If we think back to Erickson's theory, the developmental inadequacy that results then becomes the platform from which all other relationships develop.

Personal insecurities, poor communication, poor insight and a lack of empathy are just a few of the issues that manifest when these people begin the search for an intimate partner in their twenties. For some Gen Ys, relationships can become a window to these unresolved inner conflicts. The common experience of 'always attracting Mr or Ms Wrong' is a perfect example of this, as having a trail of unsuccessful relationship experiences is an obvious symptom of inner conflicts being played out in relationships with others. For example, while 'they' may be initiating the hurtful behaviour, 'we' are allowing it to happen. Although it's important to assert healthy boundaries with regard to the behaviour we accept of *other* people, it's equally important to reflect on why *we* allow certain people into our lives. This self-reflection and increased awareness then empowers us to make different choices.

The developmental milestones that form the psychological basis for Gen Y relationships are in many ways no different to the developmental challenges previous generations faced. Understanding these challenges is critical in interpreting how Ys make sense of and respond to their environment. The only way we can begin to develop *realistic* expectations is by understanding these challenges. After all, Gen Y is a generation in the midst of negotiating some pretty major developmental challenges, within a uniquely fast-paced environment.

Gen Y and mental health

In their report on the 2007 Australian National Survey of Mental Health and Wellbeing, Tim Slade, Amy Johnson and their colleagues reported that mental ill-health is the number one health issue facing young Australians. Mental disorders are more prevalent for young people aged 16 to 24 than for any other age group, and affect 26 per cent of young Australians in any year.

While young people today have the highest rates of mental health problems, they are *less* likely than any other age group to seek professional help. The survey found that only 31 per cent of young women and 13 per cent of young men with mental health problems had sought any professional help.

The reasons for this come down to a combination of two factors for Gen Y: over-valuing self-mastery and interpreting help-seeking behaviour as a 'weakness', and an under-developed capacity for self-reflection and insight. Adapting to a fast-paced culture means maintaining an 'outward' focus. One of the consequences of this is that many Gen Ys do not have *time* for self-reflection. As with any skill, practice makes perfect — and so this skill is underdeveloped for many Millennials.

What this means is that while previous generations also experienced limitations in terms of their developing brain and emerging sense of self, today's cultural and social context create unique challenges.

In 2000, Professor Jeffrey Arnett, author of *Emerging Adulthood: The Winding Road from the Late Teens through the Twenties*, identified changes that have occurred over the last several decades for young adults. Specifically, both genders have many more choices than they did several decades ago. Past generations usually followed a predetermined script with clearer role, family and social expectations — which helped them find their path more quickly. Expectations about what the next step should be after completing education are far less clear for Gen Y. The diversity of roles and opportunities available is both a blessing and a curse. Today, it takes much longer for young people to find their own path. This is a process fraught with anxiety for some, especially as they are subjected to the pressure of making a decision and 'committing' to it before they are ready.

One of the other challenges facing Gen Y is the rate at which their environment is changing. Although Millennials are the instigators of change in many ways, many find that they are unable to get off the treadmill. *Keeping up* has become a challenge. Members of previous generations could leave school or work in the afternoon and return the following day with very minimal changes within the peer group. Today, things can be radically different between leaving school at 3 pm and returning the following morning. Social networking, instant messaging and FaceTime have resulted in a fast-moving peer culture. Some members of Gen Y can experience overwhelming anxiety from not having access to technology. In severe cases, the 'fear of missing out' can lead to technology addictions.

The proliferation of technology, especially social networking, has also contributed to a generation that experiments with 'identity' more than previous generations. Facebook, Tumblr, Instagram and countless other sites, apps and technologies are all vehicles for young people to construct identities according to how they want others to see them. Sometimes, this occurs at the expense of being true to the *real* emerging self, especially if a young person has unresolved conflict about 'who they truly are'. In such circumstances, the young person may get caught up in the world of virtual identities – one where they feel forced to keep up with their online persona rather than develop a true sense of self. In some cases, they may even have more than one online identity – each a representation of an aspect of personality seeking approval and validation.

In a society with such unclear expectations, young people are seeking reassurance and validation through a *sense of belonging* now more than ever. Many see technology as one way of achieving this connectedness. The problem occurs when this reassurance presents conflicting ideas or represents something unattainable or unrealistic. In this situation, internal conflict often results.

Consider a young woman whose negative body image is driven by comparisons with airbrushed and digitally enhanced media images. The inner conflict that results from seeking reassurance from unhelpful sources can trigger significant mental health issues, including low self-esteem, anxiety and even depression. In order to resolve this conflict, the young woman must realise her inner strengths – a difficult feat for someone constantly focusing on external sources of reassurance.

When young people are confronted with pre-existing generations' values or expectations, they often experience conflict with parents and other authority figures. Young people who successfully master this have learned to seek reassurance from the inner confidence that comes from collaborating with those who value their individual strengths.

There are several reasons behind the rising rates of mental health problems in our young population. While the developmental challenges Gen Y face are part of the story, they are not the only things that account for these problems. We can discern a lot of differences between this and prior generations in the environment – specifically, how Gen Ys interpret and respond to a fast-paced and diverse culture. Many

Gen Ys see their environment as having abundant opportunities for growth, whereas others find it to be a very difficult and complex world to negotiate.

We know from Erickson that conflict represents an opportunity for growth – *if the conflict is resolved*. However, in order for Gen Ys to identify and capitalise on their individual strengths, they need to know where to look – and to value the strengths once they find them. To do this, they need to learn about the value of self-nurturing and the benefit of self-reflection.

People seeking to understand Gen Y must take the time to understand their inner psyches and adjust expectations accordingly. Parents and educators must aim to understand the unique social and cultural pressures that these young people are exposed to. The best way to do this is to connect with young people around their experiences instead of judging their reaction to them. This means reflecting on personal values and understanding how they influence the development of certain expectations. For example, a father may be frustrated with the fact that his 21-year-old son doesn't want a university education. This frustration comes from his own personal experience, specifically the fact that *his* decision not to attend university has led to him being unable to provide adequate financial support for his family. He feels that he does not want his son to make the same 'mistake'. By understanding the real source of his frustration, this father can then allow himself to connect with his son's experience. From here, he is in a much better position to provide support and guidance to his son.

By developing a greater understanding of ourselves, we can learn to appreciate 'difference' instead of being threatened by what it represents. Advocating and promoting acceptance and embracing diversity will allow us to build a culture in which individuals can experience the freedom to explore inner conflicts and master developmental milestones in their own unique way without judgement.

CHAPTER 4

Educating Y

Charlie Caruso

> Education is simply the soul of a society as it passes from one generation to another.
>
> *Gilbert K. Chesterton*

Generational differences have been around for as long as society has been documented. Even the Bible highlights the presence of intergenerational conflict. I'm sure there are cave paintings that reflect the same.

Once upon a time, there was a generation of parents who were certain that Elvis Presley's unashamed hip-swivelling was most certainly the end of society. In much the same way, parents today struggle to understand why their children might prefer to spend hours on interactive video games instead of playing outside with their friends.

Our world today is very different to that of our parents and grandparents, as has always been the case. So it stands to reason that generations adapt to the changing environment as well as influence the one that they inherit.

In today's digital age of abundant information, it is almost unheard-of to get information from a single source. Educators are facing a reality where those they were traditionally expected to inform are challenging their ideas. Gen Ys are bringing new theories to their education, and alternative expectations about how learning occurs and how and what they expect to be taught. Because Millennials have lived their whole lives surrounded by technology, those charged with their edification are involved in an incessant effort to keep them engaged in learning. As stated by Jenny Devine, author of 'Five Myths and Realities about Generation Y':

> Gen Y are drawn to new information as if it were a bright shiny object. Their connected world gives them ease of access to information and material on demand. The quick access to material leads to a 'cut and paste' methodology.

The need to constantly re-invent teaching methods to include blogs, e-portfolios, web 2.0 tools and more to meet the needs of the digital natives in the classroom is a struggle that Linda B. Nilson, author of *Understanding Your Students and How They Learn*, knows only too well:

> Millennials view higher education as an expensive but economically necessary consumer good, not a privilege earned by hard work and outstanding performance.

> They (or their parents) 'purchase' it for the instrumental purpose of opening well-paying occupational doors on graduation, [causing them to] feel entitled to their degree.

> As many of them did little homework for their good grades through high school, they anticipate the same minimal demands in college. [They often resent] the amount of [work] that [lecturers] assign them [as well as] the standards we hold for their work. Those whose grades slip in college feel their self-esteem threatened and may react with depression, anxiety, defensiveness, and even anger against us. In addition, we bear a lot a 'bad news': that they didn't learn enough in high school to handle college, that knowledge bases are full of holes and unsolved mysteries, that their beliefs and values are subject to question and debate, and that both college and the real world demand that they work and prove their worth.

> Despite the difficulties Millennials may present, this generation can be easy to reach if we make a few adjustments. After all, they have career goals, positive attitudes, technological savvy and collaborative inclinations.

GenY.edu

Growing up in a world dominated by the internet, many of today's students were raised alongside the humble PC. Alison Black, author of *Gen Y: Who They Are and How They Learn*, suggests that Gen Y is far more comfortable using a keyboard than writing in a notebook, and happier reading from a computer screen than from paper.

Gen Ys think and process information differently from previous generations, a proposition that Alison Black has validated in her research which suggests there *is* a physiological difference between digital natives' brains and those of previous generations. Black discovered that the early exposure of infants and young children to various stimuli can affect neurological development. As such, children reared in a media-rich, interactive digital environment tend to think and learn differently because they are physiologically different from those reared in a non-digital environment.

Jenny Devine explores this point further in her previously mentioned article. Devine highlights the fact that, from the moment a student makes the choice to attend university, their life is directed, shaped and transformed by technology:

> They are required to look up course information on the university website [and] apply for a position via an electronic enrolment system. Their phone enquiries are responded to by [an] automated response system and their email queries are met with a highly efficient automated email response. They enrol in the unit of choice via an electronic system and receive an email from their lecturer welcoming them to the unit. When they finally attend their first class and meet a human, they are told to refer to all their unit requirements on the Learning Management System (such as Blackboard), prepare their assignment using the impressive library database and be sure to submit their assignment electronically via a plagiarism detection system (such as Turnitin).

In this microcosm of human experience one can truly appreciate the extent to which Gen Y has been shaped by digital technology – transforming our brains and behaviour. Richard Woods, writer and former editor for the UK's *The Sunday Times*, has stated that digital input might have rewired the human brain – helping it to respond faster, sift out information and recall less. The sheer mass of visual, auditory and verbal information in today's world forces digital natives to edit, sift, and filter more. For example, the brevity of text messaging has spread to email and other communications, compelling many to rewrite English with simpler spelling and symbols. In addition, Gen Y processes information in narrative images, with text supplemented or even supplanted by symbols and visuals.

However, it has been questioned whether the gains in technical expertise and informal knowledge are facilitating short attention spans and negatively impacting students' depth of comprehension. Although Gen Y may be proficient in obtaining data, there is the possibility that they might lack the sophistication to understand and evaluate the information they retrieve.

And then there is Dr Jean Twenge's *Psychology Today* article, titled 'The Revenge of the Insulted Narcissist', which hit on a point that has sat uncomfortably with me for some years. Admittedly, I have some beef with the current standards of our education system. I am often left with the feeling that our education system has been recently 'dumbed down'. Twenge points out in her article that today's students are indeed pumped up by a system that rewards mediocre performance with As. In 1976, only 17 per cent of US high school students graduated with an A average. Now it's 34 per cent. Twenge states:

> Today's college students are significantly different from previous generations. On average, they are overconfident, have high expectations, report higher narcissism, are lower in creativity, are less interested in civic issues, and are less inclined to read long passages of text.

Dr Twenge's article 'Teaching Generation Me' explains that the rapid pace of technological change has further exacerbated the general 'disconnected-ness' that faculty members feel from their students. The faculty want to know how to bridge the generational gap and best understand those they teach. But are these really true generational differences, or simply perceptions biased by age and experience?

Dr Twenge chooses to respond to such questions by turning to empirical data, preferably time-lag data that can separate the effects of age and generation. Her results certainly challenge some of the myths and common misconceptions about Gen Y:

> Entering college students are increasingly likely to believe they are above average in attributes such as academic ability, writing ability, intellectual self-confidence, and drive to achieve … One reason for students' inflated self-perceptions might lie in the more subjective feedback they receive in the form of grades: Twice as many high school students in 2010 (vs. 1976) graduated with an A average. This also means that high school students have been given better grades for doing less work.

Is this kind of 'inflation' meant to protect young people from the cold, hard reality of failure?

This trend seems to involve a complex set of agendas and scenarios. Tertiary institutions need to generate income in order to continue to provide education – which no-one would disagree is a vital service. But does 'lowering the bar' have more to do with 'revenue positioning', and less to do with protecting the feelings of aspiring Gen Y thought leaders?

Whether or not universities around the world are indeed lowering the bar is up for debate. I'm sure there is strong evidence to suggest this is the trend for certain universities, much as I'm sure there will be strong evidence to suggest otherwise for others. How this is affecting Gen Y is unknown, as surprisingly little research has actually been done on it. For Twenge at least, there is evidence to suggest that the various education systems have been (and should be) modified to cater for the 'unique' needs of the Millennials. As she states in her article 'Generational Changes and Their Impact in the Classroom: Teaching Generation Me', it's necessary to alter the approach to education in order to cater for the 'Generation Me students [who] have high IQs, but little desire to read long texts'.

For others, there is a real concern that the introduction of the computer (and, in high school, the internet) into the classroom has radically changed the way people learn. Researcher Betsy Sparrow of Columbia University has looked at the internet's effect on cognition. She found that people were much less likely to remember particular facts if they believed that the information would be accessible to them in the future. The Centre for Information Bureau and the Evaluation of Research paper 'Information Behaviour of the Researcher of the Future' also suggests that despite Gen Ys' familiarity with computer technology, students rely heavily upon search engines, view rather than read, and may lack many critical or analytical skills needed to evaluate the information they find. Perhaps this 'new skill' is nothing more than the symptomatic presentation of the learning evolution.

Furthermore, Dr Twenge notes other generational shifts that she feels may have implications for classroom teaching: 'Scores on a standard measure of creativity have declined, particularly since 1990.'

Such a claim seems to me to be in stark contrast to an ideal commonly associated with Gen Y that paints Ys as 'creative innovators'.

Let's clarify what 'creativity' actually means. Although there are many variations to the description of creativity, for the sake of this discussion let's agree that creativity describes the ability to conceive new ideas. But creativity is still subjective, making it virtually impossible to accurately measure. In contrast, innovation could not exist without the ability to think creatively about the problem the innovation is able to resolve. As Theodore Levitt said, 'Creativity is thinking up new things. Innovation is doing new things'.

So how can members of Y be 'known' for innovation, yet simultaneously not be considered 'creative'? How can one even measure something like creativity?

When I challenged Twenge on this point, she directed me to the research conducted by Kyung Hee Kim, as published in the *Creativity Research Journal* in 2011 – which found, using the Torrance Tests of Creative Thinking (TTCT), that fluency (children's ability to produce ideas) has decreased in young Americans (kindergarten through to sixth graders) since 1990.

Research indicates that children's ability to produce new ideas steadily decreased from 1990 to 1998; scores remained static between 1998 and 2008. What is interesting is that the bulk of Gen Ys were in primary school (kindergarten to sixth grade) from 1990 through to 1998.

The research concludes that younger children are tending to grow up more narrow-minded, less intellectually curious, and less open to new experiences. It's interesting that they say Gen Ys are 'growing up' less creative – as opposed to being born 'less creative'. So what is happening to children as they grow up? In 2006 Sir Ken Robinson, English author, speaker and international adviser on education in the arts, presented a TED talk called 'How schools kill creativity'. Robinson says that children in their natural state are always willing to take a chance. If they are unsure of something, they will usually attempt it anyway, because they're not afraid of getting it wrong.

> What we do know is, if you're not prepared to be wrong, you'll never come up with anything original...And by the time they get to be adults, most kids have lost that capacity. They have become frightened of being wrong. And we run our companies like this. We stigmatise mistakes. And we're now running national education systems where mistakes are the worst thing you can make.

Sir Ken Richardson is right. But what does this mean for Gen Y? I'm not so sure.

I do accept that Gen Y's a new breed of student: a cohort that requires an updated approach to education. I know we're different; I am a Y student myself. But lacking in creativity? #notconvinced.

I still believe Gen Ys are innovators and problem-solvers at heart, and there are many examples of Millennials already applying that innovative spirit to their education. I don't need studies, statistics or academic research to prove that, either. Ys themselves are the best testament!

Take the founders of Zookal, the largest student portal in Australia, providing a variety of service lines that make students' lives easier. Five university friends formed Zookal by pulling together some start-up funding from their parents that they used to buy 300 textbooks in time for the start of first semester in 2011. They planned to rent the books to students and focused on their classmates in the business faculty at the University of Technology, Sydney. This year, Zookal will begin utilising drones to make its deliveries in Australia, with ambitions of bringing the unique, unmanned delivery method to US customers by 2015.

Zookal co-founder and CEO Ahmed Haider discusses the limitless opportunity for innovation in the education 'space':

> There has been more disruption [in education] in the last five years than the previous 50 years. I think a more digital and connected generation will emerge and universities will [become] places to facilitate and spark debate and ideas and the focus will move towards networking and practical experience instead of a theory-based approach with Gen Y at the helm of education.

Skillshare – a global online community where you can learn real-world skills from many incredible teachers – is yet another great example of Gen Y's role in the revolutionary approach to education. Skillshare founder Michael Karnjanaprakorn explains how traditional education is a one-size-fits-all solution that forces people down a predetermined path – and how their approach is different.

> Our mission is simple. Reunite learning with education and make it accessible to every single person on this planet. Anyone can learn anything, at any age, at an affordable cost, anywhere in the world. Learning has no roadblocks, prescribed paths, tests, quizzes, or outdated majors and degrees. It's driven and powered by students. Here, students never 'graduate' because they are lifelong learners. Teachers are passionate. Students stay curious—because curiosity is the compass that leads us to our individual passions.

Gen Ys, like the founders of Zookal, Skillshare and the thousand others like them, will increasingly dominate the workforce and redefine professional work ethics and values. As such, institutions for higher education must redefine the learning landscape. They must concentrate on honing good values and habits and promoting lifelong learning among this generation.

The education game

Like today's students, I grew up in a world of instant gratification. I have little patience for lectures and step-by-step instructions. Compared to my experiences with digital technology, I find traditional teaching methods dull, and constantly crave exciting new approaches to education.

Likewise, besides my first six months as an internal student at university, I have continued my undergraduate degree externally, only heading onto campus for exams. I have always logged online to download lecture notes and assignments, and have only communicated with my tutors via email (and the occasional Skype call). This system has worked for me – for nearly ten years!

If this has been my experience of a 'digital education', what might the future of an education adapted to Gen Y's preferences look like?

Kevin Wheeler, founder and chairman of the Future of Talent Institute, doubts that learning will look at all like we think it will.

> Today's virtual learning [will look] more like what you see at skillshare .com — [a site] where anyone can teach and anyone can learn. Students evaluate teachers and each other. [They see] classrooms as boxes that close you in and limit you. The idea of a structure, a formal design to learning is increasingly foreign, as is the notion of chronological progression through grades — as well as the idea that you need to be a certain age to learn something.

> I doubt future learning, at least the stuff that will be successful, will come in packages. People will learn 'on the fly' as other learners and software interprets and suggests alternatives. And learning experiences will be much more social, video-based and game-associated than we can even imagine. People will learn by experimenting and by being challenged to achieve levels of proficiency. Peers will provide ideas and stimulate creative solutions. Feedback will be immediate.

> The ability to perform will be the basis of further challenges and growth. Games, even non-educational ones, probably are the right idea and teach more than we think.

Games – even 'non-educational ones' – that's the future of learning? Perhaps their popularity with Dr Sheldon Cooper is a clue to their power?

In his book *Everything Bad is Good for You*, author Steven Johnson states that IQs have risen as a result of games and online activities – and that even the process of watching television is more complex and multilayered today than ever before. It requires greater attention spans, better concentration and the ability to hold several plot elements in your mind at the same time.

Such claims are embraced by the countless developers of online brainteasers and other IQ games promising to boost intelligence and improve mental function. But is there tried and tested truth to these promises?

According to lead researcher Randall Engle of the Georgia Institute of Technology, such claims are misleading and only tell part of the story. While games might improve mental dexterity (predominantly where memory is concerned), they do not and cannot improve overall intelligence. The confusion seems to lie in the difference between the definitions of intelligence and memory.

Though improved memory may help a person recall events, information or people, improved intelligence would help a person better understand relationships between items or solve complex problems. So perhaps saying games increase IQs is a bit of a push. That's not to say that online games won't play a major role in the future of education; they have and will continue to do so.

As noted by R. F. Mackay in the article 'Playing to Learn' for the *Stanford Report* in March 2013, games can assist in the development of non-cognitive skills, which are as important as cognitive skills in explaining how we learn and in determining our probability for success. According to James Gee, a professor of literacy studies at Arizona State University, skills such as patience and discipline (which one should acquire as a child but often does not) correlate with success better than IQ scores do. And those non-cognitive skills – that is, not what you know but how you behave – are far better suited to a game context than to a traditional classroom-and-textbook context.

In her paper 'Engaging by Design: How Engagement Strategies in Popular Computer and Video Games Can Inform Instructional Design', Michele D. Dickey says:

> Although the primary purpose of games is entertainment, the underlying design employs a variety of strategies and techniques intended to engage learners in 'gameplay'. Strategies … may differ depending on the game genre, but may include role playing,

narrative arcs, challenges and interactive choices within the game, as well as interaction with other players.

Depending on the genre and individual game, players may be required to analyse, synthesise and use critical thinking skills in order to play and execute moves.

In their paper 'Motivation and Learning Progress through Educational Games', Ulrich Münz and his co-authors noted that instructors face difficulties when teaching complex *theoretical* material to students who are mainly interested in solving *practical* problems. As such, a lack of motivation may impede students' optimal learning. Their research shows how educational games can help to motivate and teach undergraduate university students:

This becomes obvious if we recall that motivation is a cornerstone for good learning. One way to close this gap between theory and practice is educational games.

The use of pedagogically sound interactive digital game-based learning (DGBL) resources has also been explored by Susan Salter and her co-authors in an effort to engage first year biological science students in recalling, linking and applying foundational knowledge and improving their learning outcomes.

The results of their study suggest that their 'creatively designed resource' was effective in enabling a mixed cohort of students to retain, link and extend foundation knowledge. Their study, as published in the journal *Creative Education*, proposed that DGBL resources have a valid role in enabling many students that are considered as digital natives to demonstrate positive learning outcomes by successfully recalling and transferring unit content into new learning domains.

The Millennials' 'special' approach to learning

Gen Y was the first generation to be taught 'computer lessons' or have the ability to study the subject 'IT' — but has the introduction of the computer and internet into the classroom made any difference to student Y when compared to their predecessors? Table 4.1, supplied by Alison Black, author of *Gen Y: Who They Are and How They Learn*, compares the students of today to their parents.

Table 4.1: comparison of Boomer and Gen Y students

1969	2009
Politically more liberal	Politically more conservative or independent
General learning orientation	Vocational/career orientation
Family/self-financed	Government/family/self-financed
Academically prepared	Lacking basic skills
Competitive	Collaborative
Worked and studied alone	Group work, team work
Lack of experience with diversity	Acceptance of diversity, more tolerant
Unsure of self	Assertive and confident
Low debt after college	High debt and defaults on loans after college
Friendships bound by proximity	Friendships not bound by geographical limits
Idealist — any problem can be solved	Cynical — aware of global warming and other world issues but still hopeful
Rejection of organized religion	Growing importance of spirituality and religion
Took responsibility for self	Growth of helicopter parents who hover and assume responsibility for college–age children
Acceptance of institutional structure (i.e., food, dorms, etc.)	More demanding consumers with customer expectations of immediate service
A privilege to attend college	An expectation to attend college; entitlement
Family stability	Family instability
Physically fit	Growing problem of obesity
Rejection of values of parents and society	Sharing values of parents and society
Mentally healthy	Less mentally healthy
Dependent upon note-taking: paper and pencil	Dependent upon technology; digital natives

The comparison seems to paint the picture that there *are* in fact significant differences between Gen Y and Boomer students. As students, are Ys really more assertive and confident despite the fact that we lack the basic skills our 'academically prepared' parents displayed?

Like many other Millennials, I accept that spelling and grammar are not my strong points. There once was a time such limitations might have prevented me from aspiring to be a published author; of course, the fact that you're reading this book proves that this is no longer necessarily the case. But my parents are strong in both.

I never did memorise my times table chart – I never needed to. I grew up with calculators. Did that prevent me from doing well in calculus in high school? Not one bit!

As a Millennial, I don't feel limited by my shortfalls in spelling and grammar. I am not so sure it matters anymore. Spell check is a tool I rely on, and I don't believe it's going anywhere soon.

A study carried out by Adeline Lau and Lian Kee Phya from the University of Management in Malaysia addressed the emergence of Gen Y learners who come to colleges and universities with a new set of characteristics and values. These students will make up a significant part of the future workforce and the dominant social group – and will have a positive impact on it.

The changes in values that they bring will certainly create a significant change across all society. This emerging generation is increasingly calling for a greater say in how society functions, and is vocal about the importance of having their voices heard and accounted for. The study contends that institutions of higher learning play a significant role in transforming a learning landscape that could positively hone the values that Gen Y embraces, and lay the foundation for developing outstanding individuals. In order for this to happen, fundamental changes have to be made to the education system.

The results of this study support the view that teachers must cede control, and instead empower students to play a far more active role in the learning experience. As suggested by Jacqueline Brooks and Martin Brooks in their book *In Search of Understanding: The Case for Constructivist Classrooms*, teachers must allow students to take centre stage in learning, and be willing to abandon familiar practices and adopt new ones.

Teaching strategies must therefore be tailored to students' responses. The focus must be on creating experiences, on triggering curiosity about the world and about how things work. The learning tasks must also be rich, sustainable and complex to provide opportunities for students to develop the desired thinking skills and dispositions.

Teachers themselves must be willing to unlearn and relearn, and to provide an arena for engagement and discovery that trespasses beyond printed text and 'chalk and talk'.

Expect much, Gen Y?

According to Dr Twenge, today's college students are now more likely to say they value becoming very well-off financially and are attending college to make more money. She also labelled them as 'overconfident', with 'high expectations'. But like so many of the characteristics we discussed in chapter 2, these are less specific of Y than really just a basic description of a typical young person.

I don't doubt that members of Gen Y do indeed have high expectations. A great deal of research validates this claim. Most recently, Deloitte's third annual Millennial Survey found that, across the globe, 70 per cent of tomorrow's future leaders may reject what traditional business has to offer, preferring to work independently through digital means. (More on this in chapter 16!) This and other findings in the study point to significant talent challenges facing business leaders if they are to meet the Millennials' expectations. But is having high expectations a bad thing?

Surely Y's tendency to 'dream big' is a critical element in their ability to one day 'achieve big'. So, while I am perplexed as to the concerns about 'high expectations', I admit that they can lead to great disappointment, which could lead to serious challenges as Ys adapt to their realities. But if they keep on dreaming, they might just achieve their dreams.

Aren't drive, hunger and the energy needed to succeed in this 'big bad world' fundamentally derived from high expectations of attaining happiness and fulfilment? Isn't that what everyone wants, expects, demands from us? Isn't that what our future employers look for?

I think so. I think having high expectations is great! So long as your feet are firmly planted on the cold hard ground of reality.

Educating Y in the workplace

The challenge of engaging Gen Y beyond what has traditionally been expected is not isolated to traditional educational institutions. Gen Ys' employers face this same need for developing Millennials' knowledge base.

Ryan Gibson, founder of Generationy.com and a contributor to this book, believes industry must find the sweet spot between bringing home the bacon and facilitating innovation. His experience in 'traditional' working environments made Ryan realise that workplace learning must be effectively enforced and suitably planned:

> Some of the best knowledge and ideas [come to light] in the evening, after work, [when I'm] browsing Twitter and finding inspiration for future projects. Unfortunately the demands of life mean this isn't a structured day-to-day or week-on-week activity. It's largely impulsive.

But should business leaders be self-educating—and proactively encouraging *employees* to self-educate?

Ryan maintains that 'the future of business' is where companies begin to facilitate innovation by inspiring their employees to learn by formalising the learning process, making it part of a job role to learn and develop. The changing nature of work, production and processes due to globalisation has focused attention on the relationship between workplace learning and organisational performance.

Thus far, some companies have begun to implement 'formalised learning' by giving time back to employees for formal education. One company in particular is HighSpeedTraining, an e-learning course provider with a smart, agile approach to developing the business. Technical director Dan Jordan has begun this formalised learning process himself after fearing he wasn't moving forward with the demands of owning a fast-paced online business. He realised that 'the most efficient way of learning for me is to purchase a book on the subject'. His unique situation in growing a business led him to realise 'many of the skills that enable you to start a business are not the skills that can help you to grow one'.

After doing some research, Dan realised that most of the books on which modern management theory is based were written by a guy called Peter Drucker. He read them in his spare time and found that:

> ...being separated from the business [allowed me to] think much more clearly about what I wanted to achieve. I always came back with a sizeable list of actionable items that made a good difference.

Unfortunately, this motivation never lasted very long. Even after reading, he 'jumped straight back into programming without checking the notes [he] had made'. Eighteen months later he found those notes, which he had done nothing with.

Dan realised that if only he'd actually done something with this knowledge, he'd have faced a lot fewer problems than he did. So he decided to formalise the process of learning about and thinking about the business, rather than just working in it. 'Each Monday I stay at home and read something from the list of books I keep, while making notes about what I want to achieve that week.'

Dan's story highlights a common opportunity cost facing the vast majority of workplaces that haven't yet implemented any formalised workplace learning or development strategy. Employees are being under-utilised. Companies are not activating their knowledge and potential in a beneficial, revenue-producing way.

According to research conducted by Bersin for Deloitte, companies are spending increasingly less on learning and development. This drop is largely due to the emergence of 'social learning' – an area where, according to Bersin, large businesses have tripled their spending in the past five years. So what exactly *is* social learning? And how does it work?

Social learning is a derivative concept of Albert Bandura's social learning theory, which posits that learning is a cognitive process that takes place in a social context and can occur purely through observation or direct instruction, even in the absence of motor reproduction or direct reinforcement.

The process can be extremely effective when incorporated into a more structured program, such as combining a formal course with a learner discussion forum. In addition, high-impact organisations are creating employee networks, connecting novices to experts through expertise directories, and sharing knowledge through communities of practice.

Social learning theory is applied in the workplace to encourage employees to help manage or lead themselves. It's one of the many factors the Gen Y labour force is looking at when appraising prospective workplaces. Innovative companies are using methods like these and others instead of a 'pay reward' to attract, motivate and retain Y personnel.

In a press release about their recent study, lead analyst Karen O'Leonard of Deloitte Consulting LLP pointed out that both US and worldwide organisations have to commit more money to developing internal talent and building the desired skills for competitive advantage. Formalised learning has so many benefits to business: it enhances innovation and education, keeps employees engaged, and will hopefully prove to be a more enticing proposition for potential Gen Y employees.

As Mark Goldenberg points out in his report 'Employer Investment in Workplace Learning in Canada', the demands of the knowledge economy and the transformational nature of information technology mean that skill requirements will continue to rise and will change constantly. Collectively, these constraints point to the imperative of investing in the skills, knowledge and talents of today's workforce.

Yet in an era in which growth is the ubiquitous strategy and rapid evolution in technology, industry and market conditions is constant, learning leaders are being confronted with more responsibility than ever before.

There is a slew of reasons industries hesitate to invest in workplace learning: limitations of time and money, lack of information firms about where to get training and how to organise and provide it, as well as a lack of knowledge of what training or approach is effective for their industry and their needs.

Ryan Gibson agrees that the frequency of formalised learning is completely dependent on the sector, the speed of change and the business type.

> Fast-paced, changing industries should be looking toward implementing a learning process that enables them to keep abreast of new developments, ideas and innovation that could actively enhance the business.

Labelling workplace learning as simply 'too hard' will not attract Gen Ys. The organisations that will thrive and those that will be left behind when the Baby Boomers finally retire and the Gen Y cohort dominates the labour force will be determined by how quickly businesses adjust their current service offerings with respect to employees' needs and wants going forward.

Be it in the classroom or in the workplace, Gen Ys are facing a multitude of new environmental pressures when it comes to their education. As such, they're forcing those around them to come up with new ways to engage them, educate them and remove the barriers to accessing education.

These reforms will not be easy. They'll require an investment of time and resources that should not be underestimated. However, the return on this investment is potentially invaluable.

As Gen Y, and the generations beyond, increase their share of the workforce, professional characteristics and work ethics will be redefined, as should be the educational system that informs and moulds them.

CHAPTER 5

Reading into Y

Rob Kaldor

It does not do to dwell on dreams and forget to live.

Albus Dumbledore

Did Dumbledore know he was referring to Generation Y? His message to embrace the 'now' seems incredibly apt for the Millennial generation. The literature phenomenon known as Harry Potter not only traversed the era of Y; it was in fact a companion piece to the generation itself.

Gen Y has a very interesting perspective on literature and reading. They were born in an era before technology had saturated society, so their upbringing involved reading via a traditional narrative – no different to previous generations. Their initial reading experience pre-dates the internet, ebooks and smart phones.

However, the way they imbibe content has changed radically as Millennials have grown. Although weaned in an analogue era of traditional story structure and plot lines, their time also coincides with the technology revolution. The rollout of the World Wide Web and social media, as well as well as ebooks, ereaders and smart phones and tablets, has drastically changed the content-creation and -consumption landscape. Being at the cutting edge of this technology change, Gen Y has not only taken these new technologies on board; it has in fact steered the older generations towards them as well.

Literature has made countless attempts to change form in an effort to become more interactive and less dependent on traditional narrative structure. Probably the most famous example of recent times is the 'Choose Your Own Adventure' series (CYOAS). This series of children's books was at its peak in the late 1980s and was very popular – coincidentally during the period that Ys were reading them. This new model of literature allowed for the same book to be read in many ways, with the reader determining the pathway by making choices at the end of each chapter. As a precursor to hyperlinked books and later interactive books, the CYOAS books sat somewhere between literature, role-play and gaming. It offered classic 'what if' scenarios and encouraged repeat reads. These books were still popular as the first generation of Ys began to graduate from 'a...a...apple' to 'OMG'.

The influence of the CYOAS on Gen Ys' reading habits cannot be underestimated. The post-toddler Ys were just getting used to choices and different approaches to the traditional narrative structure. CYOAS' 'you'-centered choices have been cited as an influence in numerous games and media that followed the series. The series is credited with the heightened popularity of role-playing games, including Dungeons and Dragons. The interactive fiction community has also credited the CYOAS as being a major influence.

In addition to its mainstream popularity, numerous educators have cited the CYOAS as a uniquely effective method for helping students learn to read. The series has documented popular appeal for the reluctant reader due to its interactivity. The CYOAS has also been used specifically in technology lesson plans in elementary, high school and college curricula, as well as in professional development tools.

It's important to note that, as the series progressed, the length of the plot threads increased. Consequently, the number of endings decreased. The earliest books often contained nearly 40 possible endings, while later titles contained as few as eight. In total, over

260 million CYOA books were published in more than 40 languages, making it the fourth best-selling children's series of all time.

Themes include swashbuckling adventure, travel, mystery, fantasy, world culture, ancient civilisations, scary creatures and space. The background for ebooks, interactive books, gaming and interactivity was all set up by this series, for this growing generation attracted to interactivity by PCs and the questioning of the narrative form. And then along came Harry...

J.K. Rowling's seven-book series about a young wizard named Harry Potter had a profound effect on Gen Y. Hundreds of millions of Millennials grew up fascinated by the world of Harry Potter and his comrades. As a book series it engaged many generations, but Gen Y took this fascination to the next level as fans formed communities. The books and the movies broke publishing and box office records. Fans created a Harry Potter social network called Mugglespace. It would be hard to find a member of Gen Y that has not been touched by Harry Potter. To put things in perspective, more than 450 million copies of books in the series have been sold throughout the world. The books are available in 73 languages, and the series has been published in more than 200 territories. What cannot be gauged is the buzz around the books, the characters and, of course, the movies. The Harry Potter series was the first series where the publisher's embargoes included security attachments.

When examining the importance of Harry Potter to Gen Y, it is worth going into the relationship between equivalent influencers on previous generations. Generation X's relationship with the Star Wars movies has led to Jedi being classified as a religion in the Australian census. *Star Trek* had a similar impact. From a literature perspective, *Catcher in the Rye* and *Lord of the Rings* had an ongoing effect on the Baby Boomers (and following generations). Research by Anthony Gierzynski and Kathryn Eddy in their book *Harry Potter and the Millennials: Research Methods and the Politics of the Muggle Generation* have found that Potter aficionados are generally more accepting of difference; that is, they have a more liberal and tolerant political attitude towards others. They are more supportive of egalitarian goals, and opposed to violence and torture – which they see primarily as the tools of the antagonists throughout the series. Gierzynski and Eddy argue that this series is a key element that shaped the Millennials' political prerogatives. Other 'books of the generation', such as the Twilight and Hunger Games series, back up this overriding liberal attitude.

The other main change to occur during Gen Y's era is the emergence of ebooks. Ebooks appeared on the web, were easily shared and stored on a hard drive or storage disk, and quickly began to proliferate. Early ebooks were written about specific interest topics, and tended to have a technical focus. This fractured market of independents and specialty authors resulted in a lack of consensus on the best way to package, sell, or read ebooks. Numerous formats and platforms emerged, some supported by major software companies (like Adobe's PDF format), and others supported by independent and open-source programmers.

Multiple readers naturally followed multiple formats, most of them specialising in only one and thereby fragmenting the ebook market even more. The result was a lack of an overriding message to the public regarding ebooks, which kept them from becoming a mainstream product.

The moment that pushed ebook readers into the mainstream was the day in 2008 that the US's richest woman, talk show host Oprah Winfrey, announced the Amazon's Kindle digital-book reader was her 'new favorite device'. Winfrey called the ereader 'life changing'. As an avid book reader with a following of millions, Oprah's influence cannot be underestimated. Her book club recommendations have turned obscure authors into bestsellers.

The Kindle's revolutionary reading interface, backed by the power and range of Amazon, led to year-on-year increases in uptake. It was estimated that by 2012 the ereader market equated to nearly 25 million annual sales of units. Interestingly this is the year that uptake of devices peaked, as the rollout of tablet devices such as iPads and the explosion of the app market allowed readers to use their tablets to read books. Eventually publishers agreed on formats and a pricing methodology. Ebooks now represent over 15 per cent of the total book market, and Kindle, Apple, Google,

Nook (Barnes & Noble's ereader), Kobo and Sony all have stakes in the ebook markets.

Ebooks have also reflected two of Gen Ys' typical traits – a desire to be heard (via self-publishing) and a shorter attention span (ebooks tend to be shorter and more episodic).

Amazon Kindle Direct Self-Publishing – along with online self-publishing sites like Smashwords and Lulu – offer authors the opportunity to get their unique perspective out to the public easily and efficiently. An extension of blogging, self-publishing via ebooks (and physical books if there is a following for the ebook) offers the opportunity for voices to be heard. The ebook form is also appropriate for shorter fiction.

As keen up-takers of technology, members of Gen Y have not only embraced ebooks; they now have a new book category that's specifically ebook-focused and aimed straight at them. The New Adult fiction (NA) category gives readers content expectations, but it does not dictate genre-based criteria. A novel is categorised as NA if it encompasses the transition between adolescence (a life stage often depicted in Young Adult fiction) and true adulthood. Protagonists mostly fall between the ages of 18 and 26. NA characters are often portrayed experiencing rites of passage, including going to college, living away from home for the first time, being deployed by the military, working in apprenticeships or a first steady job, engaging in their first serious relationship, and so on. Common themes in NA include identity, sexuality, race, alcohol abuse, drug abuse, bullying, empowerment, familial struggles, loss of innocence, fear of failure, and so on.

Two leading NA book series have dominated the genre. The Hunger Games and Twilight series have all of the classic NA traits. The category has often been summarised as 'Harry Potter meets *50 Shades of Grey*'.

The Millennials have not only traversed the analogue–digital precipice with ease; they have embraced reading and literature in a way that has changed it forever. From zombies, wizards and ebooks, Generation Y has been part of the biggest increase in reading in history. Interactivity now takes place via social media and smart phones. Already the first Twitter novels are starting to appear as the form shortens.

The one certainty in this ever-changing landscape is that leaders from each generation will come to the forefront. If the world leaders from Generation Y follow the path of Harry Potter, then times will continue to be fascinating, glorious and unpredictable. We can only hope that Harry Potter's sensitivity, morality and empathy is manifested in tomorrow's leaders.

CHAPTER 6

Media Gen Y

Charlie Caruso

> The actions you take today not only impact you; they influence generations. Every matter matters for eternity.
>
> *Dillon Burroughs*

For the intents and purposes of this chapter, I have used BusinessDictionary.com's definition of media, which states:

> Communication channels through which news, entertainment, education, data, or promotional messages are disseminated. Media includes every broadcasting and narrowcasting medium such as newspapers, magazines, TV, radio, billboards, direct mail, telephone, fax, and internet.

It would be safe to say that Generation Y has been saturated by media, and inundated by its influence since birth.

Colour TV is all we have known. We've always had the radio, comics, magazines, newspapers and a home telephone. Most of us had mobile phones in our pockets from high school or college (despite the fact that they weighed and looked more like bricks than mobile devices). And as we've grown up, we have learned to adjust to the ever-changing ways in which we consume content, digital or otherwise.

We were exposed to LPs because our parents cherished their 'barely touched' Beatles and Rolling Stones vinyls. We listened to cassette tapes in our parents' cars when we were young, and we will be the last generation to understand the value of the lead pencil for unwound tapes. We grew up watching Disney films on VHS, yet embraced the DVD when it allowed us to skip whole *chapters* and didn't require us to keep our fingers down on fast-forward until we reached the part of the movie we wanted. And it is this transition into 'efficient' consumption that has become synonymous with changing times and the need for speed.

Members of our generation aren't exactly known for being patient; we haven't had to be. We no longer wait months for our favourite overseas sitcom to come to our screens; it's 'fast-tracked'. We now have the ability to pause, record – even fast-forward past the ads on live TV! We can buy things online with the click of a button, without even having to leave our homes or wait in line at a store. We can get movies 'on demand' – through platforms like Apple TV – while sitting comfortably on our couches, saving us a trip to the video rental store (remember those?).

And we're constantly aware of all the products and services available to us. As a generation, we have been exposed to a *lot* of advertising. The average 18 year old in today's world would have seen 350 000 commercials in their lifetime – with about 100 000 being for beer.

I could spend the rest of this book detailing the extensive statistics about Gen Y's unprecedented media consumption, but the message is: Millennials have consumed and continue to devour a *lot* of media content. One topic that does require more attention is the ways this media content has changed – the most confronting transformation of them all.

From Babe to 'Bugger' ... then Britney to Bieber?

Back in 1999, there was the 'bugger' ad from New Zealand. Most Kiwi or Australian readers will know what I am referring to immediately. For those who don't, it's worth a Google. At the crux of it, a lot of things go wrong, and everyone (including a dog) says 'bugger'. In fact, that is the *only* thing that is said.

At the time, this ad sent the complaints hotline at the Advertising Standards Authority red-hot. Back then, the term 'bugger' was thought unacceptable and it caused offense on TV. Keep that reaction in your mind. Now, go watch your latest music video show. You know the kind that kids these days are eating their cereal to? Because somehow we no longer have the need to keep the R rated clips for the adults at midnight. It's pretty much porn... isn't it?

Where was sex on TV for Baby Boomers when they were growing up? Well, besides the fact there was barely TV at all – what they were exposed to was programs showcasing wholesome family entertainment. They grew up watching programs like *Gilligan's Island*, *Little House on the Prairie*, *Popeye* and *The Brady Bunch*.

Gen Xers – the so-called 'MTV generation' – experienced the emergence of music videos, the new wave, punk rock and Madonna. What they witnessed was much less graphic than what the youth of today see on a regular basis.

Before I go any further, I'd like to inform you – I'm no prude. I don't necessarily want to see what some of today's celebrities are offering up, but that's what remotes are for – right?

Wrong. Melinda Tankard Reist – Canberra author, speaker, Fairfax Media columnist and media commentator, blogger and advocate for women and girls – corrected me here, and was right in doing so. Melinda is well known for her work on the objectification of women and the sexualisation of girls, and works to address violence against women and is a co-founder of Collective Shout, an advocacy group for a world free of sexploitation (www.collectiveshout.org). And she has the following to say:

> They're hardly doing it in private. It's part of mass-market saturation of limited and stereotyped messaging about [what] women are good for. It's not just the physical 'seeing', it's also lyrics which celebrate male domination ... You don't need to be a 'prude' to be concerned about this — and it's not just children who are impacted. We all have to live in a porn culture.

Melinda is correct. None of us should have to feel like we need to prove we're 'not prudes' and avoid protesting the portrayal of women in the media. I find it offensive that children are constantly exposed to inappropriate lyrics and images. There seems to be no limit on the sexualisation of *everything* nowadays.

According to a new report in *The Archives of Paediatrics and Adolescent Medicine*, one in three popular songs contains explicit references to drug or alcohol use. The research found that the substance use depicted in popular music is frequently motivated by peer acceptance and sex, and it has highly positive associations and consequences.

Of course, most of us are aware of this. We can all see the drastic change in the way media manufactures and promotes its content. My concern is just this: that we're being desensitised. And I'm not alone.

Melinda Tankard Reist spends a considerable amount of her time presenting 'reality checks' to parents, educators and the general public about the recent trends in the objectification of women in media.

I show over 200 images to people of the way women are represented, the kind of games or toys offered to girls—and it honestly shocks them. I have noticed a shift over the past couple of years. It's not enough to present women violently; the next step has been to show women enjoying the violence, wanting it, inviting it even.

The vast majority of people [to whom] I present have no idea how bad things are in the media. Most admit that they had stopped noticing. The cumulative total of all of these things put together forms content that is so common, so entrenched, so embedded in mainstream culture that it does become normal. And that's what I am working hard for, to get people to start noticing again—to start waking up.

I asked Melinda what she thinks some of the biggest challenges we're facing as a society are, due to the media's proliferation of sexual images:

[I'm primarily] concerned with how entrenched and extreme the objectification of women and the sexualisation of girls has become.

People have become used to such images dominating the public space and have started to think that it's normal.

As a result, girls have very limited and stereotyped ideas about themselves, their bodies, their relationships about sexuality. Boys are being socialised and conditioned to think about girls existing for one purpose: to provide male sexual gratification and pleasure…Whether it's in music, advertising, magazines, TV and film, pretty much everything is a medium or conduit for these limited messages.

This is a stark contrast to the portrayal of women throughout the Baby Boomer years. The representation of women in the notoriously misogynist advertisements of the 1950s and 1960s depicted women as sub-human, not intelligent, belonging in the home and as mere servants to their husbands. This makes a significant contrast to the D&G advertisement depicting a woman pinned to the ground by the wrists by a bare-chested man, with other men in the background looking on, which, to many, suggested a gang rape scenario (and which was been banned in many countries – rightly so!). The ad (easily Google-able) offended the dignity of the woman, as she was portrayed in a degrading manner, immobilised and subjected to a man's will. It was deeply offensive – it was disgusting.

Women who grew up with the 1950s misogynist attitude, who were told that women couldn't work, fought hard to defend their position in the world – and in many ways won that battle.

More recently the lines of the battlefield shifted to much darker territory, and the internet changed the number of combatants we had to fight. Not only are the images that represent gender roles infused with adversely sexual and often violent messages, the internet has brought us a growing problem that relates to the consumption of a media that previously had been well restricted – particularly to young children. Pornography is rapidly becoming one of the single most serious issues facing young people today. Gen Ys might have been the last generation to have escaped exposure to explicit pornography as children. However, our younger siblings have not been as lucky, and nor will our children. For those of you doubting the seriousness or extent of this issue, I am afraid you have been hiding under a rock that has been supplied to you by the mass media, which has chosen not to cover this issue at the level it deserves.

Melinda gave me her thoughts on this matter recently:

> The rise of the internet and the exposure to internet pornography [is another huge problem]. The average age of first exposure to pornography is eleven, [and] new research [has told us] that this is really shaping [both boys' and girls'] idea of sex and sexuality. I've heard disturbing stories from girls of how boys are expecting the 'porn experience'—the sexual activities they are watching online. And they're not asking or necessarily seeking consent to perform these acts...and there is little in the way of education to correct these assumptions of 'normal' sexual behaviour. And because those acts are so normalised in pornography, girls are left thinking 'there must be something wrong with me' when they don't want to perform them.

If you're reading this and *still* doubting the scale or seriousness of the issue, then ask your child or younger sibling if they have ever watched porn. If they tell you the truth, you will be shocked.

But it's not all doom and gloom and there are some rays of light; Melinda did point out that there are educational programs in development that attempt to help school students deal with exposure to pornography and explore respect-based relationships. But they are mostly in their infancy, and those committed to this topic are few and far between. Also, some practical solutions have recently been offered up to parents in terms of de-risking their children's exposure to inappropriate adult content on IOS devices. Apps like curbi, a breakthrough parental control technology, provide parents with a simple platform that, once installed, passes every website a child visits through a content filter. Curbi, and other solutions like it, are some of the few examples of the recent attempts to tackle this escalating issue – but we are a long way off an enduring and absolute resolution to this highly complex social issue.

Small changes and small efforts by the committed few are happening at a lag, and simply aren't enough. Besides the few individuals like Melinda, there's no action plan in place for the children being affected today – not to mention the ones who have already been over the past several years. If we take another 10 to 15 years to actually get our backsides into gear and address this issue, we'll have missed an entire generation of children! An entire generation of children who have already been exposed to this reality … a reality that has been warped in regards to perceived ideals of male and female roles, female equality, respect for men and women alike – because they are the furthest thing from what we portray in the media. We seem to expect our children to know what normal sexual behaviour is, what respect is, but we're hardly giving them evidence of these roles and ideals.

Instead we give them Miley Cyrus and Justin Bieber. We give them smart phones with unlimited access to the internet, and TVs and computers in their rooms. We hack their Facebook accounts (the ones we know of) to make ourselves feel like we are 'monitoring the situation'. We chastise young girls for trying to live up to the ideals that the media portray – the media we continue to consume and fail to condemn in any real way. Even in the cases where this hasn't directly affected Gen Y, it will affect our younger siblings, and our children – now or in the future. If Y is the generation of social change, than this should be one of the most important topics on our social agenda.

Our governments and social institutions have let us down. Allowing the advertising and media worlds to 'regulate' their own standards is absurd, and protects no-one. We can, however, do the work they haven't. The collective cohort of Gen Y is the best positioned to adequately tackle such issues. As a generation, we have some pretty good heads on our shoulders.

The media of Y

As Australian demographer and social commentator Bernard Salt previously mentioned, Gen Y is the most highly educated generation to date. Millennials are cynical about the images and messages promoted by the media, and are sceptical about media conglomerates. We're also less likely to simply believe what we read.

Adrian Cosstick, business manager at Maxus Australia – one of the fastest growing media agency networks – poignantly sums up this cynicism towards advertisements:

> Young people today have been marketed to since they were newborns because cartoons are made to sell cereal. [Consequently], they have the most sophisticated bullshit detectors of all time. The only way to circumvent that … is not to bullshit.

Because Gen Ys have always been exposed to advertising, we had to build our own protective mechanisms. Adrian is right on the money in terms of the devices we've developed to protect ourselves.

So I feel we've developed some perspective. We know (more or less) what is acceptable behaviour, and the difference between MTV porn and normal sexual behaviour. The majority of Gen Ys are smart enough to read between the lines. It's only a matter of time before those who haven't jumped on the cynicism bandwagon read one of the many thousands of social media pages and websites popping up around the world that are offering a new voice, a more transparent point of view – and asking the questions that previous generations did not have the opportunity to so effortlessly do.

These sites *do* ask questions, and their creators *are* tomorrow's leaders. We are embarking on a new age for mass communications, and for once they're not being wholly manipulated by the media conglomerates. I'm going to give some of these sites a shout out…because I feel they deserve it. Whether you're a Gen Y or Gen something-else, they provide a valuable insight into the psyche of the next generation – and it's worth taking note, and appreciating what's making our cohort tick.

Upworthy

With posts that have titles like 'See Why We Have an Absolutely Ridiculous Standard of Beauty in Just 37 Seconds', Upworthy is social media with a mission that is making important content 'as viral as a video of some idiot surfing off his roof'.

www.upworthy.com

New Statesman

This is Britain's leading weekly political, cultural and current affairs magazine, which has been celebrated for its progressive politics, boldness, independence and scepticism.

www.newstatesman.com

The Representation Project

This project is a movement that uses film and media content to expose injustices created by gender stereotypes, and to shift people's consciousness towards change.

www.therepresentationproject.org

Collective Shout

This grassroots campaigning movement speaks out against the objectification of women and the sexualisation of girls in media, advertising and popular culture.

www.collectiveshout.org

TEDx

If you're looking for inspiration, motivation and education – TEDx is the place to go. TED is a nonprofit organisation devoted to Ideas Worth Spreading, and began as a four-day conference in California over 26 years ago. TED has quickly become THE destination for world's leading thinkers and doers who give the talk of their lives in under 20 minutes.

www.ted.com

Wikileaks

Understandably, this is a contentious inclusion; yet I feel it's an important one. Wikileaks represents the changing demand for transparency that resonates with Gen Y. The ethics, moral or otherwise, around releasing confidential documents and information to the mass public is open for debate. There is doubtlessly an issue with any individual or organisation assuming the role of gatekeeper. Yet governments already hold that power and position, and I'm not sure they're doing such a great job at it.

www.wikileaks.org

Anonymous

This is a loosely associated international network of activist and 'hacktivist' entities. The group became known in 2004 for a series of well-publicised stunts, and distributed denial-of-service (DDoS) attacks on government, religious and corporate websites. Broadly speaking, Anons oppose internet censorship and control, and the majority of their actions target governments, organisations and corporations that they accuse of censorship. Anons were early supporters of the global Occupy movement and the Arab Spring. In 2012, *Time* magazine gave Anonymous the title of one of the '100 most influential people' in the world.

www.anonnews.org

The media revolution

Sites like those just mentioned send a clear message: The revolution is coming, and Gen Y seems to be leading the pack. The time when our generational predecessors paid for the privilege of consuming the media dished out to them will become akin to the era when prisoners actually paid to stay behind bars.

No longer will Millennials be spoon-fed sloppy journalism mixed with the agendas of scheming editors, and accept it for truth. The sites listed above have given us platforms to meet up, vent and to share the truth and better communicate stories. I believe we are on the brink of a media revolution.

Yes, I work in the media industry — and I love it because I have come to work in this industry on my own terms. It's a new phenomenon where disruptive media models are tracking power and influence – and, to me, it sings the same song my beloved Bob Dylan sang all those years ago: the times are a-changing.

The consolidation of bulk media outlets under one owner is a clear impediment to a free and independent press. And despite the fact that this has been the primary media business model for the last few decades, it's clear that this approach is no longer working. The internet and the escalating battle for 'face time' has forced the entire media industry to re-think its ancient (and previously highly successful) market-share strategies.

Consumers in today's digital age have more power – and we know it. We are demanding change through our actions. By choosing to consume less of what traditional platforms offer us, we are instead making independent decisions and consuming *what* we want, *when* we want to and *how* we choose to view, read and listen to it.

Consider the uptake of Netflix, an American provider of on-demand internet streaming media, which gained 2.33 million American streaming subscribers in the fourth quarter of 2013 (to total 33.1 million US subscribers) – implying year-over-year growth of nearly 14 per cent. According to eMarketer's latest estimate of media consumption among adults, the average time spent with digital media per day will surpass TV viewing time for the first time this year. The most noticeable growth area is mobile media consumption – scary news for the media heavyweights of the world.

We live in a world with an intense amount of media clutter. As a result, Gen Ys have grown accustomed to approaching media at a surface level only – simply to keep our heads above the water. The increasing prevalence of multi-screening behaviours has encouraged Gen Y (and Gen everyone else, for that matter) to be more passive consumers, and has shortened our already-short attention spans. Traditionally, newspapers, TV and radio had to sell advertising so they could pay (poorly) for the journalism used to form their content. When these same outlets moved to online distribution, their advertising revenue was weakened. If consumers continue to consume more media content online—and at the current levels we are—there is less market share, and, therefore, less revenue, for the traditional media platforms.

Another brick in the (pay) wall

It seems one of the media giants' initial defensive strategies has been to sack a load of their journalists in an effort to reduce costs. The obvious problem with this, of course, is that they are in the business of *creating engaging content* that consumers *want* to buy and consume. They supplemented their incomes by placing adverts around that content. If they get rid of all of the decent journalists writing that content, then they won't have decent content to advertise around—and those advertising dollars will simply disappear.

So some of these traditional outlets have started sharing their stories. If you browse news content online, or even in the physical papers, you might have noticed this new trend to 're-purpose' content from other newspapers. Unfortunately, people get tired of reading the same story over and over. That's not news; that's recycled words.

Some have introduced pay walls in an effort to secure revenue for their content. In February 2013, Jack Matthews, CEO of Fairfax Media Limited, one of Australia's largest media companies, presented to the constituents attending the Australian Broadcasting Summit (myself included) their latest, greatest defence strategy: making consumers pay for their articles.

I'll admit it—I sat there and quietly sniggered.

I wondered what exactly made Fairfax's content *so superior* to all the other online news content providers that consumers would *pay* to access their content.

I sniggered because I hadn't expected the 'big five' to follow Fairfax's lead, all putting up pay walls. But I'm glad they did. I support paying journalists to write good content. If consumers want quality content for free forever, then they are dreaming. Professional journalism is a vital pillar of our society; we need to fight for and protect it – that means we as consumers have to pay for it.

There is doubtlessly logic behind the notion of pay walls. As consumers, we get to choose which media outlet's content we value most, and can then opt to pay its creators. The good news for the media industry is that pay walls seem to have worked, and in some part are recouping content creation expenses. But it's not the miracle cure – far from it.

In August 2013, the *San Francisco Chronicle* removed its pay wall after only four months, with many more outlets expected to follow suit. This only added fuel to the growing speculation that the end for media pay walls may be near.

But it's not all bad news. The quick to act – those who position themselves to leverage the latest trends in the media industry – will be the first to benefit. These include Gen Ys like Rakhal Ebeli, a former journalist and presenter who founded Newsmodo after having seen a rapid shift in the news landscape first hand. After more than a decade of working with one of Australia's highest-rating broadcasters, Rakhal is of the new breed of media leaders. He developed Newsmodo to facilitate new opportunities for freelance journalists in the media industry:

> The global news landscape is shifting and there are new ways that freelancers can position themselves to maximise their potential in this market, which is shifting rapidly in their favour.

Newsmodo is not alone. Look at the impact and growth of sites like oDesk and Freelancer and you will see that change is upon us. In late 2013 these two largest online marketplaces for freelancers announced their intention to merge, making the 'freelancing' model hot property right now.

'Together, [our] companies have done $2 billion in a market that's more than $422 billion', says oDesk CEO Gary Swart. 'We're not even scratching the surface of the disruption that's ripe for the 1.0 way of working.'

Breaking (up with) news

With so much disruption in this area and only one chapter in this book to discuss it, I thought I might briefly touch on one aspect of the media business that has been disrupted more completely than any other: the concept of 'breaking news'.

Mathew Ingram, senior writer at GigaOm.com, recently wrote a post titled 'You Can't Play a New Media Game By Old Media Rules' where he commented:

> Just as television devalued the old front-page newspaper scoop, the web has turned breaking news into something that lasts a matter of minutes — or even seconds — rather than hours. If your business is to break news, your job is becoming harder and harder every day.

Ingram points out that breaking news has been disrupted because of social media — specifically, Twitter. The disappearance of Malaysia Airlines flight MH370 in March 2014 provided yet another example of how powerful Twitter, and other platforms like it, is in times of disaster, and how it is changing the way media is produced, distributed and consumed. User-generated pictures or video clips shot from the handy iPhone regularly lead television bulletins and feature on the front pages of newspapers around the world.

A 2009 report by Nic Newman for the Reuters Institute for the Study of Journalism focuses on the rise of social media and its impact on mainstream journalism. The research concluded that social media and user-generated content (UGC) have fundamentally changed the nature of breaking news due to their contribution to the compression of the 'news cycle', which has put more pressure on editors over what to report and when to report it. It seems that news organisations have responded by abandoning attempts at 'breaking news', instead focusing on being the best at 'verifying' and curating news content.

Conversely, the Pew Research Center examined the role that news plays in social media and found that Redditors — that is, individuals using Reddit, a social news and entertainment website where registered users submit content in the form of links or text posts — are the most news-obsessed people around. Sixty-two per cent of Redditors receive news via the platform. Twitter wasn't far behind, with 52 per cent of its users getting news from it, and Facebook came in at third place with 47 per cent of users accessing news content on their timelines. Yet the same report found that Facebook is the strongest for news delivery, simply due to the fact that there are many more Facebook users than reddit users. So in terms of numbers, Facebook is still delivering the most news to the largest pool of people.

None of the findings, including the fact that Gen Y was leading the pack in terms of the consumption of news via social media, were particularly surprising. Countless studies support this proposition, and a recently published study from L2, a consumer think tank for digital innovation, revealed how rapidly Millennials are moving away from traditional media consumption. The report stipulated that, of the Ys surveyed, four out of five who access newspaper content daily did so digitally.

Blogonauts

Something else the L2 study highlighted is the emergence and significance of blogs to Gen Ys, as well as their media consumption behaviour. If Baby Boomers were the TV generation, then it's safe to say that Gen Y is the blogging generation. Nearly half of the Ys in the L2 report admit to reading at least one blog daily, making blogs as popular as newspapers for Millennials.

As a whole, blogging has become more relevant for business as a way to enhance their online presence and improve their Google rank. Yet, as Alicia Strusa and Lauren Dow from *Truth Leaders Magazine* explain, Gen Y has taken blogging to a whole new level.

> There are hundreds of platforms (including some of the more popular ones like Wordpress, Blogger, Squarespace, and Tumblr to name a few) that have brought people together through online communities where they can express themselves by more than 140 characters. The most important part about blogging for Gen Y isn't the money that could be involved or the exposure that could be associated with it on the internet ... [rather], it is feeling involved in a community of individuals who share the same ideas, dreams or beliefs that you do.

I have heard countless Baby Boomers ask: Why blog? What makes you think that the words you type on your blog are worth reading?

If you're writing good content about topics people enjoy reading, then people will read your blog. A blog is a simple content distribution platform – instead of glossy magazines, we have email updates and online browsing.

Many people have made careers out of blogging. This form has reduced the barrier to entry for those who have always yearned to write for a living – and has allowed millions to find their voice online.

The Huffington Post is a clear example. Launched in 2005 as a liberal/left commentary outlet and alternative to news aggregators such as the Drudge Report, by 2011 the Huffington Post was valued at US$315 million. Notably, the site became the first commercially run United States digital media enterprise to win a Pulitzer Prize.

American author and freelance journalist Rob Walker believes that the blogging phenomenon's strength comes from being able to report on the 'strange and wonderful, or merely strange…things you are likely otherwise to have missed' in the mainstream media.

But how many 'bloggers' actually make a full time living from it? Darren Rowse, founder and editor of ProBlogger Blog Tips, believes earning a full-time wage is achievable; but it's slow-starting and certainly not attainable for everyone:

> I've been blogging for just under ten years, and [have been making money from it] for nine of those. It started out as just a few dollars a day but in time it gradually grew to becoming the equivalent of a part-time job, then a full-time job, and more recently into a business that employs others.

Yet while Rowse admits that most bloggers aren't making money, the blogging phenomenon has produced some of today's most innovative and engaging writing.

It's natural to wonder what impact this might have on journalism. What happens if those with the power to inform and communicate to the world are not bound by the 'canons of journalism' – that is, the basic guidelines on how to conduct yourself as a journalist: responsibility, freedom of the press, independence, sincerity and truthfulness and accuracy, impartiality, fair play and decency?

Regardless of some journalists' quality or integrity, the emergence of bloggers presents an interesting issue. While still protected by the freedom of the press, it appears that not all bloggers are bound by such standards and ethics. Some may have never even received training or education on how to adequately protect themselves or the people they discuss in their online content. Judge Kermit Lipez in the US Court of Appeals recently noted that these protections don't just apply to professional journalists. He said in his decision:

> ...changes in technology and society have made the lines between private citizen and journalist exceedingly difficult to draw. The proliferation of electronic devices with video-recording capability means that many of our images of current events come from bystanders...and news stories are now just as likely to be broken by a blogger at her computer as a reporter at a major newspaper.

Such developments make clear why, in the US at least, the news-gathering protections of the First Amendment cannot turn on professional credentials or status.

Some acknowledge the need to establish a code of ethics for bloggers. In 2007, Tim O'Reilly, the founder of O'Reilly Media (formerly O'Reilly & Associates), and a supporter of the free software and open source movements, proposed The Blogger's Code of Conduct with the intention of enforcing civility on blogs through bloggers' actions, and moderating comments on blogs.

The international reaction to the proposal went viral among bloggers and media writers. *The San Francisco Chronicle* reported that the blogosphere described the proposal as 'excessive, unworkable and an open door to censorship'. People landed on both ends of the spectrum: while author Bruce Brown approved of the code and reproduced it in *The Secret Power of Blogging: How to Promote and Market Your Business, Organization, or Cause with Free Blogs*, technology blogger Robert Scoble went as far as to state that the proposed rules 'make [him] feel uncomfortable' and 'as a writer, it makes [him] feel like [he lives] in Iran'.

The specific code O'Reilly put forward doesn't matter as much as the fact that he publicly acknowledged the need for one. As yet, no code of ethics applies to bloggers; yet with the existence of over 320 million blogs as of April 2013, there seems to be a growing need to introduce one. It's clear that blogging won't be going away anytime soon – so it's preferable for it to be regulated in some way, and perhaps better appreciated and recognised for being the internet's answer to the ineptitude of the corporate mainstream media.

In the end, blogging is simply the result of the existing quality of media communications: we have solved the problem of the lack of meaningful content by writing it ourselves. J.D. Lasica – entrepreneur, social media strategist, author, journalist, blogger and co-founder of the early social media community Ourmedia – published his thoughts on this matter in the Online Journalism Review and stated that the movement 'may sow the seeds for new forms of journalism, public discourse, interactivity and online community'. He goes on to say that blogging represents Ground Zero of the personal webcasting revolution. Blogging will drive a powerful new form of amateur journalism as millions of net users – young people especially – take on the role of columnist, reporter, analyst and publisher while fashioning their own personal broadcasting networks.

There is clearly a movement for the bloggers of the world becoming the new media players; they've provided a much-needed challenge to traditional media outlets. However, if bloggers are presenting their writing under the pretense that they're promoting their own opinions when they are actually getting paid to promote products – then how exactly is that different from the 'cash for comments' paradox? And what repercussions might this have for everyday people differentiating truth from advertising messages?

I do not have the answers to these questions; I am merely reiterating the points many before me have made. I do feel that the new trajectories that the media industry has been taken on, by the internet and the development of social media networks, are, overall, a good thing. At the same time, there are a lot of ugly aspects of the new media – now, and most likely in the future.

The celebritY

I feel a great example of the ugliness of today's media is the strange, almost perverse celebrity obsession society seems to have. A recent documentary, *Teenage Paparazzo*, presented by *Entourage*'s Adrian Grenier, highlights this strange fascination. They interview actor Matt Damon, who points out that, in recent years, fans and the media have stopped asking him, 'What is it like to be an actor?' or 'What is it like to make movies?' Instead, these questions have been replaced with 'What is it like to be famous?' – like the actual reason you're famous is no longer important. Damon's words resonated with me. Haven't we all got a little carried away? What is with the fascination we all have with the concept of the 'celebrity' – especially with their private lives? What I find especially ugly is how this relates to the *children* of famous people.

Many of us are guilty of occasionally flipping through a magazine and absentmindedly checking out photos of a celebrity with their kids. You might not give it a second thought, but those 'celebrities' whose kids are being terrorised by strange men hounding them with cameras when they leave their homes have! Wouldn't you? Dax Shepard, his wife Kristen Bell and a procession of American 'celebrities' have recently made a point to call this ugliness out, tweeting using the hashtag pedorazzi. This group includes the likes of Halle Berry and Jennifer Garner, who have recently dedicated themselves to developing the California Senate Bill 606, which has now made it illegal to photograph a child because of their parent's employment in a manner that 'seriously alarms, annoys, torments, or terrorises' them. In late January 2014, Dax Shepard posted 'Celebrity Orgy', a blog post that was reposted by The Huffington Post and re-titled 'Why Our Children Should Be Off Limits to the Paparazzi'. Dax stated:

> I personally believe, and I understand a lot of people differ on this point, that protecting [my daughter] includes keeping her life private until the moment she decides otherwise. I think she is entitled to

that. I think every minor is entitled to that. My wife and I, ever the approval-junkies, made a decision to get into show business and become public figures, but she has not. She hasn't even decided if she prefers pureed carrots to peanut butter.

So we took to Twitter urging consumers to stop buying magazines that print unsolicited photos of minors. We recognise that the odds of this happening are exceedingly low. We are not naive.

Why should they be low? If media is considered the 'mirror' of modern society, then society looks pretty unsightly.

But there is always hope. We could fix our disfigured exterior if we chose to. We hold the power to achieve this; we influence the media by choosing what we consume or watch. In the end, they will produce what sells.

So if we only buy what we want to read, and what we want our children to be exposed to, then we'll have at least part of the answer. Even given its adverse effects, media is a not something we could live without. Fortunately, each of us has the power to change the shape of our world through the media we consume. And perhaps Gen Y, with our scepticism and knowledge of our collective power, might be the generation that does create the change we so desperately need.

CHAPTER 7

Millennial Communications

Charlie Caruso

Wise men talk because they have something to say; fools, because they have to say something.

Plato

I'll never forget entering my grade one classroom, eagerly anticipating my new journey as a 'big kid'. I still remember the smell, the luxury of nap times in the afternoon, playing 'heads down thumbs up', and that getting your name on the board was *a big deal*. One thing in particular happened that year that still, to this day, seems like a *big deal* for me: I learned how to write.

Our teacher set a class game: we were instructed to write our first names as many times as we could in one minute. My full name is Charlotte – and I was sitting next to a young boy called Hal. That's right: H-A-L.

How on earth was *that* fair?

Of course, it wasn't, but it was *one game* over 21 years ago – so why do I remember it so clearly? The truth is, from that point on I formed the basis of my handwriting style on a need for speed – to compensate for that game I was never going to win.

The decline of handwriting

As a Gen Y born in 1987, handwriting was a major part of my primary and high school education. In school, we were forced to follow a handwriting rule book, which commenced the formation of our own personal writing style – a style so unique that, to this very day, I can look at a collection of handwritten letters from girlfriends (and boyfriends) of the past, and be able to tell you, at a single glance – ten or 15 years later – who wrote which letter. My friends and I used to write notes... every day.

We'd fold them up all funky, like a cryptic code that only a special few knew how to crack. I can't remember how to fold them now; I've forgotten the secret codes. I cannot pass them on to my daughters.

We used to pour out our hearts into those letters. We would share our secrets, and make plans for the weekend, for sleepovers – for our future weddings. We'd laugh out loud (before 'lol'), gossip and share our journeys on these handwritten pages of our childhood. We grew up in those letters.

Then one day, the letters stopped, as mobile phones and the internet had entered our lives. We started texting our plans, and re-pinning pictures of our aspirations. Now there is Whisper to type our secrets to. I miss those notes and the innocence and simplicity of the time they were written. Those folded letters are nothing more than relics of my childhood – remnants of a unique form of communication that has been replaced. This has been the consequence of the changing face of communication. These changes have affected our lives, our relationships – perhaps even our happiness?

The role of the computer and computer-based technology in reshaping our relationship with both the written and the printed word is undeniable. But is there any truth to the claims that handwriting might soon become an art form, much like calligraphy once was? Have keyboards replaced our need for the pen and pad? And if so, what effect will this have on communication, now and into the future? Are we at risk of losing something sacred, or are these concerns as over-hyped as the 'Millennium bug'?

The written word seems to hold a special place in Baby Boomers' hearts, perhaps because it reminds them of their 'inkwell' days: times of love letters and drawn cheques, when one's handwriting was a signature identity and insight into the writer's personality.

Gen X enjoyed writing letters too. Most members of this generation did not have computers at school, and have always felt safe with a pen and pad. They were the last generation to entirely hand-write papers and notes.

Gen Y's predecessors consider handwriting in any form to be far more personal than the printed word; it takes time and careful consideration to write someone a letter. Baby Boomers (and some Gen Xers) seem to feel that such an effort displays a level of politeness, respect – even generosity, perhaps. Most consider it to be a refreshing act of kindness that they appreciate.

But as the Boomers age, will the use of paper and pen become rarer and rarer? What will happen when there are no more Boomers to write letters to? Will it be then that the handwritten letter be derelict as Morse code, woodblock printing and cuneiform tablets? As Gen Y parents send their young children to school with a single iPad instead of a back-breaking assortment of textbooks, will they be waving goodbye not only to their children for the school day, but to the value of handwriting and its significance in the world?

In a post on digitaltrends.com, journalist Jam Kotenko says the biggest reason handwriting and other related practices are considered archaic is because ... well, they *are*:

> If you compare the ancient practice of written words to the constantly developing, next-gen-ness of technology, there's no argument over efficiency and ubiquity. Digital wins, hands down. People are more prone to type on a keyboard because it's easier and quicker, and online communications [are] simply faster and ... accomplish more.

Is this a good thing? I am not entirely sure. We rely so much on the internet, on our PCs, smart phones and everything driven by power – what would happen if some natural event or disaster occured that rendered our laptops, tablets and PCs useless? What kind of world are we preparing for, when we now use digital signatures instead of handwritten signatures?

I was pondering this question when I came across Professor Naomi S. Baron's article 'The Future of Written Culture: Envisioning Language in the New Millennium':

> Whatever eventually becomes of modern written culture, its material manifestations aren't disappearing any time soon. People will still read and write … and manufacturers can count on making bookshelves for years to come.
>
> Printed books that continued to be produced might become more collectors' items than objects for daily use; concerns about spelling and punctuation could slacken (following the present trend) without denying the importance of writing as a cultural artefact. That is, we can imagine a society in which many of the values of print culture would be maintained without relying primarily upon familiar print technology and editorial assumptions.

We can all breathe a sigh of relief that the written word is safe for now. Yes, things are changing; Gen Ys might focus on the 'efficiency' of delivery instead of the art of expression. But that doesn't necessarily mean we can't – or won't.

Talking Y

Extending one's vocabulary used to be a sign of a well-read, intellectual type. These days, you might as well be speaking Latin if you use big words. If no-one understands you, you're not smart – you're obsolete.

I felt obsolete when I didn't know what YOLO meant. I was mortified when I notified a fellow Y that he had accidentally misspelt 'crazy' on his website, because it said 'how cray is that' – and discovered that 'cray' is a shortened form of 'crazy' that is very commonly used in Y pop culture. I felt old when I heard a fellow Gen Y literally *say* 'lol' instead of use it for the purposes it was originally intended! I am a member of Gen Y, and even I have struggled at times to communicate with my kindred demographic.

So how does one communicate with Gen Y?

It is a popularly held belief that, while Boomers prefer 'face time', Gen Ys prefer to communicate through SMS, email, Instant Messaging (IM), blogs and Skype rather than on the phone or face-to-face. In fact, Gen Y accounts for a whopping 74 per cent of the total SMS messages that are sent.

Millennial Branding, a leading Gen Y research and management consulting firm founded by Dan Schawbel, cites statistics that in-person meetings and email trump technology at work:

> Despite new technologies like Skype and social networks... 66 per cent of managers say that in-person meetings are [still] their preferred way of communicating with Gen Ys and 62 per cent of employees feel the same way about how they communicate with their managers.

> The second most popular way of communicating between managers and Gen Ys was email—preferred by 26 per cent of managers and 25 per cent of Gen Ys.

What is interesting about these findings is that there is barely any difference between Gen Ys and their managers in terms of their preference for in-person communication. Gen Ys do seem to prefer to chat in person, something that has been supported by PricewaterhouseCooper's comprehensive Next Gen study, which proposes that Millennials' aptitude for electronic communication *augments* but doesn't *replace* face-to-face interaction. Since personal interactions are the preferred method for Gen Ys – especially when it comes to performance and career discussions – why are non-Ys so hung up about communicating with the Ys? Do we really need a 'special' approach to communication, or is this notion overinflated hogwash?

As stated by Australian social researcher Michael McQueen, author of *The 'New' Rules of Engagement*:

> There's an idea that Gen Y want older generations to be like them; we hear the phrase 'generational transvestite', [indicating that] older generations are trying to be like the younger generation they are dealing with—which isn't effective.

You don't have to be like them or dress like them or talk like them—just be yourself. That's just a relief for a lot of leaders, because they can be themselves—and it is far more endearing for Gen Y if you're authentic.

The Centre for Generational Kinetics published its 'Top 5 Rules for Gen Y Communication', which includes the following information:

Gen Y can go through a ridiculous amount of emails in an hour because [they] apply the 'twitter filter' to [their] inbox—only reading an email's subject line. [They] gauge importance at a glance, and will only open an email if [they] know that it demands a response.

They state that the best way to get Gen Ys to read an entire email is to explicitly write, 'Read this entire email' in the subject line, and if you manage to crack the open, then the pointier the bullet, the better.

Now that we've opened your email, the first thing we look for are quick bullet points. Millennials will try to discern the contents of an entire message from the first two bullet points they scan across. We refer to paragraphs as 'Walls of Text'. If you really, really need us to read every word, lead your Walls of Text with bold opening sentences. We will decide if said Wall of Text is pertinent to our situation based on those words, so choose them carefully.

Never, ever put critical instructions at the end of a paragraph.

I'll admit it: I do this *daily*. And I'm not so sure it's a 'Y' thing; I think it's a mere reflection of the *amount* of email communication we receive. Gen Ys aren't the only ones email-bombed on a daily basis. All of us receive too much spam, too many potential viruses, too many email subscriptions (that we keep forgetting to unsubscribe from). But the difference may be in the preference of a punchier bullet-point email to an hour-long meeting—especially in cases when both approaches will provide the same end result.

Doesn't everyone want to avoid wasting precious time?

According to the Centre for Generational Kinetics:

Generation Y is the guru of group projects. [They] never call a meeting if an email would spread the information just as easily. On the other hand, Baby Boomers call meetings just in case something worth discussing comes up. Generation Y wants to call a meeting only if [they] are certain that a decision must be discussed by the group.

Productive meetings are great, but just meeting for meeting's sake is a waste of everyone's time. Yes – there are situations when face-to-face contact is vital. We all get to the point where the emails back and forth become too much and someone *has* to pick up the phone and make the time to discuss.

Emails are great; there's a reason that they're most people's main source of correspondence. Our compulsion to over-commit to almost everything nowadays often leads us to forget the little (and sometimes big) things. When we're able to search emails, we get an instant reminder.

If we spent our time calling the people with whom we correspond daily, we would literally have no time left in the day to do any work. Emails are essential. But we have to acknowledge their limits – which can occasionally lead to damaging communication breakdowns.

There's been a general loss of tone that not only applies to email exchanges, but to any non-verbal or non-visual communication. Anyone who has endured SMS warfare over a misinterpreted text knows exactly what I am referring to.

Psychologist Nicholas Epley of the University of Chicago, who conducted research with Justin Kruger of New York University, reported that people misinterpret an email's tone *50 per cent of the time*. Furthermore, 90 per cent of people *think* they've *correctly* interpreted the tone of the emails they receive, making for a potentially dangerous gap in communication.

The lack of tonal and nonverbal cues have made email, IM, SMS and social media posts/tweets a haven for misconstrued statements eventually resulting in flame wars. The study attributes much of the misunderstanding to egocentrism, since readers have a difficult time 'detaching themselves from their own perspective'.

This seems a significant problem for Millennial communication – whether or not Gen Ys actually are involved. Everyone older than Gen Y was first exposed to communication devices such as text messaging, instant messaging and email while they were at work, which might be why they perceive these devices as productivity tools. In contrast, Millennials were exposed as children, so for Gen Y, these devices are lifestyle tools. While Millennials might prefer face-to-face communication, when on devices, it's casual Friday. With cybercommunications, Gen Y prefer the efficiency over formality.

Great conversationalists are able to adjust their conversational style and language depending on their audience. Employees will only give their optimum value in the workplace if they feel they're being understood – which usually means that the workplace must accept that every generation communicates differently. For the non-Ys out there – perhaps a stronger, more efficient relationship with Gen Y may be just an SMS away – at least you'll get a faster response than to all those voicemails you've been leaving.

Yet, many have questioned whether 'lowering' their standards of communication to 'accommodate' Gen Y – that is, accepting texting over calling, emailing about an issue rather than meeting face-to-face – only contributes to this deterioration of the communication process. Many feel that these 'new' communication styles that Gen Y embraces pave the way for further sacrifice of conversation – for the sake of mere connection.

There have been many instances when I have been with family or friends and looked up from my phone due to the silence surrounding me, only to realise that I am not alone in my 'screen sneak'. The people around me might have been checking the news headlines, weather forecast, their emails, or their Pinterest account – but what was that 'screen time' replacing? What conversations weren't being had – and what is the cost of our plugged-in lives?

Have smart phones' ability to keep us constantly 'connected' (which has now become our compulsion) completely destroyed the main attribute that makes us human – our ability to communicate?

We can't blame the smart phones; all they've done is be used by their creators. Smart phones aren't the reason for our social sickness; we are.

Millennials are not the *sole* consumers of smart phones, and we're not the only ones with our faces in our screens on buses and trains, and while walking in parks around the world. We are *all* guilty of forgetting there are conversations to be had with actual people sitting next to us, every single day. Yes, Gen Ys undoubtedly account for a significant proportion of the individuals I have just described, but it's likely more a reflection of the change in the way society communicates; those in the younger spectrum of the population have naturally adapted to 'the new way' much faster than the rest. However, this tendency doesn't necessarily nurture the skills Gen Ys need to succeed in a world that is still dominated by Baby Boomers and Gen X.

A survey of *Fortune* 500 vice presidents conducted by the *Journal of Business Communication* showed that 97.7 per cent 'believed that communication skills had affected their advancement to a top position'. Paul E. Madlock, author of *Organizational Communication: Strategies for Success*, published a paper called 'The Link Between Leadership Style, Communicator Competence, and Employee Satisfaction', and concluded that a supervisor's communication competence was the greatest predictor of employee job and communication satisfaction.

This is where the communication gap is appearing.

The proliferation of Gen Ys' online interaction and subsequent reliance on online communication likely means that many Millennials have missed out on valuable face-to-face interactions. Some Gen Ys are admittedly inept at speaking in a polished manner, unable to listen attentively or read other people's expressions and body language. Ronald Alsop, author of *The Trophy Kids Grow Up*, presented a piece for the website BBC Capital that explained that, as a result, employers are finding that their young hires are awkward in their interpersonal interactions and ill-prepared to collaborate effectively with teammates and develop relationships with clients.

It seems there is a widening gap between the communication standards managers expect from Gen Ys and what Gen Ys *think* is expected of them. Hopefully, this gap will not be permanent. Gen Ys' predecessors and the business world at large have succumbed to the reality that both parties must find middle ground. Baby Boomers and Gen X need to restrict their harsh judgements on Gen Ys' 'new' communication style if they want a labour force to replace them. And it seems that Gen Ys are making efforts to acknowledge the rules of engagement (if they want to be employed). There is no point ignoring the fact that the internet and the multitude of communication platforms it has provided has revolutionised the way we interact. But that doesn't mean that we can't merge the old with the new.

Gen Ys are absolutely capable of deep, meaningful conversations. However, I concede we do seem to prefer to reserve this sort of engagement for personal friends and family.

GrammaticallY

As the uptake of the English language continues to increase globally, the digital age – and the subsequent communication revolution – has not only impeded vocabulary extension; it also seems to have side-tracked the fundamental rules by which the English language is formed. Rules that, while complex and in many ways contradictory, are cornerstones to its function.

And a commonly held belief is that Gen Y is to blame. They are the generation of bad spelling, poor grammar, terrible punctuation. (That's what spell check is for – right?)

Other generations' workers tend to see Gen Y as too casual in general. They think we're too informal too quickly in the workplace, use informal language and misspellings in written communications, and are lax in our time commitments.

But are these tendencies our fault?

I was able to write and edit this very book with medium to average spelling skills. Y? Because I am from the generation that typed and then right-clicked in high school. And that makes a big difference to the skills formed for accurate spelling.

Has anyone ever asked you how to spell an uncommon word and, after attempting to do so from memory, you can only figure it out when you 'write it down'?

It's a fairly common experience – and here is the science to back it up.

In 2012, Karin H. James, associate professor at the Department of Psychological and Brain Sciences at Indiana University, and Laura Engelhardt of Colombia University, presented evidence in the *Trends in Neuroscience and Education Journal* that highlighted the fact that brain activation during letter perception was influenced in different and important ways by the previous hand-writing of letters, versus previous typing or tracing of those same letters.

In their paper, 'The Effects of Handwriting Experience on Functional Brain Development in Pre-literate Children' they state:

> A previously documented 'reading circuit' was recruited during letter perception only after handwriting—not after typing or tracing experience. These findings demonstrate that handwriting is important for the early recruitment in letter processing of brain regions known to underlie successful reading. Handwriting therefore may facilitate reading acquisition in young children.

Millennials as a whole were perhaps less affected by keyboarding in the early years of language development; however, they were most certainly exposed to the effects of typing in the middle to later years of schooling, formative years that Baby Boomers and many Gen Xers spent preparing essays with a pen and pad. So it is very likely that the 'essay writing' period was when the spelling and grammar gap for Gen Y first appeared.

Gen Ys could 'right-click' throughout essay preparation – something that probably stunted the development of our spelling, grammar and punctuation skills. This developmental 'growth stunt' is something that our predecessors seem to find particularly frustrating today.

I have emphasised to many senior executives—particularly those who have been annoyed by Gen Ys' less-than-desirable spelling and grammar skills—that they need to stop focusing on the negatives. Instead they should embrace the enhanced typing speed and multitasking nature of the digital native.

Gen Ys were raised during a time when education systems were forced to evolve and allow for new technology. We adapted to these altered circumstances, which has in turn affected the way we interact and utilise language.

There is no argument that language is ever-evolving. Consider this: if Shakespeare were alive today, would we understand his tweets?

Or would it look more like this?

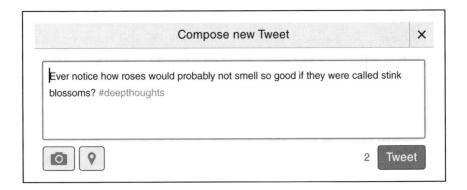

Gen Y has more in common with Shakespeare than one might imagine. Shakespeare invented over 1700 words by changing nouns into verbs, changing verbs into adjectives, connecting words never before used together, adding prefixes and suffixes, and devising wholly original words. Shakespeare didn't always play by the rules – and almost 400 years later, he is revered as the greatest writer in the English language. YOLO ...

Yet the language of the great poet is *very* different from today's. It might be an 'evolved' version, having had countless 'updates' throughout the years – but what of the languages that are simply being lost? We understand the historic, cultural and spiritual role that our language plays in our existence; but how many languages might Y see disappear over their lifespan?

Payal Sampat, a research associate at the Worldwatch Institute, produced a compelling account of this very phenomenon in his piece 'Last Words: The Dying of Languages'.

> It's believed that the human faculty for language arose at some point between 20000 and 100000 years ago. Many languages have come and gone since then, but it's unlikely that the global fund of languages has ever before gone into so extensive and chronic a decline...
>
> English is rapidly gaining ground as the primary international medium of science, commerce and popular culture. Most of the world's books, newspapers and email are written in English, which is now spoken by more people as a second language (350 million) than as a native tongue (322 million).

Clearly, language is ever-evolving. It makes sense that as we increase our global connectedness, a centralised language becomes critical in enabling effective global communication. We must also focus on developing skills that enable clear and open communication. A pressing issue is the potential retardation of interpersonal communication skills in the Gen Y and younger cohorts, due to the proliferation of social media and digital communications. The ability to effectively communicate with each other, both in person and online, is of critical importance, and something that society at large must address.

I am still a big fan of all things digital – for efficiency, for spell check, and for other factors involving expediency and ease of use. However, we need to teach our children basic communication skills, as well as the beauty and eloquence of the spoken and written word.

The current 'new way' of communication is largely focused on efficiency – and in the process we sacrifice the ability to extend ourselves and fully exploit the stupendous verbosity that our language offers us. But Gen Y isn't to blame here; we are nothing more than a product of our education, our environment – something provided to us by our predecessors. The challenge for all of us going forward could be to reintroduce our brilliant words into everyday dialect, resurrect a 'vocabulary extension fad' if you will.

If only we had a popular figure, someone Millennials might revere...

Enter actor Russell Brand and his Messiah complex. Russell Brand, an unexpected but delightfully candid and articulate voice, has gained significant popular following in recent times. It seems that Mr Brand understands how to communicate with the Y tribe.

In October 2013, Brand became the guest editor for left-wing political magazine *The New Statesman*. His extended piece citing the need for revolution led well-known political journalist Jeremy Paxman to question him on *Newsnight* in Britain – an interview that received over 9 million online views in the first week.

So how does Brand communicate so well? I thought I'd examine Paxman's interview in a little depth and analyse the particular points I feel encapsulate Brand's canny ability to excite and enthuse Gen Y.

During the exchange, Paxman highlighted the fact that Russell Brand has never before voted, and questioned Brand's authority to edit a political magazine.

Brand's response was quick witted, and humorous – that he was asked to by a beautiful lady – and, perhaps most critically, it was honest. Brand doesn't take himself too seriously, and is the first to admit he doesn't 'know much about politics – thus [he is] ideal'. Furthermore, when continually probed about his authority in commenting on politics, Brand's response was something that struck a chord with many Gen Ys worldwide:

> Well I don't get my authority from this pre-existing paradigm which is quite narrow and only serves a few people. I look elsewhere for alternatives that might be of service to humanity. Alternate means, alternate political systems.

The viral jousting match between Brand and Paxman publicly launched a conversation that had previously been only whispered. Brand called for a revolution and encouraged others in refusing to vote, not out of apathy, but out of weariness and exhaustion from the lies, treachery and deceit that has been imposed on us by the political class for generations. He claims that this trend has now reached fever pitch, and we face a disenfranchised, disillusioned, despondent underclass that is not being represented by that political system—thus rendering voting complicit with the system that is failing.

Brand's words are strong; his points seem to have resonated with the Millennial generation (and others) who are now charged with creating the change we feel is needed. And *that's* how you communicate in this day and age—speak truth, be humble, be angry and go viral.

It's not hard to communicate with the Y cohort. We don't speak any special language; we're simply not that different. We're online, we are connected, and we have an excellent bullshit radar. We are drawn to honesty, and respect candour and people who get to the point. The rules of engagement are that simple. If you want tips on how to engage us, look to those who grab our attention. They will reveal more than this book could ever attempt to do, through their actions and the subsequent reactions of their Gen Y audience.

CHAPTER 8

Political Y

David Burstein

> What nobler employment, or more valuable to the state, than
> that of the man who instructs the rising generation?
>
> *Marcus Tullius Cicero*

Nowadays, there seem to be crises everywhere we turn. Leaders around
the globe have abdicated their responsibilities and, by most objective
standards, there is a growing mess being left for my generation—the
Millennial generation—to clean up. Yet despite the adversity that we
face, we are ready to step up. There are countless examples of our
eagerness to solve problems and address challenges in our communities,
countries and around the world.

Politicians urge their colleagues to embrace change 'for the young
people', but Millennials have already started acting. We're a
generation of pragmatic idealists seeking to incite significant change,
aware that we can only do so with a practical approach.

Millennials have been organising online and offline for years. But
nowadays there are more instances of Gen Ys gathering specifically
to tackle certain problems. They came together in this way just
a few years ago at the second edition of a conference called One

Young World in Zurich, Switzerland. Over 1200 young people from 170 countries – including often-underrepresented nations like Iran, Libya, Iraq, Egypt, Tunisia and Saudi Arabia – all congregated, ready to share, collaborate and problem-solve.

Did the conference end with solutions to all our world's problems? No, of course not. But two things made this event valuable to the 1200 young people who participated – and, potentially, to the world. It is truly the only global *youth* summit, and the only one that brings together not just leaders but also regular citizens. The mere act of having such individuals connect and work in concert could tip the balance on some of our most pressing global challenges.

One Young World is representative of something I think we'll see a lot more of in the coming years. This generation has come of age in a rapidly globalising world. We're not only comfortable with it; we're excited about it. Millennials have embraced the need to globalise by becoming the first generation of truly global citizens. This might be due to the fact that we're also the first to spend all of our grown years in a world where instantly and constantly connecting to people from all over the globe seems normal and natural.

While young people may not be organising on a specific issue, we draw inspiration from each other. One of the highlights of this event was a conversation between Oscar Morales – who created the Facebook group One Million Voices Against FARC in 2006, which set off the collapse of the Colombian terrorist network FARC – and Wael Ghonim, the Google executive who created a Facebook page called We are All Khaled Said in 2010, which started the Egyptian revolution. Though the two met for the first time at the event, they'd always been 'together' as members of a generation fighting the same fight, taking advantage of the tools they know so well, offering a fresh approach to long-standing forces in their respective countries. There are hardly any problems today that *cannot* be considered global – and we can only confront these issues globally and in solidarity. As a result, younger generations are joining hands across the world to rise to the challenge.

Educating the Y voter

When supporting a recently defeated bill in New Hampshire that would have prevented college students from voting in their college towns unless their parents had been residents there, State House speaker William O'Brien claimed that young voters were not qualified to vote because they had no 'life experience'. They 'just vote their feelings'.

There are ignorant young voters, just as there are ignorant older voters. Ignorance isn't contingent upon age. And how would one even discern *who* an ignorant or foolish voter was? What criteria would you even use? Is it merely someone who has little life experience? Many young people have rich life experiences; many over 30 have quite empty life experiences, and vice versa. Does someone earn the right to not be considered foolish just by having lived a certain number of years?

Who should get to decide what a foolish voter is? It would undoubtedly have to be lawmakers. But in the unlikely event that a group of politicians could agree on a definition for an informed versus a foolish voter, how could this be enforced?

Ignorance is a major issue—truly, a bipartisan epidemic—facing democracy, and it reaches far beyond voting behaviour; it is present throughout our political system. It's not a problem tied to age, nor one we can solve by changing voting laws. The real culprit in creating political ignorance is our education system, which has failed to inform young people adequately about civics and current affairs. If we want to accomplish this critical mission of creating a better and more informed electorate, we have to actively work to give young people the tools and background to think about politics critically and to make informed political decisions.

There is crucial work to be done in middle and high schools; once students graduate, it's often too late to introduce them to basic political participatory concepts. Several states in the US don't allow students to graduate without passing a civics course. While it is a positive step to have every student in such a class, these classes are usually watered down to learning the basics of government, memorising the Bill of Rights, and the like.

What we need are enriched civics classes and curricula that ask students to discuss the meaning of citizenship and democracy, the role of voting, the process of elections, and one of the main questions at the centre of this: what are the criteria for deciding how to vote? Teachers should not tell students how to vote or tell them what their criteria should be. Rather, teachers should start a discussion that encourages students to develop their own criteria. This should be the hardest and most important class every high school student takes.

It's concerning to have an electorate with a large number of ill-informed or uninformed voters. Addressing this issue requires that we take a long-term approach that includes enhanced civics education and a national conversation. Despite this being a specifically US-based example, it's still important to keep in mind that introducing laws that remove voting rights from some would be a huge step backwards for democracy around the world. Every generation has its faults; but this one has plenty of members who are ready, willing, able and eager to participate in civic life. We shouldn't be denied that chance on the basis that some of us may be foolish.

Solution Y

Our clear lack of trust in politicians and religious leaders speaks to the current dearth of respected authority figures in societies around the globe. With these traditional sources of immutable 'truths' removed from the equation, parents wield greater influence. The dismal scores reaped by religious leaders also are in keeping with what appears to be a broad movement away from religiosity. According to Euro RSCG Worldwide's Prosumer Report, 'Millennials: The Challenger Generation', only 16 per cent of Millennials surveyed agreed that religion will be a more important part of their lives than it was for their parents, while nearly two-thirds (63 per cent) disagreed, including 43 per cent who disagreed strongly. Just more than two-thirds of the sample (67 per cent) believe the world will be less religious in 2030 than it is today.

For this first post-ideological generation, change is a lot less political and a lot more personal. This is because members of the Millennial generation see myriad ways in which they can make some small contribution to change on their own – through their spending, eco-conscious behaviours and persuasive blogging, for example – and also because the change they seek has everything to do with people and very little to do with political ideology. Their concept of change is not about rioting and power grabs, but rather gradual improvements brought about by incremental changes in behaviours and attitudes. The Prosumer Report found that only 39 per cent of Millennials agree 'there will be no change without a revolution'; 29 per cent disagree with the notion and 32 per cent are neutral. And, in fact, 42 per cent say they don't believe in revolution at all. For them, change is something that's gradual – slow but enduring. They adhere to the Gandhian notion that they must 'be the change you want to see in the world'.

So what steps do Millennials believe they need to take in order to bring about this change? While 58 per cent (ranging from 48 per cent in France to 70 per cent in India) believe 'starting new political movements' is key, the most popular responses were decidedly more personal and aimed squarely at economic and environmental sustainability: 63 per cent believe people should drive less, and 62 per cent say people should consume less.

The idea of reducing consumption is particularly valued in the hyperconsumerist cultures of the US and UK (chosen by 75 and 78 per cent of those samples, respectively). Not surprisingly, respondents from India – poised to overtake China as the world's most populous country – were most likely to agree (85 per cent) that having fewer children is the most important change people can make.

Despite the fact that young people turned out in some of their largest numbers in US elections in 2008 and 2012 – and that they will represent a third of the electorate by 2020 – Millennials are still portrayed as 'apathetic' or 'politically disengaged'. Yet Millennials are deeply engaged as citizens, generating surges in volunteerism, Peace Corps applications, and the number of young people starting businesses and organisations. As a generation that grew up in the midst of the Monica Lewinsky scandal, numerous terrorist attacks around the world and lived through two highly politicised wars in Iraq and Afghanistan, this generation has never seen the political system at its best, so it's not surprising we are not deeply engaging with it beyond the vote. A recent study by the Harvard Institute of Politics found that just 35 per cent of Millennials believe running for office is an honorable thing to do. It is likely that we won't see this generation's true political power until more of them start running for public office but, when they do, their leadership will transform the political landscape for all generations.

Note: The contents of this chapter have been derived from David Burstein's many contributions to this topic, including 'What Happens When Millennials Come Together' and 'What's So Wrong with Young Voters?', which he previously published on The Huffington Post.

CHAPTER 9

Engaging Y

Scott Broome & Stacey Taylor

> Each generation imagines itself to be more intelligent
> than the one that went before it, and wiser than the one
> that comes after it.
>
> *George Orwell*

In recent times, Gen Y has emerged as one of the most complex demographics to engage. Compared to previous generations, the critical Gen Y audience has become seemingly anesthetised to traditional modes of engagement. However, by understanding the various motivations that drive the Gen Y segment, strategic rules of engagement can be employed in order to communicate with them effectively.

Securing the undivided engagement of a person or group has always been a complex and arduous task. When engaging a specific person or group, an accurate understanding of their motivations is crucial. Recognising and understanding a person's motives is necessary to spark their interest and involvement. Inspiring them to participate in a particular task or activity will strengthen and deepen the subject's initial interest. When a person contextualises information in a meaningful way, they form a relationship with that content – and want to demonstrate a level of commitment to it. Establishing this commitment stimulates an underlying need and is considered a form of effective engagement.

The methods used to engage Gen Y are often manipulated to suit varying environmental settings. Capturing Gen Y's attention in the workplace will require a starkly different approach to engaging Gen Y in a consumer landscape. The overall goal is the same; but the strategies employed will differ.

In order to understand how to engage Gen Y in a workplace environment, it's necessary to develop an understanding of their predecessors, Baby Boomers and Gen X.

Most people view Baby Boomers as work-centric individuals; they're generally regarded as a generation of hard workers who invested long hours building reputable careers. Characterised by their willingness to sacrifice a personal life, Baby Boomers strive for professional stability. Baby Boomers are, for the most part, resourceful and process-driven. They are heavily influenced by rules and regulations and comply with hierarchical constructions in the workplace. They are usually reluctant to change, and therefore may have a hard time adapting to new-age working environments – in particular, those influenced by the technological revolution.

Gen X employees, on the other hand, value the flexibility of work–life balance. Unlike the Baby Boomers, who are more likely to comply with unsatisfactory working conditions, Gen Xers will change roles as required in order to achieve a personal and professional equilibrium. Despite being less inclined to work traditional working hours, the Gen X employee strives for professional success and will often demonstrate complete dedication to their professional projects. Capable and highly practical, Gen Xers respond positively to workplace changes and show a keen interest in learning new skills and abilities.

Gen Y is the fastest growing group in today's workforce, and they demonstrate a reliance on technology as a daily process. They're constantly connected to all forms of digital communication, and embrace email, text messaging and social media over traditional forms of workplace interaction. Unlike Baby Boomers, Gen Ys are characterised by their casual approach to work. Favouring a relaxed and open working environment, the Gen Y employee will opt for casual attire and reduced workplace restrictions. Blending their professional and personal lives into a single sphere, Gen Ys are happy to create social relationships with co-workers in both online and offline settings. This trend supports new-age collaborative movements in the workforce. Compared to their predecessors, Gen Y employees are the most educated and possess the most diverse skills, due to their enthusiastic embrace of new technologies in the digital landscape.

As a significant proportion of today's consumers, the Gen Y populace serves as one of the retail industry's biggest growth opportunities – and also acts as one of its biggest challenges. To date, Gen Y represents 25 per cent of the Australian population, and is predicted to become the most significant retail spending group in Western nations by 2015.

Notoriously fickle Gen Ys are subject to more experimental marketing programs than any other generation. As a result, Gen Y consumers have become immune to traditional sales strategies and tactics. As a critical consumer group, Gen Y despises advertising messages that conform to conventional formulas.

The Y cohort is susceptible to all forms of traditional and new-age media, and it is important for marketers to avoid cookie-cutter approaches to content. As a rule of thumb, Gen Y responds to vibrant visuals, sharable content, celebrity endorsements and scenarios that reflect their values and lifestyle. The rise of a digital culture has made it necessary for marketers to explore new and unconventional ways of engaging Gen Y in order to maximise message transmission via online channels.

Most Millennials are willing subscribers to modern technological practices; indeed, 81 per cent of Australian Gen Y consumers prefer to buy goods and services online. This evolution from traditional modes of consumption has changed the way businesses and brands engage with younger consumers. A TH?NK Global Research study in 2013 found that, on average, Gen Y spends 31 to 60 minutes per day on the internet. The online space has become a repository of knowledge that provides the Gen Y consumer with a vast inventory of reviews and word-of-mouth content. Gen Ys refer to their online social networks for guidance and support. Therefore, retailers must converse with the Gen Y audience in an online setting via interactive forums and engaging social media content.

In a world that encourages traditional workforce practices, 41 per cent of Gen Ys choose to work full time. Having entered the workforce during secondary school and opting to remain at home for longer, the Millennial generation's disposable income makes it an especially attractive consumer market. This means that marketers must also influence consumer behaviour by engaging Gen Y on a financial level. Gen Ys are more inclined to accept additional credit when a product reflects their personality and lifestyle. Some institutions have had some success through introducing coloured credit cards and relevant loyalty programs, including holiday incentives and free technological gadgets. Moreover, with online shopping threatening the traditional retail landscape, businesses must steer away from conventional sales promotions and look at new and exciting ways of engaging Gen Y, such as creating in-store and out-of-store social experiences. Gen Ys are more inclined to attend an end-of-season sale if it takes place in an imaginative and original space – such as a secret location. Companies can integrate these features into an interactive online social media campaign to attract Gen Y audiences en masse.

Corporate Social Responsibility (CSR) serves as an equally enticing marketing tactic. Gen Y is more environmentally and socially conscious than previous generations, and they rank sustainable efforts to preserve the environment as important. According to an environmental poll by TH?NK Research Group in 2013, 22 per cent of the 156 respondents ranked ecological concerns as their maximum priority. In comparison, 64 per cent of respondents classified the environment as a moderate to high issue.

Given their preference for ethically sourced products – such as free trade coffee beans and brands against animal testing – there is significant potential for retailers to engage Gen Y by aligning their brand to the generation's core values. Incorporating CSR messaging as a marketing tactic serves to capture the Gen Y consumer's attention and provides an attractive and noble reason to engage with a brand on a long-term scale.

Engaging Gen Y is a complex and strategic task that requires a thorough understanding of the segment's motivational priorities. Understanding Gen Y contextually, as individuals and consumers, plays a pivotal role in forming an effective communications strategy.

Companies and brands must consider the following tactics before devising a communications plan for the Gen Y segment:

- Understand the key drivers that motivate Gen Y.

- Create a *social experience* that sparks curiosity and interest.

- Develop unique, *sharable* content.

- Streamline communication messages to embody *core Gen Y values.*

- Converse with Gen Y across multiple communication mediums.

- Communicate using vibrant and relevant visual materials.

- Most importantly, *have fun!*

Desensitised to traditional modes of engagement, Gen Ys prefer new and innovative experiences that transcend the physical world and infiltrate the digital sphere. It's a generation that evolves daily, and marketers must constantly remain one step ahead by anticipating trends in the Gen Y community. After all, in the land of Gen Y, today's status update is last minute's news.

As a special shout out, we would like to thank TH?NK Agency for all their insightful research. You guys rock our world!

CHAPTER 10

Y the Social Media Mania?

Charlie Caruso

Engage, Enlighten, Encourage and especially…just be yourself!
Social media is a community effort, everyone is an asset.

Susan Cooper

There has been a fundamental shift in the way we communicate over the past five years. Though members of Y have largely generated this trend, members of all generations have embraced it.

The way I distinguish between a Y and a member of another generation is very simple: if you had a mobile phone in high school (and a Nokia brick still counts), then you're a Y. But if you had Facebook in high school, then you are a Z. My methods of classification might be questionable, but it seems these two social developments have carved out very different cohorts of youth.

Of course, Y also embraced social media – but we did so in our twenties, and without the worry of cyberbullying. Social media isn't just for Gen Y – it's a new tool that the whole world is using to communicate. Consider, however, that Mr Youth's report 'Meet the

Class of 2015', researching the attitudes of 18 year olds, found that 76 per cent of Gen Y spends over an hour on Facebook every day.

Social media acts as a platform for Millennials to efficiently engage, share and participate in a conversation about the things that are relevant in our lives – anything from having a bad experience at a restaurant to what we think of Miley Cyrus's latest antics.

Gen Y has embraced social media because it ticks all our boxes: it's efficient, it's inexpensive, it keeps us connected and informed – all the while using technology, something we feel at ease using. Connecting online comes naturally to a group that has grown up with multiple social media channels as varied as MSN chat, Bebo, Myspace, Facebook, Instagram, Tumblr, Twitter, Snapchat and many, many more.

Those who do not understand and have never used social media simply cannot wrap their heads around Gen Y's incessant use of hashtags and acronyms. They wonder why we need to photograph our food at restaurants before eating it, or post updates on the hour every hour while travelling. To them – and admittedly, to some of us – this new way of communicating seems cray cray.

It's easy to feel a general sense of dismay seeing countless members of my generation worry more about what is on their phone than the beauty and potential of the world around them. But it's easy to judge, and harder to think about the broader changes that are taking place with the social media phenomenon. Sure there are two sides to the social media story – and about a hundred shades of grey in between.

Really, social media is simply a new medium for communication. And communication is nothing new, nothing scary, nothing overtly different. We used to have wondrous cave painting, then scriptures in stone, ancient writings, the Bible and the Quran. Shakespeare communicated stories in the plays he wrote; literature in fiction and non-fiction expanded and developed. Newspapers and the mass production of current affairs commenced in the nineteenth century, a time when the international postal system allowed us to correspond via letters to loved ones around the world. We broadcasted news and communicated through radio programming and, shortly thereafter, telephones allowed us to stay in touch with our friends and families more often – both locally and internationally.

The 1930s brought the introduction of TV programming, a seemingly futuristic tool at the time. And when we thought we couldn't imagine anything more advanced, home computers, mobile phones, texting and the internet proved that notion wrong. Today, social media is just another new communication platform to fulfil the human need to communicate stories and connect with one another.

Social media just happens to suit the fast-paced, instant gratification Gen Y lifestyle. We are communicating more but, perhaps for the first time, we are personally communicating with *more people* – in a faster, cheaper and more efficient way than ever before. Francois Gossieaux, author of *The Hyper-Social Organization: Eclipse Your Competition by Leveraging Social Media*, believes that social media has allowed us to behave in ways that we were originally hardwired for. As he states in his book, 'We can get frank recommendations from other humans instead of from faceless companies'.

Social media + news

According to the the PewResearch Center's 'Millennials: Confident. Connected. Open to Change.' report, social networking sites are now the top news source for the Millennial Generation (see figure 10.1, overleaf).

News organisations have been confronting the problem of a declining audience for more than a decade, but recent trends strongly indicate that these difficulties may only increase over time. Today's younger and middle-aged audience seems unlikely to ever match the avid news interest of the generations they will replace, even as they eagerly transition to the internet as their primary source of news. Not only has social media affected the way we consume our news; it has also altered the *content* we consume, much of which is now user-generated. As we discuss in chapter 6, we have essentially become our own reporters.

Figure 10.1: Uberflip's infographic of news consumption in 2013

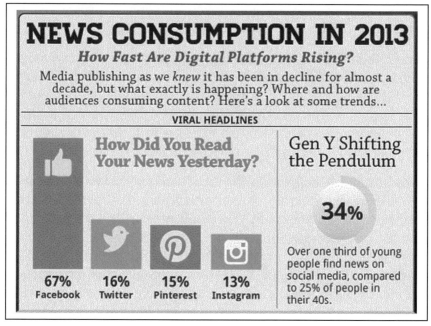

NEWS CONSUMPTION IN 2013
How Fast Are Digital Platforms Rising?

Media publishing as we *knew* it has been in decline for almost a decade, but what exactly is happening? Where and how are audiences consuming content? Here's a look at some trends...

VIRAL HEADLINES

How Did You Read Your News Yesterday?

67%	16%	15%	13%
Facebook	Twitter	Pinterest	Instagram

Gen Y Shifting the Pendulum

34%

Over one third of young people find news on social media, compared to 25% of people in their 40s.

Source: Created by Uberflip, www.uberflip.com

Social media + politics

One of the brighter outcomes of social media is the potential for social change that this seamless interaction and communication has the power to incite.

According to the findings of a report from the Pew Internet Project, there has been evidence to suggest that social networks may be encouraging younger people to get involved in politics. According to Brian Solis, author of *Engage! The Complete Guide for Brands and Businesses to Build, Cultivate, and Measure Success in the New Web*:

> Social media spark a revelation that we, the people, have a voice, and through the democratisation of content and ideas we can once again unite around common passions, inspire movements and ignite change.

Social media has created an atmosphere with a heightened sense of political engagement – a time where spin is harder to pull off and citizens demand accountability from their leaders.

A great example of this occurred in 2013, when a rally for marriage equality spread throughout social platforms as the US Supreme Court heard cases regarding same-sex marriage. Even brands took to the trend by creating products branded with the movement's red equality symbols. Although the Supreme Court still has not reached a decision in the ongoing debate, justices were aware of the public support.

The Kony video was a recent game changer that gave us a brief insight into the mighty power that social media has the potential to wield. In 2012, this video was launched as part of a campaign to bring Joseph Kony – the leader of the Lord's Resistance Army (LRA), a guerrilla group that used to operate in Uganda – to justice and make people aware of his crimes. Filmmaker and narrator Jason Russell posits, '99 per cent of the planet doesn't know who Kony is. If they did, he would have been stopped years ago'.

The Kony video had over 97 million views on YouTube within its first few months online. Never before have initiatives such as the Kony movement received so much attention with such speed.

Social media in emergencies

Social media provides the best way for most people to connect across vast distances. Many of us are now able to connect with friends and relatives without having to waste money paying for international phone calls. These networks and platforms allow us to share pictures and glimpse into one another's lives. When we can't physically be with the people we love, these sites are the perfect complement to other communication formats like email and Skype.

Another interesting contribution that social media has made toward the wellbeing of our society is that it has become a platform for support and safety information during a crisis. There have been several recent disasters during which social media provided the only viable avenue of communication. Most people in the north-eastern United States didn't have power when Superstorm Sandy hit in October of 2013, but some mobile networks and wifi towers were still operational. Many people used Facebook to detail the destruction and reassure friends or family that they were safe. The tragic 2013 Boston Marathon bombings mobilised the worldwide social media community to offer support and information for those affected. According to *Ad Week*, Twitter donated a promoted hashtag (valued at an estimated $200 000), #OneBoston, to lend support to victims. More importantly, networks like Twitter proved to be a safety tool for people in the area. The Boston Police Department tweeted up-to-the-minute news describing injuries, death tolls and areas to avoid. In an effort to keep phone lines clear, police asked people to use social media to communicate.

According to a study conducted by the American Red Cross, during an emergency, nearly *half* of those surveyed would use social media to let loved ones know they were safe. Sixty-nine per cent agree that emergency response agencies should regularly monitor their websites and social media pages so they can respond promptly.

I definitely acknowledge the benefit of social media in emergencies – but I also think there are potential risks. The facts mentioned highlight how a message can be manipulated once it is released. There is the potential for network overloads during a crisis – preventing important calls and data transfers during a time when they're needed most.

Another risk is fearmongering, and digital lynch mobs attacking those accused of being perpetrators via malicious social media rumour spreading. With the creation, manipulation and distribution of 'breaking news' at the hands of anyone with an iPhone, extensive, thorough investigation of suspects, victims and the story itself can be twisted and contorted by those wanting to 'break news'. Misinformation at times of heightened emotion, pain and anguish is extremely dangerous. #MH370 springs to mind.

Yet I acknowledge social media's potential for *good* in these circumstances too – something that the horrific Boston Marathon bombings highlighted. Social media seemed to shape every aspect of the live response, from eyewitness testimonies on Facebook, to authorities using Twitter to tweet live updates, to *The Boston Globe* temporarily converting its homepage to a live blog that pulled in tweets from Boston authorities, news outlets, and ordinary citizens.

So, we have to take the good with the bad. Social media is the latest platform for society to communicate, so it can facilitate the positive aspects of our humanity as much as the negative. That 'negative element' isn't restricted to the potential spread of false accusations during times of crisis. Rather, as many parents around the world fully appreciate, the serious danger of social media is its facilitation of bullying behaviour.

The cyberbullY

Because it allows anonymity, social media can act as a portal for bullies who hide safely behind their screens. These individuals can hide from the cruel effects of the words they have the courage to type but perhaps not the heart to speak. This has serious negative impacts on our society and this generation of young people. Recently, cyberbullying has reached disturbing heights, with 49.5 per cent of students reporting having been victims in 2012.

Social media has allowed cyberbullying to escalate previous forms of harassment to a whole new level, and has transformed social interaction forever. And it's thrived due to the lack of accountability accompanying our online actions. There is no authority in control of online harassment and bullying. Mobile phones, laptops and tablets make the opportunities infinite.

Bullies used to have to witness the effects of their abuse and deal with the intervention of onlookers. Nowadays, they can impose traumatic abuse without such concerns. They are not obliged to enter their real details when registering for an online profile. Though it would be hard to enforce a system that ensured authenticity, the current one allows its users to exploit anonymity, acting under pseudonyms and avoiding any potential direct repercussions. Users who would ordinarily avoid confrontation for fear of physical or legal reprisals find themselves free to insult and harass others online without consequence.

Admittedly, we cannot blame social media in and of itself for the emergence of cyberbullying. People are the problem; this platform has just given them another venue to be cruel.

Social media's effect on communication

Bullying isn't the only unfortunate side effect of social media's sharp rise. A 2012 study by the Center for the Digital Future at the USC Annenberg School found that the percentage of people reporting less face-to-face time with family in their homes rose from 8 per cent in 2000 to 34 per cent in 2011. Thirty-two per cent of those surveyed were on social media or texting during meals (47 per cent of 18-to-34 year olds) instead of talking with family or friends. Many health professionals around the world have raised their concerns for those who spend a lot of time online and seem to develop poor interaction skills, often resulting in feelings of social isolation.

According to Stanford political science professor Norman H. Nie, quoted in Kenneth Dixon's article 'Researchers Link Use of Internet, Social Isolation', the internet is but the latest in a long list of technological developments that have improved quality of life and negatively affected social interactions. Nie states:

> It's a history that began with the Industrial Revolution, when the male started to leave the house to earn a living and was not teaching his son how to carry on his craft. Now we have very few remaining institutions that are face to face.

Social media sites have altered the speed and effort we put into our communications. Instead of putting effort into accurately conveying our feelings, we focus on reducing the characters and posting what we think others would 'favourite', 'like' or 'share/retweet'. This 'new' direction of communication not only enables our short attention spans, but also encourages the expectation of instant gratification, which in turn fosters self-centredness in young people.

I'm not alone in my concern that the online social world is destroying real communication, dumbing down society and leading to a community of people who have no idea how to actually function in the real world. Many scholars, bloggers and social commentators have emphasised that more people need to put down their phones, turn off their computers, and learn – or re-learn – to communicate face-to-face. As the famous American writer Gertrude Stein once said, 'Everybody gets so much information all day long that they lose their common sense'.

One major indicator of the chilling decline in communication values was discussed in an article that Ethan A. Huff posted on NaturalNews .com. The article cited the case of Simone Back, a Brighton, UK, woman who announced her suicide on her Facebook status. None of her more than 1000 'friends' contacted her in response to the posting, and many simply argued with one another back and forth on her 'wall' about the legitimacy of her posting and whether or not Back had the freedom to choose choice to kill herself. As Huff says:

> This sick display of meaningless Facebook 'friendship' is only fuel for the fire to the many who say it represents the 'writing on the wall' of worse things to come. If individuals cannot learn to interact and develop meaningful relationships outside the narcissistic, soap-opera environment of the Facebook 'News Feed', then society is in for some major trouble down the road.

Our society may be well connected, but we are indeed lacking in any real form of accountability. As we make more connections online, we seem to be losing our humanity – our sense of *what is real* in terms of how our actions, online and otherwise, affect others' lives and feelings.

After all, what do our 'statuses' really mean – and what makes us post them? Imagine trying to explain to an alien – or someone from the nineteenth century – what social media is and why we post. There must be something from which we derive satisfaction, right? Why else would we be spending so much time on these platforms? What are we trying to portray about ourselves?

Are you a 'Boaster' – the type who showcases the 'highlight' reel of their lives, posting a collage of filtered Instagram pics of themselves at the beach, drinking cocktails at the pool, or hiking up Everest? Are you a social media 'Whinger' – someone who constantly takes carefully constructed digs at those they expect to be stalking their pages, playing a constant political game? What about the social media 'Stalkers' – those who rarely post, but always look at everyone else's pages? Then there is the 'Check-in assailant'! You might have turned down an invitation to the local lawn bowls tournament, citing a severe cold, but as you relax with a few wines at your local bar, suddenly the 'Check-in assailant' strikes again, and BAM – your cover is blown. See the next section for more on the check-in phenomenon.

Of course, not everyone uses social media in this way – some simply re-post pictures and statuses that make them smile or think. Some share funny moments; some even share sad moments. But it's a thought-provoking question to consider: what story are we painting of our lives via our social media pages – and more importantly, *why*?

In a study published in 2013 in *PLOS ONE*, scientists at the University of Pennsylvania examined the language used in 75 000 Facebook profiles. They found differences across ages, genders and certain personality traits. This allowed the researchers, led by computer and information scientist H. Andrew Schwartz, to make predictions about the profile of each user. Remarkably, the researchers found they could predict a user's gender with 92 per cent accuracy. They could also guess a user's age within three years more than half of the time.

Are we really that predictable and that transparent?

The psychology of social media

Why are we so drawn to social media, and what are we *really* getting out of it? Michael Poh, freelance blogger and regular contributor for Hongkiat.com, published an article titled 'The Psychology of Facebook' attempting to answer this question:

> The satisfaction comes about when our statuses get acknowledged, or even better, 'approved'. Deep inside, we users know that each time we update our statuses, many of our 'friends' will get to see it and possibly react to it.
>
> It is this awareness that makes us want to shout out our statuses. Thereafter, it gradually becomes a conditioning process where the user gets rewarded with acknowledgement and approval each time his or her status receives feedback from 'friends'.

Something clicked when I read this. There is no question that I feel a slight elation when something I post attracts many likes or comments, as well as a slight pang of discomfort when a post gets no attention. Not one measly 'like'! I get the vast majority of my social satisfaction and the core of my happiness from my family, my friends and my career – so it's a millisecond-long emotional experience. But it helps me appreciate how, for the young and impressionable, the lonely and those going through tough times, the acknowledgement and approval that social media can offer might make a significant impact on their lives.

A study on social networking sites by Pew Internet revealed that commenting on and 'liking' other users' posts makes up the majority of what users do on Facebook on any given day. Perhaps since we appreciate having others acknowledge us or 'like' our posts, we do the same to others as a sign of goodwill.

Poh's article also discusses another activity that is a trademark of the Facebook platform: checking in. 'Checking in' refers to the phenomenon of self-reported positioning – where an individual, via their chosen social media platform (Foursquare, Google+, Facebook,

Jiepang, GetGlue, and so on) 'checks in' to a physical place to share their location with their friends. Users can 'check in' to a specific location by text messaging or by using a mobile application on a smart phone – the application will use the phone's GPS to find the current location. Once users have checked in, they have the option of sharing their location with friends on services such as Twitter or Facebook.

Checking in carries the risk of becoming a tool for stalkers in the offline world. Even though Gen Y (and Gen other) users are aware that their privacy is at stake, they are still willing to compromise it just to share their present location with others. This begs the question: how powerful is the satisfaction we get when we tell others where we are and where we've been to, that it overrides our safety concerns? Do people simply not care that this unwise for personal safety reasons? Don't Y desire the same level of privacy that their parents had?

Ah, privacy: the grey area we all accept we are uncomfortable with. The death of our privacy through our engagement with social media faces continuing scrutiny, but rarely any *real* action. There's a chance that we've underestimated just how addicted Gen Ys are to their social media accounts – so much so that privacy doesn't even matter much to them anymore. It has been said that young people are now so connected to social media via mobile devices that they feel as thought they have lost a limb when they don't have them.

Social media addiction

A 2013 study by Ethan Kross and his co-authors, called 'Facebook Use Predicts Declines in Subjective Well-Being in Young Adults' in *PLOS ONE*, revealed that excessive use of social networking sites makes people miserable. Conducted among young adults with an average age of 19, the survey shows that the more they access these sites, the less satisfied they feel with their own lives.

Research from Sydney's Happiness Institute has supported such findings. They have discovered that Australians could have problems with 'mental obesity', or an overexposure to social media. And clinical psychologist Dr Tim Sharp has stated that overexposure to high volumes of useless information could affect our level of happiness. He cites that psychological symptoms of 'mental obesity' could be likened to anxiety, depression and stress.

Researchers at Chicago University concluded that addiction to social media can be stronger than to cigarettes and booze. They conducted an experiment where they recorded the cravings of several hundred people for several weeks. Social media cravings ranked ahead of cravings for cigarettes and alcohol. It also seems those suffering from social media 'addiction' are struggling to keep it under control at the workplace. There are countless reports of employers across Australia and internationally reviewing their social media policy in the wake of dropping productivity due to continual Facebook 'hits'.

Working social media

And it's not just productivity that is being affected. As social media continues to grow, so does the debate regarding its application within the realm of business. Employers are facing the new reality that the Y cohort expects their workplace to be social media–friendly. Members of Gen Y consider the use of the internet and social media websites to be a major condition of employment. Organisations that fail to proactively embrace this new technology are likely to have a hard time attracting and retaining younger employees.

This sentiment has been supported by findings from a study carried out by the US-based IT trade association CompTIA, which interviewed 700 office workers from a cross-section of different age groups. The findings uncovered that two-thirds of Generation Y employees judge employers according to their technology prowess, and expect workplaces to provide access to the types of technology that they use outside work. Since Gen Y and younger employees will eventually become the dominant workforce group, any problems that come as a result of falling behind with technology will become more serious.

The potential loss of productivity shouldn't be the sole factor companies consider when assessing the use of social media in the workplace. Many organisations use internal social media systems to effectively encourage employees to share 'tacit' knowledge (that is, knowledge that may have remained obscured in old-fashioned, hierarchically managed, silo-based organisations).

An example of 'tacit' knowledge is the complex social skills that are extremely difficult to teach, such as leadership. There is no process or training that can be guaranteed to make someone a leader – leadership skills extend from experience and shared learning.

Sales is another example of this. Great salespeople are commonly described as 'naturals' because it's difficult to transfer their skill to others. Yet tools like social media give people the ability to extend their knowledge 'socially' on a platform that many can access.

A study carried out by Millennial Branding identified that Gen Ys are using their personal networks and profiles as an extension of their professional personality. Even though they see Facebook primarily as a way to socialise with family and friends, they are inadvertently blending the two – increasingly blurring the lines between personal and work life.

Studies have shown that utilising this trend can help build positive external business communications. McKinsey's survey on web 2.0 usage showed that social networking and blogs are the most common networked enterprises. They report measurable business benefits, including increased marketing effectiveness, reduced communication cost and increased speed of access to knowledge.

Yammer is an in-house social media tool that more than 200000 leading companies are currently using. It brings together all of a company's employees inside a private and secure social network with the intention to drive business objectives. In 2012 the National Australia Bank introduced an internal social network using the Chatter platform as part of its online academy, and has found it to be positive in improving employee engagement.

In contrast to traditional workplace communication like emails and intranet posts, social media tools are becoming increasingly valuable in encouraging employees to actively create and distribute content. Yet according to James Griffen, head of digital strategy for social media monitoring company SR7, the rapid spread of individual voices and opinions, and the potential to generate influential groups, is one of the biggest risks social media poses:

> Social media represents a powerful shift in favour of stakeholders, enabling employees to share their grievances with an unlimited audience as soon as the grievance occurs.

Griffen believes that reducing such risks will require companies to quickly identify the 'small lone voice' and deal with any legitimate issues from within the organisation before the situation 'snowballs'. He reinforces the need for businesses to devise their own social media usage guidelines, so that staff are clear about what the organisation deems acceptable – and, more importantly, unacceptable.

There are things about work that clearly bother us all from time to time and, once in awhile, we need to let off some steam. Social media, however, isn't the wisest place to do so. As tempting as it is to 'share', Facebook and Twitter aren't the correct platforms for sharing your disagreement with one of your employer's policies or decisions. Outbursts like these could have potentially damaging effects on a company's reputation. Even when comments are 'deleted', it doesn't mean they go away entirely. (Screenshots, anyone?) Remember: the internet is forever. Organisations must develop and express very clear frameworks concerning what employees can and cannot post on social media about the company and its internal decisions and workings. When there are no rules in place to keep them from doing so, employees won't think twice about posting – or about the potential repercussions.

Gen Y and social media are collectively changing the face of communication in organisations. With increasing demand for the uptake of emerging technologies, the process of looking for jobs is changing fast. An increasing trend has been the use of blogs, Twitter, Facebook, LinkedIn and even YouTube to enhance potential applicants' presence. With more than 80 per cent of companies using LinkedIn for recruitment purposes, it seems there are countless ways that social media is interacting with today's working environment.

In the current business climate, companies will need to develop well-rounded strategies to manage social media use in the workplace. While a majority will still prefer to block social networking entirely, a growing number will expressly permit and enable these platforms for work-related purposes. And so they should, especially as social media is playing such an important role in brand extension and as part of an effective integrated marketing mix. As Sarah Timmerman, founder of online clothing retailer Beginning Boutique, has said, social media has revolutionised brand engagement:

> Social media transformed the marketing industry. A new BIA/Kelsey report says social media ad revenue will reach $11 billion by 2017. Brands have the ability to personally engage with customers like never before and it's showing in sales. People like to see brands respond when they comment on a Facebook post or mention the company in a tweet. The use of social media to handle the bulk of customer service inquiries is slowly becoming standard practice. Interaction fuels sales and social media agencies know that it is the key to brand success in a digital world.

Social media as a business strategy

For businesses, social media is so much more than a place to post a link to your website; it is an opportunity to interact with members of Gen Y. We are active participants, now in constant conversation with the brands who appeal to us. As Timmerman states, businesses are now realising that social media users are active participants that are in constant conversation with the brands that appeal to them:

> Given their severe fear of missing out—or FOMO, as the acronym goes—social media is Gen Y's go-to place for planning the best wardrobe, weekend or catch up. Businesses need to keep that in mind as they attempt to figure out how to deliver awesome places for connection online.

Sarah is one of the many Gen Y social media success stories. Her savvy social media expertise and effective marketing strategies have seen Beginning Boutique's collective social media network exceed well over 500 000 fans from around the world on Facebook, Instagram and Tumblr, making Beginning Boutique one of the emerging success stories from Australia's online fashion scene. Timmerman continues:

Gen Ys will have you in their social media life to be entertained. The internet has created an abundance of awesome content that makes us laugh, cry and cringe. Members of this age group are now able to have conversations with business owners and staff—immediately making those businesses part of their lives, and not just a shopping or commerce experience. This ultra-personal movement of media use has created an incredible opportunity for businesses to go viral—which, of course, is every brand's dream.

Like anything, social media has its benefits and its drawbacks. It's truly a mirror of society; it has never been, and never will be, anything more than the cold hard truth of humanity. Some of that is hard to watch, and easy to ignore. Yet it also shows us our more beautiful parts. Our compassion, our sense of mortality in times of tragedy, our support for the sick and helpless and the everyday heroes who have gone viral for simple acts of heartwarming humanity.

Social media is here to stay. The question is: How it will be used by Y in the future? The answer lies with Y.

CHAPTER 11

The Digital Umbilical Cord

Professor Mary Quigley

> Before you become too entranced with gorgeous gadgets and mesmerising video displays, let me remind you that information is not knowledge, knowledge is not wisdom, and wisdom is not foresight. Each grows out of the other, and we need them all.
>
> *Arthur C. Clarke*

Are Millennials misunderstood? They have been branded lazy, entitled, disloyal, tech-addicted social morons – but has it been too easy to plaster judgement over a generation who are only now settling into adulthood?

To understand Gen Y, consider their obsession with technology not as an addiction, but simply as the process by which they discover, understand and experience the world around them. Author Douglas Adams perhaps put it best:

I've come up with a set of rules that describe our reactions to technologies:

1 Anything that is in the world when you're born is normal and ordinary and is just a natural part of the way the world works.

2 Anything that's invented between when you're 15 and 35 is new and exciting and revolutionary and you can probably get a career in it.

3 Anything invented after you're 35 is against the natural order of things.

Gen Y never needed directions to get to where they were going; thanks to GPS, all they needed was an address. They have never really needed to go to their friend's house so they could study together, because Gchat and Facebook group messages allowed them share their assignments online. They find the CD player in their parents' car to be a useless piece of equipment. Having a 'chat' has seldom involved talking, and a tablet is no longer something you take in the morning. And if they're arguing over something trivial, there is the ultimate problem-solver: the answer is a click away, thanks to Google.

And yet, it's so easy for people who have not been incubated in the technological cocoon to misinterpret Gen Y's tech preoccupation as inattention or rudeness.

I learned recently that when they bring smart phones to class, it doesn't necessarily mean that they are texting. Like many professors, I don't allow texting in class. So when I noticed one student deeply engrossed with her phone, I was about to ask her to put it away when she suddenly referenced a line in the magazine article we were discussing. She was reading a 3000-word article on an iPhone screen.

This is the trend nowadays – and why would we ever keep students from using tools that *enhance* their education? As cited by Ashley Wainwright in her post '8 Studies Show iPads in the Classroom Improve Education' on the SecurEdge Blog, 86 per cent of student tablet owners believe tablets help them study more efficiently, and 76 per cent claim that tablets allow them to perform better in class. Additionally, more than one-quarter of students listed their laptop as the most important item in their bag – almost three times the number of students who chose textbooks.

So exactly how much do Gen Ys rely on technology in their daily lives? Well, consider that recent surveys have found, according to

Ekaterina Walter's article 'Number Crunching: The Top 51 Stats for Generation Y Marketers', that:

- 62.7 per cent of US undergraduates surveyed had an internet-capable handheld device.

- 67 per cent access Facebook from their smart phone.

- 59 per cent visit Facebook during class.

- 73 per cent earn virtual currency. Facebook Credits (36 per cent), Farmville Cash (25 per cent) and Microsoft Points (17 per cent) rank among the most popular.

- 75 per cent upload photos via their mobiles.

- 80 per cent use two or more devices simultaneously while watching TV.

While many Baby Boomers can type, text and tweet ad infinitum, we were not born digitally connected like the under-thirty, Gen Y crowd. We are new arrivals in a land where the natives can't imagine being disconnected even for a few minutes, as a journalism professor colleague and friend of mine found as she strolled around her seminar of 15 students as they discussed a reading. She noticed one student typing furiously on her laptop, so she peered over her shoulder. 'What are you doing?' the prof asked. 'Buying airline tickets', replied the student. 'No you're not', said the prof as she shut the laptop, leaving the student aghast.

This professor has won awards for teaching excellence; her class discussion was not boring. Instead, she found herself straddling the generation gap that separates digital immigrants from digital natives.

The classroom now translates to the office, where a recent survey conducted by security firm Fortinet canvassed 3800 twenty-something employees in 15 countries and found 'a critical mass of users who maintain they would go or have gone against company policy in order to use their own mobile device for work'. This survey showed the latest manifestation of this generation gap: Gen Y assumes the office welcomes BYOD (bring your own device). Of course, allowing employees to use their own smart phones, tablets and laptops to connect at work opens the door to data and security breaches and IT problems. But members of Gen Y view digital connectivity as a basic right.

At the office, school, home and elsewhere, Gen Y goes online whenever and however they want. A lawyer friend recently went to court to watch a cross-examination in a triple homicide case. He noticed a group of law students in the courtroom gallery, texting away during the testimony. They stopped only when the judge interrupted the witness and gave the students a lecture on courtroom courtesy and demeanour. Apparently the digital natives (and yes, some of their elders, too) are clueless about basic human courtesy.

I asked my students about why they feel the need to be online constantly, even during class. One admitted that he felt compelled to surf if the browser was open: 'I'm addicted', he said. While several students complained that it was distracting to sit next to other students who are on Facebook or typing away, they didn't want to say anything for fear of being judged by their fellow Ys; whatever other students want to do in class is their business. Another student tried to justify checking her email occasionally during class for 'important' messages – an 'important' message being anything from Kim Kardashian giving birth, to a Supreme Court ruling, to an internship posting.

Much has been written about Gen Ys and their need for constant connection. Some experts posit that it's possible to multitask and absorb the content of a lecture or a meeting while reading celeb gossip. Others disagree, arguing that when we do several things at once we do none very well. Some experts chastise digital immigrants to 'get over it' and accept the new world order. Still others argue that the Gen Y mind is wired differently and can easily switch between online and offline in a way that Boomers' minds can't.

The frequency of texting among all teens has now overtaken the frequency of *every other common form of interaction* with their friends. Fully two-thirds of teen texters say they are more likely to use their mobile phones to text their friends than talk to them – a statistic emphasised by figure 11.1.

Figure 11.1: going online wirelessly, by age group

Young adults 18-29

Adults 30 and older

All adults 18 and older

	By laptop	By cell / handheld	By another device
Young adults 18-29	55%	55%	28%
Adults 30 and older	34%	30%	10%
All adults 18 and older	38%	35%	14%

Source: Pew Internet & American Life Project, September 2009 Tracking Survey, August 18-September 14, 2009. N=2,253 and the margin of error is ±2%, based on all adults age 18 and older. Interviews were conducted in both English (n=2,179) and Spanish (n=74).

A study by the Pew Research Center titled 'Teens and Mobile Phones' showed that half of teens send 50 or more text messages a day, or 1500 texts a month – and one in three send more than 100 texts a day, or more than 3000 texts a month. The same study found that boys typically send and receive 30 texts a day; girls typically send and receive 80 messages per day. Globally, there are 1.8 billion mobile-phone owners aged under 30. The global youth mobile market is worth $360 billion annually – 10 times the size of the global recorded music industry, according to Graham D. Brown's article 'mobileYouth® - Youth Marketing and Mobile Culture'. See figure 11.2.

Figure 11.2: percentage of teens who own a mobile phone, by age

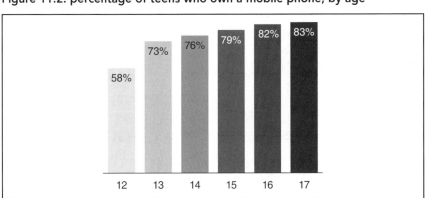

12	13	14	15	16	17
58%	73%	76%	79%	82%	83%

Note: September 2009 data.

So where does that leave us Baby Boomers, in whatever tiny part of the world where we still hold sway? Will we be forced to ban digital devices in our classrooms, offices and homes? A few professor friends have done just that. 'If they want to take notes, let them use pen and paper', one told me. Another suggested letting students use laptops during lectures, but then mandating 'top down' during the discussions.

These issues are not restricted to the classroom. If you think holding an office meeting is distracting now with people glancing at their phones, now that Gen Ys are flooding the workplace, will eye contact become a relic of the past? Where do we draw the line in digital sand?

Interestingly, Gen Ys themselves aren't the only ones living in fear of digital disconnect. There is evidence many of their parents are suffering from the effects of the electronic umbilical cord.

A long time ago, in a pre-digital era far, far away, college students called their parents once a week, using a phone card – and, before that time, they used an artefact known as a payphone. Except for health or money emergencies, that was the extent of contact with parents: once a week.

Not anymore. First it was mobile phones; now texting and instant messaging have replaced that weekly call... and replaced it and replaced it. As students head off to college, parents – many accustomed to keeping tabs on their teens via mobile phones – won't have to worry about losing contact. In a study conducted at Middlebury College and the University of Michigan, Professor Barbara Hofer found that college students text, phone and email their parents an average of 13 times a week.

Professor Hoffer refers to texting as an 'electronic tether'. She finds that all this digital hand-holding is counterproductive, especially for college freshmen. The first year of college is the time when these fledgling adults should be learning to make their own decisions about such pressing matters as classes, partying and how to do laundry – not constantly texting Mum to find out what she thinks.

And this habit of continuous contact doesn't end after the student makes it successfully through freshman year. A discussion among my class of NYU juniors and seniors got lively when the topic of texting came up. Many students admitted that they text and talk to parents – mostly mums – several times a day. What do they text about?

- 'My mother texts all the time asking questions like 'Did you go to the gym today?''

- 'My mom texts just to see what I am doing.'

- 'If I don't answer the cell phone, my mom texts to see if I am okay.'

It's understandable that parents are concerned about how that hard-earned $50 000 annual tuition and board is being spent. But is all this texting good or bad? The students were unsure, and were resigned that there was no way to stop parents from texting, short of turning off the phone – and they certainly weren't going to do *that*! Several mentioned that they preferred texting to talking on their phones to their parents, as it was less intrusive and took less time. Another plus: no-one knows you're texting a parent instead of a friend, so it's less socially awkward.

Of course, texting is just one form of electronic umbilical cord. Many students keep in contact with parents via Skype or iChat, especially when they are on a semester abroad – supposedly learning to make their own way through foreign lands. I iChatted with my daughter several times a week when she was in Italy last spring semester. For one, it was cheaper than talking on the phone, and it was so reassuring to be able to actually see her while we talked. Most of my NYU students had the same routine, except one who stopped because it made her too 'homesick' to see her family gathered around the laptop in their comfy living room while she lived in a tiny bedroom in a host family's house.

Some psychologists, like MIT professor Sherry Turkle, argue that the electronic umbilical cord needs to be cut. In her book *Alone*

Together: Why We Expect More from Technology and Less from Each Other she writes about the 'Huck Finn' moment when young adults are supposed to sail off alone down the Mississippi. But technology keeps them bound to their parents, hindering them from developing independence.

Gen Y has been connected to a technological umbilical cord for as long as they can remember. Technology has been one of the few constants in their external environment. Members of this generation are comfortable with technology; they adapt well when it changes, and are the very people who are taking it to the next level.

Though the complexity of the relationship between the Millennials and technology is extensive and multidimensional – and one that we cannot fully realise, discuss or understand in a single chapter – it's crucial to grasp the following: technology is a way of life for Gen Y.

For a connected generation – a generation that will be inevitably blamed for the ruin of formal language, and who is as young as the technology with which it has grown up – Gen Y is proving to be as complex as ... well, *every other generation.*

CHAPTER 12

TechnologY

Charlie Caruso

The production of too many useful things results in too many useless people.

Karl Marx

Meet June.

June has the potential to change the world – and the power to save our skin.

June isn't alive yet, and never will be.

June is a bracelet – a very clever bracelet that connects to your smart phone to let you know exactly how much sun exposure you've had each day.

The June bracelet, developed by 'smart product' maker Netatmo, keeps track of UV intensity, and will work out the exact amount of sun exposure you need according to your skin type. June reveals the full extent of how the sun is affecting you daily, and will accordingly provide you with skin care tips.

June isn't the future; she is the now.

Clever people around the world are developing devices like June every day. Companies like Netatmo are focused on meeting our growing gadget-obsessed needs.

This love of gadgets is not necessarily a Gen Y phenomenon; we all seem to jump on board when there's a cool new tech invention. Gen Ys might be the first digital natives – but compared to an average four year old, our technological uptake is relatively slow.

Gen Ys grew up alongside the computer. But the life story of the humble PC is like Benjamin Button's: it started life very, very big and comparatively slow. As the PC grew older, it progressively got smaller, thinner, quicker and more 'agile'. One day soon, it might disappear entirely.

The internet, by its birth year, is another member of the Y clan. It blossomed at about the same time, too, with the number of websites reaching a million around the same time that Gen Ys were transitioning through adolescence.

Technology has made the world seem a much smaller place. A single text, email or status update can connect you with a friend or family member regardless of where they are in the country or world. It's rare to walk down a bustling city street these days without witnessing a procession of smart-phone zombies, eyes glued to their screens – a scene that only ten years ago would have been regarded as closer to fiction than reality.

The downside of technology

Today's technology-driven environment has also brought continued concerns about health risks that were previously inconceivable. The recent concern for the youth of today is mobile phone addiction. The Japanese have termed this '*keitai-izon*', which literally means 'mobile phone dependence syndrome'.

As discussed in chapter 10, the explosion of social media, the booming smart phone market and the notable increase in the time many of us are spending online have continued to rouse concern regarding the broader implications of this new social trend. A considerable amount of research has been conducted over the past few years with respect to the true psychological impact of this emerging phenomenon.

Intel Labs released a survey in 2013 of 12 000 individuals aged 18 and older that found that 61 per cent of young adults feel that technology is 'dehumanising'. Despite popular belief, this research indicates that Millennials are currently the group *least* enthusiastic about technology.

'It seems at first glance that Millennials are rejecting technology, but I suspect the reality is more complicated and interesting', says Dr Genevieve Bell, director of interaction and experience research at Intel Labs, in an interview for Intel's Newsroom. '[It just] might be that Millennials want technology to do more for them, and we have work to do to make it much more personal and less burdensome.'

Many believe technology has distorted human interaction; we lose subtle nuances through our digital interactions. The complex processing and signalling of tone, gestures and body language are masked when communicating online. While these subtle signals might seem insignificant, they're vitally important in everyday communications.

As is so often said, technology makes us more 'connected' but less in touch.

But that doesn't mean we have lost our *humanity*. Far from it. Technology is enabling Gen Y to transform the world and lives every single day.

Gen Y tech inventors

Take Ryan Farris, a 29-year-old engineering manager at motion and control technology company Parker Hannifin. Farris co-invented the first lightweight and portable exoskeleton. Packed with sensors, it enables paraplegics with severe spinal cord injury to stand up and walk. It also enhances rehabilitation for people who have suffered a stroke.

Or Kelvin Doe from Sierra Leone who, at 13 years of age, used acid, soda and metal parts that he found in the trash to build his own battery because he found it too expensive to buy batteries for a project he was working on. He then constructed a generator to light his home and operate an FM radio station that he also built. He now employs his friends at the radio station.

Doe's inventions caught the attention of MIT Media Lab doctoral candidate David Sengeh. Doe participated in a solutions challenge Sengeh launched in 2012 asking students 'to invent solutions to problems that they saw in their daily lives'. Twenty-six-year-old biomechatronics researcher and fellow Sierra Leonean Sengeh wanted to enable youth in developing countries to find solutions to local problems. So he arranged for Doe, one of three winners, to become a resident practitioner at the MIT Media Lab. As if that weren't enough, Sengeh also happens to be working on a design that aims to offer the perfect fit for every prosthetic socket. He is also the cofounder of Lebone Solutions Inc., a company that won $200 000 from the World Bank to produce microbial fuel cells in Africa.

And it's not only Y men who are kicking some serious technological innovation butt, either. Erie Meyer, 29, and Aminatou Sow, 28, were growing tired of the constant refrain that there are seemingly no women in technology. So Sow — the New York–based digital engagement director for IAVA, an organisation that supports veterans — and Meyer, a senior adviser to the White House's Chief Technology Officer in D.C., took action. They created Listserv, a membership group for women in tech to talk about their accomplishments, brainstorm on projects, exchange tips and, importantly, *prove that they exist*. They called it Tech LadyMafia, and it currently includes more than 750 women who live in locations everywhere from California to Hong Kong.

Women are making other cool things, too. For example, take the smart clothing hanger that conveniently doubles as a dry cleaner. Yeah, you heard right: you hang your clothes on a hanger that *dry cleans* your clothes instead of just…hanging there. Developed by designers Beom-Seok Lee, Dong-Il Kim, Wan-Il So and Ki-Won Song, this device uses volatilised air that removes unpleasant smells and kills clothing germs and moulds without causing any damage to clothes.

Earlier this year, 18-year-old Eesha Khare from California's Lynbrooke High School made headlines with her device that can fully charge a smart phone battery in 20 to 30 seconds. She developed a tiny super capacitor that contains a special nanostructure, allowing for greater energy per unit volume.

Tech-savvY

Not only are Gen Ys some of technology's most voracious consumers; we are also leaders in developing it. The other great thing for this generation is that we are young enough to buy cool tech like Samsung's Get Smart wearable technology watch, *and* old enough to afford it.

But are we digital natives really all that different in terms of our digital proficiency and technological knowhow? Or do we just have the advantage of accessing such aids in the early years of our career and our lives?

There is research to discredit the theory that Gen Y has grown up immersed in technology, and therefore thinks and acts differently to previous generations. BC Institute of Technology associate dean Mark Bulle and faculty members Tannis Morgan and Adnan Qayyum published new evidence of this assertion in their multi-year, multi-phase research project, 'Digital Learners in Higher Education: Implications for Teaching, Learning and Technology'. Their research explores the validity of the claims that Gen Ys are significantly different from previous generations in their uptake and interaction with technology.

They found that there are no meaningful differences between students in Gen Y and older generations in the way they use technology, behave or prefer to learn.

As reported in the article 'Growing up Gen Y: The Impact of Being Immersed in Technology' on CLO Media's blog, the research team concluded that there is little conclusive evidence to prove that Gen Y have any distinct characteristics as a result of their increased technology use, including that of distinct preferences (especially for immediate feedback and experimental learning). They noted that the few studies purporting otherwise were based on speculation and lacked substance in the methodologies used to select, distribute and collect data (often as a result of being privately funded).

They also hit back against the myth that the increased immersion in technology has distinctively influenced the way Millennials learn and behave, specifically by changing the physical structure of the brain. They concluded that the few studies that support this proposition are again, lacking in substance and seem to lack empirical support and valid explanation to the connection between the data collected and the hypothesis proposed.

With the lack of any real evidence to prove otherwise, it appears that Gen Y is really no different from any other generation in terms of how we interact with technology. A sound theory is that you tend to understand whatever aids, tools and technology you had access to up to the age of 15. For some, that might have been skateboards; for others, Gameboys. But whatever it was, the tech you had up to that age is likely the tech that you pick up easily and are most comfortable with. After that, you're as slow on the uptake as the rest. So perhaps our relationship with technology and the digital age defines Gen Y less, and our proficiency has a lot more to do with timing, and our ability to use the technology on offer at an earlier part of our lives.

Technology and, at the core, the internet, has made what might have been impossible for the Baby Boomers, and unattainable for Gen Xers, easy to do for Gen Y. Sometimes it only requires a click of a mouse and tap of a keyboard.

The new frontiers of tech

Gen Ys are now at the age where we are building or planning to build our own homes. So new green tech like the innovative Window Pane

Plugs – power plugs built into windows to extract the energy from the sunlight and provide electricity – appeals to us. And it affects, in some part, the decisions we make.

Additionally, we might just be the first generation to embrace a new currency, one that is entirely free of government control. Enter Bitcoin, an experimental, decentralised digital currency. A purely peer-to-peer version of electronic cash, it facilitates online payments to be sent directly from one party to another without going through a financial institution.

Bitcoin is designed around the idea of cryptography (the art of writing or solving codes) to control the creation and transfer of money, rather than relying on central authorities – those big, bad 'banker' types.

The original Bitcoin software was developed by Satoshi Nakamoto, who released the Bitcoin IP as an open-source code. ('Open source' meaning that, instead of restricting others from stealing the intellectual property, the code was published to encourage others to further develop the technology.)

In order to effectively control the currency, the developers of Bitcoin ensured that the 'coins' are in limited supply; thus they must be 'mined'. Mining is done online, and 'miners' set their machines to run a series of complex calculations that tally up and certify all the transactions of other global Bitcoin holders. If the miner's computers complete these calculations and solve a complex mathematical puzzle before anyone else, they earn about 25 Bitcoins as payment.

When I initially discovered this, I felt it was a bit rough – probably because I knew there was a whole lot of no chance I could ever 'mine' Bitcoins. But then logic kicked in and I realised that there was zero chance of me single-handedly having the skills to mine gold (or any other precious trading metals, for that matter) – so I made my peace with the rationale behind Bitcoin mining.

As exciting as the burgeoning Bitcoin trade is, it isn't without risk. In February 2014, Mt. Gox, once one of the largest Bitcoin exchanges, closed after losing hundreds of millions of dollars' worth of the digital currency because of transaction malleability. Basically, a hacker was able to manipulate the code that makes a Bitcoin transaction happen, so that it looked like it didn't go through. The closure of Mt. Gox, which once claimed to account for 80 per cent of Bitcoin trading volume, has emphasised the technological and regulatory risks of this experimental (yet incredibly exciting) digital currency.

All potential risks or teething problems aside, if introducing a new currency to the world isn't the greatest representation of just who Gen Y is – and how significant the role technology plays in their identity (and potential) – I don't know what is.

eCareers

Millennials have every reason to assume that they can gather any and all necessary information with the touch of a button on a 24/7/365 basis. If they require raw market data, they can instantly access extended social networks and obtain immediate feedback. This is precisely why Y's relationship with technology has changed the way they relate to the world.

This applies to their careers, too. Nowadays, you need relatively few skills to 'move up the chain'; it's really about your resources, connections and being able to see beyond your immediate clan. The internet enables Gen Y to do that – incredibly quickly. LinkedIn is a perfect example. We have all heard the expression, 'It's not about *what* you know; it's *who* you know' – because it's true. Connections, networks, getting the chance to approach the next person up the rung where you need to be, is what enables career progression.

Once upon a time, you had to be a member of a well-connected family to be working in the circles that could 'make things happen'. Or you'd have to attend university with such people – or somehow beg, borrow or steal to get noticed by them.

Gen Y, however, has resources like Inmail. And I can assure you that this book would not have existed without LinkedIn. I might not have even had the inspiration to think of it.

Y? Because LinkedIn was how I approached the majority of people I interviewed and the authors who contributed to this book.

Digital dependence

It's not just the ability to connect to people you might have never had the chance to; it's the inspiration and knowledge required to get to 'the next step' that Gen Ys use to *make things happen*. Gen Ys are exposed to new content and ideas on a daily basis. We are a generation of people who, pretty soon, will have 100 per cent mobile penetration and internet access, and the ability to consume information and ideas at an unprecedented rate.

And because we can end an argument quickly thanks to Miss Google, there has been a marked change in the priority of information we store versus what we can always Google. Gen Ys are often surprised by how much they *don't* know and how much they rely on external aids to function every day.

Mark Caruso, an Australian mining entrepreneur (aka my father-in-law) once told me that intelligence is simply the ability to manipulate the environment at hand, with the resources available, in the most efficient way possible to achieve a desired outcome, much faster than everyone else. This seems a good analogy for why Gen Ys don't put in any real effort to hone skills that might be required to 'survive' without the aid of the internet and technology. One of our 'resources available' is the internet; why would we try to survive without it? If all other generations were to ship off to Mars and take Google with them, leaving behind Gen Y to run the planet and feed themselves, would enough of us be able to sustain ourselves? Would we have enough 'real life' skills to be able to last without Google?

As technological devices, search capacities and cloud-enabled content-retrieval continue to evolve, Millennials will have the advantage of instinctively understanding and building upon emerging technologies. Because the opportunities these provide are just so immense, it won't be long before we have built *new* technologies that mitigate any consequences of our lack of 'real world' knowledge and dependence on the internet – simply because we may have solved the potential 'real world' catastrophes.

ParticipatorY culture

The availability of technology has created a heightened ability to connect and collaborate with others. New technology creates new rituals of behaviour, new belief systems and new rites of passage – and new challenges, many of which will likely be ethical. Technology happens not only within the current social context; it also creates new cultures and new social contexts.

A great example of this is the new phenomenon of 'participatory culture', a trend that's essentially the opposite of consumer culture. Participatory culture is where people (the public) act not only as consumers, but as contributors or producers (*pro*sumers) as well. This trend is most commonly applied to the creation of some types of published media, like on social media. Recent technological advances have given individuals the power to create and publish such content, usually through the internet and over social media platforms.

Paul Willis's article titled 'Foot Soldiers of Modernity: The Dialectics of Cultural Consumption and the 21st-Century School' describes this new culture as it relates to the internet and Web 2.0:

> [In participatory culture] young people creatively respond to a plethora of electronic signals and cultural commodities in ways that surprise their makers, finding meanings and identities never meant to be there and defying simple nostrums that bewail the manipulation or passivity of 'consumers'.

Technology and the innovation that has led to the development of the internet have come to play a significant role in the extension of participatory culture – simply because it has enabled individuals from around the world to work collaboratively; generate and disseminate news, ideas and creative works; and connect with people who share similar goals and interests.

The argument about whether or not digital natives interact with and embrace technology any differently than our predecessors is relatively insignificant. What is exciting, unique and special to Gen Y is that we just might be the right generation, positioned in our prime at the right time, to use our newly accessible 'superpowers' to transform the world. Being a generation privy to the mistakes of generations gone by – and one less motivated by power, greed and competitiveness – Gen Ys might just be the 'chosen ones', empowered to transcend, reshape and redefine the world that we will one day leave behind.

The potential is limitless.

CHAPTER 13

EnviromentalY

Dr Samantha Smith

Never mistake motion for action.

Ernest Hemingway

Generation Y has grown up surrounded by talk of the environment and the many pressing threats to its sustainability. Issues like the greenhouse effect, reducing the vast hole in the ozone layer, saving the whales and preventing deforestation were, for many, common discussions in the classroom and at home. This exposure has resulted in an assumption that Millennials are more sensitive to environmental issues and concerns than previous generations.

In July 2013, 1500 young people came together in Melbourne to take part in Power Shift, the largest climate summit in Australia's history. Coordinated by the Australian Youth Climate Coalition and featuring a number of inspirational young environmentalists, the summit began with Australia's first-ever meeting of the Youth Climate Cabinet in the City Square. Stopping the traffic, participants then proceeded en masse to the federal government offices with a banner demanding politicians 'Aim higher on climate because our future is your mandate'.

Power Shift made it clear that there are some real standout members of Gen Y who are incredibly passionate and active when it comes to getting action on climate change. But are these vocal activists as common among this generation as we'd like to think?

Ladies and gentlemen, please shed a tear for the planet because – contrary to popular belief – it would seem not.

American psychology academics Jean Twenge, Elise Freeman and Keith Campbell recently examined young adults' life goals, their concern for others and their civic orientation in a paper published in the *Journal of Personality and Social Psychology*. They found that some of the largest declines appear to be in taking action to help the environment.

To isolate generational or time-period effects due to age or development, the researchers examined data from Boomers, Generation X and Generation Y at the same age. When it came to the environment, three times as many Gen Ys (15 per cent) than Boomers (5 per cent) said they made no personal effort at all to help it. Likewise, Gen Ys were less likely to say they made an effort to flick off the switch to save energy (51 per cent of Gen Ys reported making an effort, compared to 68 per cent of Boomers and 60 per cent of Generation Xers).

And Australia's Millennials appear to be no different. The Australian Bureau of Statistics' 2012 report 'Environmental Views and Behaviour' found that 18-to-24 year olds were less concerned than *any other age group* when it comes to environmental problems in general – or even about issues closer to home such as water shortages in this drought-prone land.

Perhaps most revealing is the difference between the *perception* of Gen Ys as being environmentally sensitive and their actual *behaviour*. To demonstrate the case, consider how they act when it comes to electricity consumption. Nationally, the majority of Australians reported to the ABS that they took steps to limit their personal electricity use. However, once again, Gen Ys were less likely to claim that they were doing this, with only 79 per cent of 18-to-24 year olds having taken steps to be energy efficient, compared with 92 per cent of Australians aged 35 to 74 years.

It is worth noting that a large portion of Millennials still live with their parents, and are therefore not yet financially responsible for their personal consumption of energy. According to the Australian Bureau of Statistics' 2009 report into the living arrangements of young people, almost one in four (23 per cent) people in Australia aged 20 to 34 years were living at home with their parents in 2006, compared with 19 per cent two decades earlier. Almost half (45 per cent) of people aged 20 to 24 who had never left home said that the main reason for this was financial.

Over to the US, and Pew Research Center's 2012 analysis of young adult living arrangements by their senior economist Richard Fry found that 36 per cent of 18-to-31 year olds were living in their parents' home. That number rises to 56 per cent when looking specifically at younger Millennials' (aged 18 to 24) living arrangements. With these living arrangement stats in mind, relying on parents to finance the cost of electricity in the home – and therefore not having the monetary incentive to consume less – may influence Millennials' individual electricity consumption habits.

An interesting environmental contrast came about when looking at climate change concerns. The ABS found in their environmental views and behaviour research that 61 per cent of Australians aged 18 to 24 highlighted concerns about climate change, compared to only 40 per cent of Australians aged 75 and older. What has been a prominent political issue in the Australian media is no doubt set to further affect Gen Ys in years to come.

So why does Generation Y appear on paper to be concerned about the hot topic of global warming – yet also seem averse to pitching in and switching off electricity to attempt to cool down the earth?

To explore the relationship Gen Ys have with the environment and delve into what they see as their environmental challenges and green behavioural motivations, I conducted a qualitative research study with Gen Y students from a Melbourne university. Eight focus groups were held with a gender mix and equal representation from Gen Ys living with their parents and Gen Ys living out of home.

On the topic of electricity use, the majority of those living at home confirmed that they were not responsible for any percentage of payment of the electricity bill. Not surprisingly, when it came to what impact their disposable income had on how much electricity they used in the home, close to 90 per cent of those who lived at home noted that it had either not a very strong impact or no impact at all. In contrast, over half of those who lived out of home said it had either a fairly or very strong impact.

When asked what attitudes they had towards the concept of 'living a green life', a common theme raised by both sets of focus group participants was the degree of 'effort' required:

- 'You have to put in heaps more effort [to live a green life]; just for example turning off all the power points – ten minutes a day of your life.'

- 'For a little bit of effort I would do it; but if it's going to cost me a lot [of effort], then I don't think I would [act in an environmentally friendly way].'

- 'I think the first step [to being green] is always the hardest step; putting in the effort to change your lifestyle.'

- 'What do you actually get in return for the effort you put in?'

With the exception of a few participants who came from households with a reportedly strong environmental conscience, the majority of Gen Ys in the focus groups *did not* appear to be concerned about the environment – and did not strongly aspire to 'live a green life'. Responses to the question, 'What does it mean to you all to live a green life?' varied dramatically:

- 'I suppose it would be minimising your daily impact on the environment.'

- 'Recycle everything.'

- 'A better future.'

- 'Just being conscious and aware and taking reasonable measures to limit your usage of electricity, water and natural resources.'

- 'When you buy stuff from the market, always go for local produce, eating less meat.'

- 'I think it's another way of putting more worry and stress into your life.'

In general, the majority of Gen Ys represented in the focus groups appeared to dismiss the impact that they have on the environment. Many lacked any sense of personal ownership about the environment and seemed to believe that businesses and developing and developed countries are the key culprits of environmentally damaging practices. They deemed anything they personally did as insignificant:

- '…If we are the only ones that are going to [live a green life], and on a larger scale not many people are going to do it, then what is the point?'

- 'Any effort we make is really futile, because if the countries with huge populations aren't going to do anything, we are not going to suddenly stop climate change – assuming that there is climate change. We're not suddenly going to stop it because Australia is energy efficient.'

- 'I think businesses use more energy than households… they're the ones causing more greenhouse gases.'

- 'If they are directing [energy saving campaigns] to the household, I don't think it's the right people [to focus on]. I think it's the big companies that it needs to be directed to. If I compare my electricity usage with my workplace, I'm surprised you can even see the use. They turn things on all the time which do not need to be turned on.'

- 'I don't feel it's households that are wasting the most electricity. I think it's companies, factories and stuff. So I feel if I do a little bit, it's nothing compared to what they waste.'

Gen Y focus group participants frequently implied the environmental issue would have to directly have an impact on them in order to elicit a response:

- 'You see these big epic clips of rainforests being cut down and polar bears standing on tiny blocks of ice and you can't really relate to that... You know that is the reality of it, but at the same time you are thinking, 'I'm never going to see that."

- '[Older generations] worry for their great, great, great, great grandson. I'm not going to meet them, so I don't give a shit.'

- 'We don't really care because we don't have children ourselves and we don't care about their future, whereas the older generation care about future generations, so they would look after their energy.'

- 'You'll only get everyone to care [about climate change] when it directly inconveniences them. You can say it's a big problem, but it doesn't inconvenience us personally that much.'

- 'I don't know just why it's bad and what it's doing to our environment, because I don't see the bad, literally.'

- 'We can see [the impact of smoking and drinking] evidently in people's lives and on the TV all the time... Because we're not exposed to [things to do with the effects of electricity] that much... and it's not really compelling us to care, we don't see it as a big deal.'

- '... if they say living green means you are going to live ten years longer, everybody would do it.'

These comments clearly identify the lack of personal accountability Gen Ys have towards the environment and their impact on it, whilst echoing a striking message of disempowerment. Despite how well connected today's youth are, they've done comparatively little to promote positive environmental actions – possibly both as a result of their fondness for and consumption of social media.

Consider the fact that because they access so much of their news through social media, they receive urgent Climate Council warnings and alerts of devastating typhoons through the same news stream as the latest celebrity scandal. These items sit side by side, one after another in their Twitter streams. As a result, news delivery may be changing the way that they think about issues and adopt causes. It's creating a generation that knows a little about a lot but remains disengaged from the planet's problems and avoids joining a collective force for environmental change.

Furthermore, with energy-hungry technologies making our lives more connected and efficient, using electricity prudently appears to be easier said than done. It's especially challenging for tech-savvy and tech-reliant Gen Ys who favour multitasking and have a strong penchant for social media.

The question is — will the majority of Generation Y continue to keep their heads buried deep in the sand in favour of having their iPhones charged and being up to date with their Facebook news feed? If the answer is yes, how long can they possibly keep this up?

What is certain is that there is a large gulf between Generation Ys' perceptions of being environmentally friendly and the reality of their actions. In the future it will be fascinating to see if the collective efforts of groups like the Australian Youth Climate Coalition and their engaged and connected Millennials are able to influence environmental behaviour and change social dynamics.

CHAPTER 14

GloballY

Ryan Heath

> One of the fundamental questions of today's world is
> undoubtedly the question of equitable globalisation.
>
> *Janez Drnovsek*

We have come to think of the twenty-first century as the 'Asian century'. But the coming decades will not only be 'geographically different, but also generationally different', according to International Monetary Fund head Christine Lagarde. Despite lower birth rates in the world's richest nations and interventions like China's one-child policy, the world is experiencing a 'youth bulge' that will make Generation Y the most populous of all generations. This 'bubble' intersects with the world's digital transformation, indicating that the future will be shaped by different values and principles than the ones we have been used to in the Baby Boomer–led West. It follows that we need to account *globally* for this most global of generations.

Few members of Gen Y – or the 'post-eighties generation', as they are known in China, and 'Millennials' in many other places – have enjoyed the privilege that we have in Australia of coming of age in a young and rich country. Yet most of them are optimistic and connected. Young people in developing economies do not feel pushed down or sidelined because of their age. The aptly named Brazilian Dream Project, which studied 18-to-24 year olds, found that those surveyed described themselves most frequently as 'dreamers, consumers, responsible and hard-working'.

Young people are part of a thriving ascendency. Ninety-three per cent of Chinese youth say their country's best days are ahead, compared to 67 per cent globally. Contrast that with the outlook of European youth, who worry that their economies are on the wrong track and that their fate is controlled by others who will not look after their interests. A mere 6 per cent of French youth think the country's best days are ahead of them.

Wherever they live, Gen Ys are also the heart of today's global megatrends: the demand for individual empowerment within a global worldview, and the rise of Asia.

Who is Gen Y around the world?

This is the constantly connected generation: connected to technology, to each other and to the world. They spend an average of six hours a day online—starting at five hours a day in Africa through to seven hours a day in Latin and North America. When *The Australian*'s Angela Shanahan observed that 'young people treat their phones like a piece of their anatomy', she tapped the biggest driver of change of all: three-quarters of the world's Gen Ys own a smart phone. They go to bed and wake up next to their phones; they take them out at the dinner table. The internet is their preferred source of information and entertainment. Together, Facebook—created by Gen Y poster boy Mark Zuckerberg—and Twitter have more users *than China has citizens*. No-one can deny the presence of this pervasive use.

Ninety per cent of Gen Y agrees technology has made them better informed about political issues in their country, despite the fact that 52 per cent believe their country's current political system does not represent their values and beliefs. More than 80 per cent believe technology has made it easier to overcome language barriers and get a job.

Different experiences, but equally connected = similar values

The results of the largest-ever global survey of Gen Y, 2013's Telefonica–Financial Times Millennial Survey (comprising in-depth interviews with 12 000 young adults in 15 countries), are confounding. They show the danger of assumptions about differences between rich and developing countries, left and right politics, and more.

Climate change is considered a more important issue among young South Americans than in the West. Half the world's Gen Y cohort claims that a job with good pay is a *privilege*, not a right. Though a real gender gap remains – half think that men and women do not enjoy equal rights in their lives – virtually all believe the genders *are* equal. Even those from middle-income countries tend to value experiences over possessions. Virtually all in Gen Y think they can make a local difference, but are split about whether they can make a *global* difference. European, Russian, Chinese and Japanese youth are most pessimistic, while Millennials from the rest of the world tend to have a more optimistic outlook.

What emerges strongly from nearly all literature about Generation Y is they do not like taking 'no' for an answer; that is, they are reluctant to have others define their place in the world. While this perspective seems to lead to the tendency to label them 'entitled' or 'selfish' or 'disloyal', what it really indicates is a different value system.

Christine Lagarde, managing director of the International Monetary Fund and author of the article 'A New Global Economy for a New Generation, sees the emerging values of this new generation as greater openness, stronger inclusion and better accountability. Let's explore these a little more:

- *Greater openness.* Gen Ys are open to the world, and to the idea of a common global community. They don't expect to follow one path in life, or a set timetable. For example, many are willing to trade better pay for a position that brings them more joy. A recent MTV poll found half of Gen Ys would rather be unemployed than do a job they hate. They expect to be able to marry someone of their choosing. They are more likely to be entrepreneurial than previous generations, and they are at the forefront of trends like the development of micro-multinationals: sole traders (or very small businesses) that operate in multiple countries, often thanks to the power of the internet.

- *Stronger inclusion.* Gen Ys embrace tolerance, respect and fairness for all. The examples range from the Arab Spring movements, to intolerance of workplace bullying, to their support for marriage equality. They know that when women do better, economies do better. They are a generation whose approach to social issues is fundamentally altering the careers they pursue, the way charities operate and the methods used to conduct political campaigns.

- *Better accountability.* The new generation demands transparency. They have low levels of trust in long-standing institutions such as churches, governments and old companies. If you want their money or support, you need to allow them to interact and participate – they want answers to their questions and complaints via social networks such Twitter, Facebook and Tumblr. They want proof, not words, that you behave ethically, whether in business or politics.

Educational experiences are the great bond between youth of all generations. Logically, Generation Y is the most educated generation. Virtually all of today's youth have attended school. But while university education has exploded, educational debt has exploded along with it.

Author Riva Froymovich writes in *The End of the Good Life*, 'There was a time when the American Dream was not an illusion', before going on to detail a hollowed-out American and European middle class. America globalised its middle-class consumption-driven dream – which was snatched away from most of Generation Y, leaving them with high debt, hardly any assets and just as few prospects for fulfilling their full potential.

In the US, outstanding student loans are now greater than both national credit card loans and car loans, but rich economies aren't producing enough of the jobs needed to pay off those debts. Even doctors or lawyers have to wait until they're 30 or 35 to start building, because of the debts they incur to qualify. It is now a given that Gen Y will delay marriage, home purchases and other major life decisions until their late twenties or thirties, unlike prior generations, who passed all of these milestones at younger ages. According to the Pew Research Center, the net worth of an under-35 year old's household in the US is 68 per cent less than those same households in 1984. Whereas my parents were unusual in delaying their marriage until the age of 28, and having me at the age of 30, for Generation Y that is now the average.

It's all too common for young people today to work below their potential, or to be underpaid when that potential is used. We have higher expectations of these individuals at a time when the West's ability to support them is shrinking – when economies simply cannot pay them for their qualifications.

Consider the fact that nine out of ten first jobs in Italy are temporary jobs, no matter what level of education the job-holder has achieved. In Japan, barely half of graduates have job offers in the year they finish their studies. A graduate in India will just as likely work in an outsourced call centre as in their chosen field. And a 2011 poll by Demos found that half of American Gen Ys think they will end up materially worse off than their parents.

Those that do not find stable jobs after completing their education find themselves in a holding pattern: failing to accrue savings, not worthy of promotion, beholden to the global economy's mood swings, finding it hard to immigrate as struggling economies produce xenophobic backlashes.

And yet their underlying optimism remains. It's a basic truth in our digital world that 'one person and one action' – in the words of 23-year-old entrepreneur Ceri Davies, who suffers from both spina bifida and cerebral palsy – can effect great change. Ceri set up her own company at the age of 18, and has never looked back: 'I am permanently in a wheelchair. But this has not stopped me from living my life and living out my aspirations.' To borrow the words of my own boss, Vice President of the European Commission (the European Union's government) Neelie Kroes:

> This generation has the guts, intelligence and awareness to tell all of us some important truths. They get that technology affects everything from equality to climate change. I really take the views of these digital natives seriously, and so should smart companies and governments.

How Australia differs from others

Australia's Gen Y faces barriers, too — but they're smaller than most of their peers'. Australia is the richest country in the G20, with double the annual per-capita income of the European Union, the world's largest economy.

The global financial crisis struck in 2008 as the wave of Baby Boomer retirements was starting. Instead of Gen Ys asserting themselves in the workplace, they instead had to take a backseat to Boomers who were forced to stay in the workplace. Yet unlike in many other countries — where Gen Y workers were the first to go during cuts, or were unable to get in the front door due to hiring freezes — Australians continue to enjoy high rates of employment. We cannot say the same of countries like Greece or Spain, where more than half of Gen Y not in education is unemployed.

It is also striking how Australians have earlier opportunities for career advancement than many others. I have a smaller salary today in 2014 than I did in 2007 in Australia. Unlike nearly all my peers, I am lucky to hold a permanent role (something that the human resources department never fails to point out). And I'm even luckier than others in my team, who have more degrees and speak more languages but can't escape short-term contracts. Too many Baby Boomers won't leave and can't be sacked. Great for them as individuals, but a social disaster for unlucky Gen Y.

That personal story is indicative of a wider truth: today, many countries effectively operate a dual labour market based on which generation you belong to. In Japan, if you are young, you probably work a string of temporary contracts; in the US, you probably lacked health insurance (until Obama's health law kicked in), and probably spend most of your career paying for your education. In Europe you literally exist under different workplace rules and laws to your parents. The expensive social security net built up the decades after World War II is for others, not you. It's more like a new glass ceiling than a net if you were unlucky enough to be born after 1985.

What is next for Gen Y?

We will continue to compete against the world, and not just our compatriots. We will have to fund our ageing parents, who will live much longer than *their* parents. But we will continue to enjoy much higher material standards of living than any previous generation. In Australia the share of the population aged over 65 will rise from 13 per cent to 23 per cent by 2050 (that's 7 million people). In Europe, 30 per cent will be over 65. A flood of opportunity will arrive as the Baby Boomers do complete their retirements, starting now and lasting through to 2030. Young people will have to proactively find the opportunities. They might not always be easy to uncover, but they *will* be there.

It will not all be smooth sailing. There will be major questions about whether digital technology can deliver the sort of middle class jobs that will enable its addicted users to fund this ageing population's needs. There will be resource crunches: not enough houses and not enough water, to name just two. There will be competitive tensions, as the youth of Brazil and Asia and Africa wonder why they should fund richer countries who did not reform quickly enough or deeply enough to deal with these new world realities.

But through it all, Gen Ys will see themselves as connected to each other and able to rise to the challenge.

CHAPTER 15

Y Work?

Ryan Gibson

> Choose a job you love, and you will never have to work a day in your life.
>
> *Confucius*

You've heard about Generation Y's less-than-flattering reputation several times already throughout this book: that we're a self-entitled group who were placed on pedestals by our doting Baby Boomer parents and raised during prosperous economic times. We saw in chapter 2 how older colleagues tend to view Y as overly ambitious dreamers who don't want to pay their dues and are only concerned about higher pay and more time off.

A stark contrast to this picture is one of Gen Y as a *driven* generation – which is what our high rates of entrepreneurship, stellar education and super-connectedness suggest. We're a generation who, if we don't know how to do something, will find a way to learn it.

Millennials were born to be workplace powerhouses, and we're changing the way work happens. We arrive at the office with an active knowledge of business and strategic issues, with the goal of reforming and stimulating operations.

Millennials display a pursuit of knowledge and understanding that prior generations simply didn't show. We know this approach is transforming our workplaces and even technology by way of cloud computing and apps. Even the way we communicate via emails and Skype is informed by Gen Y values. Although 'interconnectedness' has become a throwaway term, it very much sums up the twenty-first century workplace mentality.

For example, I spent some time working for travel operator AsiaRooms .com. Though the company's head office was located in Singapore, the team had members in the UK and Lithuania — which required not just telecommuting, but doing so *across time zones*. Thankfully, tools like Google Hangout and Skype make collaboration across time zones easy — especially for a workforce comprising Millennials.

Social networking software application Buffer App has built an entire business on 'interconnectedness' with employees around the world. They use tools including Sqwiggle, Trello, HipChat, 'I Done this' and Hackpad to stay in communication with one another despite their varying global locations. Co-founder Joel Gascoigne stresses that Buffer's 'outstanding' customer support is due to this distributed workforce, and that he consciously made the decision to follow this model. Joel sums this approach up perfectly on his personal blog:

> People ask how we manage it, and I share our workflows and tools. We call HipChat our office, and a number of Google Hangouts serve as our conference rooms. I genuinely believe that [the way] we're set up will be very normal in a few years. There are certainly challenges and we're still figuring a lot of it out. It's fun and a huge privilege to be able to be part of this innovation and experiment and share our learnings.

While these all sound like positive innovations, there is another side to my generation. MTV conducted a 'No Collar Workers' study of American Gen Ys in 2012, with results that may shake some older workers to their core. One finding: 92 per cent of those surveyed feel their company is 'lucky to have them'. Seventy-six per cent of Millennials think their boss could learn a lot from them. These results make it easy to interpret Gen Y's attitudes as egotistical and self-important.

But receiving these labels doesn't pose a real threat to the Gen Y workforce; we're used to being misunderstood and branded with labels that stem from the chasm between us and our predecessors. What does matter to us, however, is the fact that Gen Ys are suffering from a considerable lack of trust in the workplace.

Older generations – particularly those in leadership positions – don't trust Gen Y. Typically, professional success has meant learning one role and showing commitment to it. However, Gen Ys are projected to have six to eight different careers during our professional lives. Staff currently aged under 30 start looking for a new role within 18 months of arriving at a given job. But businesses should be aiming to capitalise on the time they have with Gen Y – not highlight the negatives.

It's not hard to see why Gen Y might clash with other generations in the workplace; we're eager, ambitious and want to develop as much as we can. We embrace risk-taking rather than playing it safe. While other generations have been sold the story on job security, we've been brought up in an ever-changing world that values bravado.

If companies can't meet Gen Ys' expectations, not only will these youngest members of the workforce leave their jobs; there's a significant chance *they'll start their own businesses*. Across the US, UK and Australia, dissatisfied Gen Y leaders fed up with the constraints of a nine-to-five lifestyle are forming hubs of entrepreneurship.

Deloitte noted in its study 'Generation Y: Powerhouse of the Global Economy' that respect is a two-way street. Gen Y is willing to learn and deliver results to older staff, if those older staff members trust them to achieve outcomes. Companies that foster respect between generations garner better outcomes; the importance of teaching and learning becomes ingrained. For example, IBM pairs graduates with senior management. The graduates teach the senior management about social media while the younger staff learn about business strategy from their older counterparts. In this situation, everybody wins!

Twenty-first century HR shouldn't be focusing on an employee's longevity with a company or a role anymore. These days, the focus must be on *capacity* and *results*. Gen Y is eager to deliver. So how do managers 'manage' a generation so hell-bent on breaking the rules?

Managing Generation Y

Whether your business employs only Generation Y workers or has numerous generations working side-by-side, you will benefit from learning specially adapted management techniques. This becomes especially important if you have employees from different generations managing Gen Y employees. According to research conducted by the Institute of Leadership and Management (ILM), 'Great Expectations – Managing Generation Y', Gen Y workers:

- are academically talented
- are ambitious and motivated
- plan to move jobs within two years
- value both money and status
- value interesting/challenging work higher than salary
- want to be 'coached' rather than managed.

The research also discovered that 32 per cent of recent graduates were dissatisfied with their boss's performance.

So how can these very bosses effectively manage their Gen Y workers? The ILM recommends connecting graduates and leaders by focusing on the following key areas.

Progression

Gen Y workers are frequently dubbed disloyal job-hoppers; but why stay in a company where you have no chance of progression? Most businesses would improve their staff retention by offering continued learning and training to build skills as well as clear progression paths. Not only will this encourage Gen Y workers to remain within companies; it will save time and money on recruitment. Setting aside time and budget for industry-related seminars and conventions is yet another way to keep employees involved and engaged.

Coaching

The ILM discovered that 56 per cent of graduates cited their 'ideal' manager not so much as a 'boss', but as a *coach or mentor figure*. Gen Y workers benefit more from being coached than from being directed or micromanaged. The problem is that other generations aren't always accustomed to receiving – and therefore giving – this style of supervision. Therefore, it often requires specific management training.

Feedback and recognition

You only have to look at their use of social media and communication tools to realise that Gen Y places great importance on *interaction and acknowledgement* – something that translates to their work life. Giving feedback and acknowledging progress conveys to Gen Y workers that they're working towards something and *have a purpose*. Open conversations that involve the worker in their own progress are the best way to work with members of this generation.

Freedom and flexibility

Gen Y employees are used to having a number of options and alternatives right at their fingertips. They'll appreciate managers who let them work towards a goal in their own way. Managers can still retain control over projects by explaining what end result is required; but allowing employees to make choices for themselves as to *how* they will attain this objective shows they are trusted, something 35 per cent of graduates consider important.

Gen Y employee freedom and flexibility also extends further than the job role. Millennials seek freedom in a physical sense – literally removing the traditional barriers of office isolation.

Automattic – the company founded by Gen Y Matt Mullenweg – has enforced this mindset by removing 'physical office' constraints. The company has around 190 employees scattered across 141 cities and 28 countries – nearly all of whom work from home.

Mullenweg is not 'anti-office' as a rule; he simply sees himself as more 'location agnostic'. If a worker really wants an office, they are free to seek one out. Any person can get a desk at a co-location space, and Automattic is happy to reimburse employees for the expense.

What has this freedom and flexibility within the workplace afforded Automattic? The company's flagship blogging platform, Wordpress, now powers 18.9 per cent of the web and has over 46 million downloads, according to Mullenweg.

Enabling Gen Ys to make their own decisions within the workplace reaps reward. A positive culture breeds successful results.

Balance

Gen Y values a work–life balance more than other generations; our motto is 'work smarter, not harder'. Managers will therefore benefit from considering ways in which to balance the working day. For example, why have employees waste time commuting when you could offer the option of working from home? Businesses must present a more balanced environment for Gen Y. Removing the traditional working infrastructure – the very thing that prevents a sense of balance – is the first step in doing so. Allowing more flexibility creates a more balanced lifestyle for employees.

The notion of nine to five creates a situation where 'office presence' is mandatory, and performance is measured based on the amount of time employees spend in the office. The Gen Y 'work smarter, not harder' attitude would question this: 'Is it possible for all humans to be programmed where all are at their prime between these hours?' After all, might some people do their best work from 6 am through 9 am, or 5 pm to 11 pm? Allowing for these variations matches the work culture Millennials seek to be part of.

Cisco Systems is an excellent example of a large-scale global organisation that has been able to appeal to Generation Y's desires for professional and personal balance. As reported in the article 'The 46 Healthiest Companies to Work for in America' on Greatist.com:

> This multinational corporation hooks up its work-from-home employees with state-of-the-art equipment for their home office. (Nearly half of Cisco's employees telecommute full time.) To stay up on their game, 80 per cent of employees participate in professional development and education programs. For on-site employees, Cisco's LifeConnections health centre has it all—a fitness centre, primary care doctors, physical therapy and even acupuncture. Thanks to flexible hours, plus an onsite childcare centre, Cisco was named one of *Working Mother*'s 100 best companies to work for.

The whole picture

Deloitte's latest snapshot on Gen Y in the workforce finds that the labels of 'egotistical' and 'self-important' miss the story: Gen Ys are a hidden powerhouse of employee potential, critical for global business in tough times. Future-oriented, ready to contribute now, opportunity-driven: *these* are the characteristics of a generation that is already making its mark on the work world. They remain optimistic in the midst of the current economic turmoil.

But Gen Y is also very restless. Growing up in an era of rapid technological change compels members of this generation to seek greater opportunities for rapid advancement and more responsibilities at a younger age. This tendency requires that organisations change the way they attract, develop, promote and retain these talented individuals.

Members of Y are eager and ambitious. What we lack in experience, we make up for in enthusiasm about learning and a deep drive to take on new challenges. We add our own flair, make use of our technological capacities and deliver with efficiency.

We find it frustrating when our predecessors dismiss our potential value as excitable 'hype', or overzealous and overconfident potential 'risk'. We don't like hearing that we have yet to 'earn our stripes'.

I have never met a fellow Gen Y who didn't want – even crave – someone older and more experienced to 'show them the ropes'. But they don't seek this direction in a formal way. They're simply looking for someone to be a genuine mentor. It would be a great travesty of our generation if we do not retain the wealth of knowledge that has been built by our predecessors. Gen Ys love absorbing new information, processing it in our 'agile' brains and applying it to whatever challenge or problem is in front of us. It's just a matter of encouraging non-Gen Ys to see the value in the way we work. However, this transition in thinking might present more challenges than Gen Ys are aware of. Deloitte's snapshot of Gen Y workforce attitudes makes clear that Gen Y presents both a huge opportunity and a huge challenge for today's employers.

First, the benefits and opportunities. According to Deloitte's 'Generation Y: Powerhouse of the Global Economy Report':

- Ys are more eager to contribute and take on responsibility earlier in their careers than prior generations.

- Ys are seeking to advance and ready to take on tough challenges and work toward ambitious goals.

- Although they expect competitive pay, they highly value meaningful development opportunities.

- Ys are full of fresh insight on how best to reach their peers in the consumer market.

According to *The Drum* magazine, over 80 per cent of Gen Ys log onto social media daily; sharing information is high on our list of activities. Millennials operate on social media and harness its power like no other generation. We are able to use this fresh insight within the business environment.

We're a diverse and inclusive generation that's been taught to collaborate and work with teams, and have honed critical skills in a highly specialised global economy.

We welcome the chance to partner with older, more experienced colleagues and bosses. This intergenerational teamwork carries particular promise in tough economic times. With adaptation and innovation becoming an even more urgent business priority, combining Gen Ys' tech savvy and fresh insight with older generations' experience and perspective will be especially fruitful. According to Dan Schawbel, writing for MillennialBranding.com in his study of the cost of Millennial retention, 40 per cent of HR professionals cite the introduction of mentoring programs as a way to keep key Gen Y talent within the organisation. Gen Y sees mentoring as a way to integrate and understand the corporate world.

Unfortunately, most traditional organisations are not set up to recognise and harness this restless talent pool. If Gen Y isn't given clear opportunities to contribute, we're likely to move on in search of growth. Organisations must foster a culture of respect that extends to all employees, regardless of age or level in the organisation. Employers need to examine the career development and mentoring opportunities they offer to younger employees, and improve if they find these areas lacking. Companies should put effort into rethinking their traditional performance management and rewards systems. Nowadays, it's critical to encourage the rapid development of Gen Y talent and to create new incentives for seasoned workers to act as mentors to young professionals.

Interestingly, media giant Time Warner turned this traditional approach to performance management, mentoring and coaching on its head at both ends of the career spectrum. In 2009, the corporation launched a mentoring program they called 'Digital Reverse Mentoring' where tech-savvy students mentored senior executives on emerging digital trends and technologies such as Facebook, Twitter, and other Web 2.0 applications. In addition to imparting technical skills, Gen Y mentors provide Boomer mentees with a peek into their younger colleagues' values, consumer behaviours and communication styles.

This type of dual coaching and education shows how businesses can harness Millennials' knowledge to shape the future of business, thereby enabling Boomers and Gen Y to work effectively side by side.

Of course, there are some risks that come with all of this. Gen Y's energy, insight and high-tech know-how will be essential for all high-performing organisations in our current economic climate – especially companies that have downsized their workforce and desperately need to find new ways to be more profitable. Organisations that do not take advantage of the promise of intergenerational collaboration risk becoming irrelevant and obsolete.

So what does this mean for employers?

Amid the many other challenges facing organisations today, recruiting and retaining the best workers of Gen Y is vital to supporting growth initiatives now and in the future. The kinds of career and development opportunities Gen Y is seeking require significant rethinking and retooling of how organisations establish themselves, design work, and manage and reward their people.

Here is the promising information to keep in mind:

- Generation Y is *confident* during this time of high anxiety.

- Generation Y values *opportunity* over job security.

- Gen Y wants – and is receiving – *more responsibility, earlier.*

- Gen Y *trusts superiors* and wants to work with them.

Millennials are driving significant change in today's work environments. Embracing these innovations is essential for further commerce and growth. Businesses that fail to do so will be forced to say goodbye to an entire generation – and, likely, any that come after.

CHAPTER 16

EntrepreneuriallY

Paul Lange

> Because the people who are crazy enough to think they can change the world are the ones who do.
>
> *Slogan from 'Think Different' advertising campaign for Apple Inc.*

Are Gen Ys just a bunch of layabout, ludicrously spoilt-for-choice, loyal-to-no-one, delusional juveniles? Or does Generation Y hold the key to the next greatest advancement of human evolution?

It depends on who you ask – and the truth is probably somewhere right of centre. Every generation experiences the next as rebellious against the values and norms *they've* lived by. They can't – or frequently don't want to – understand life from others' perspectives.

Sure, each generation has their differences and brings about change – some more than others. But Gen Y as a group aren't buying into the old models, and they respect what they believe to be fundamental truths rather than the authoritarianism of global economics and modern world politics. They've seen early on that the systems created over the last 100 years – 'traditional' approaches – are broken, and the arguments used to perpetuate their existence are simply myths.

In her article 'Gen Y Makes a Mark and their Imprint Is Entrepreneurship', Sharon Jayson quotes Ben Kaufman, 20, founder of a company that makes iPod accessories. 'People are realising they don't have to go to work in suits and ties and don't have to talk about budgets every day', he says. 'They can have a job they like – [one they] can create for themselves.'

Donna Fenn, the author of *Upstarts! How GenY Entrepreneurs are Rocking the World of Business and 8 Ways You Can Profit From Their Success*, wrote in an article for *Inc Magazine*:

They took their baby steps during our first true entrepreneurial decade, the 1980s; watched their parents 'restructured' out of what were once lifetime corporate jobs; saw barriers to entry collapse as technology democratised the business start-up process; enrolled in newly minted college entrepreneurship programs, which have increased seven-fold in the past six years.

The chasm between Gen Y and the Baby Boomers and Gen X is one of the largest in history. Gen Y is exercising the freedom and flexibility that past generations created and provided to them from a young age. Yet the older generations are now shocked by how Gen Ys are using this very innovation and creativity.

Despite appearances, life is not necessarily 'accelerating'; what is constantly increasing in velocity is the *number of actions* a single person makes in a day, even in an hour and less, and the frequency with which things can change. This apparent infinite momentum and volatility is created by the seemingly limitless capacity of the human mind, and is facilitated by technology. There are underutilised freedoms and technologies that have opened the floodgates for Gen Ys' brains to see the infinite possibilities that can be created. They've determined how to leverage and, if need be, reinvent existing resources to achieve what they want.

This fundamentally different way of thinking is at the centre of the divide that separates Gen Y and older generations. If you can distance yourself, you'll notice that we can say the same of *every generation*.

The Cooperative Institutional Research Program (CIRP) at the Higher Education Research Institute at UCLA has been studying college students since the 1960s. Its research has revealed that Gen Ys are in fact *less interested* in becoming successful entrepreneurs than Baby Boomers were when they were the same age. The number of students who that said 'becoming successful in a business of my own' was 'essential' or 'very important' to them dropped from 47.9 per cent in 1977 to 41.2 per cent in 2012.

Conversely, survey data conducted by Gen Y research and consulting firm Monster and Millennial Branding found that 32 per cent of Gen Y workers surveyed consider themselves to be entrepreneurial. This is compared to 41 per cent of Gen Xers and 45 per cent of Baby Boomers!

So is being 'entrepreneurial' yet another Y myth? Are Gen Ys really any different in terms of their desire to build successful companies? Perhaps not. However, it might be worth scraping a little underneath the surface and looking at the issue of agenda.

Could it be that Gen Y college students (as surveyed) are less 'focused' on 'building a successful business' because that's not their driving motivation? Could Millennials simply 'fall into' entrepreneurship because they are too impatient to wait for someone else to solve an issue they encounter? What if their light-bulb moment comes *after* college? Perhaps members of Y who are attending university are more concerned with minimising their student debt – and *just studying* – at that point in their lives.

oDesk's 'Millennials and the Future of Work' report found that 72 per cent of Gen Ys working 'regular' jobs want to quit to be entirely independent; 61 per cent say they will likely quit within two years.

I'm not sure it's possible to capture Gen Ys' 'entrepreneurial spirit' by their responses to such broad questions as those posed in these studies by CIRP and Monster and Millennial Branding. Just because a group of Gen Y university students from the US were *slightly* less motivated to have a successful business of their own than previous generations doesn't prove that Gen Y are less 'entrepreneurial' than anyone else.

All of us, at some point in our lives, think of a 'brilliant solution' for a problem we encounter. What separates the entrepreneurs from the rest of us is the gumption to *convert the idea into a reality*. The ones that don't are the ones that tell their friends later, 'I had that same idea about five years ago! He stole my idea! How clever was I to think of it?' The ones that *do* are probably working on the next big thing because they are brave enough to at least give it a try. They don't just talk about it; they *do* it.

And Gen Y are doing it — a *lot*. Perhaps it's because 'failure' isn't such a dirty word these days. Perhaps it's because Gen Y thrives on questioning the status quo — 'Gen Y: The Status Quo Rebels!' Whether they realise it or not, Gen Y is the living, breathing generational example of the fact that people don't leave jobs — they leave leaders. And they act on the underlying principle of this statement in just about every aspect of their lives. Leadership is not about showing how great you are; it is about inspiring others to be great.

Millennials apply their sense that 'nothing is impossible' in as many places as they can. This too is an evolutionary change that is significant — since Gen Y has operated less according to 'how things are done' and instead asks, 'How might we change this?'

You cannot help but envy Gen Y's way of looking at the world. Like most other people, Gen Ys seek inspiration. But they don't wait around hoping it will show up. They keep moving looking for new things, and they keep running until they find it.

Take Olenka Polak, for example. In 2014, Olenka will become yet another Harvard University dropout to achieve entrepreneurial fame. Frustrated that her parents were unable to understand a film they were watching with her, Olenka and her brother, co-founder Adam Polak, came up with the solution — an app they developed called myLingo that allows ESL moviegoers to hear a film translation in their native language via headphones.

Gen Y was thrust into an inspirational desert with only a few oases from which to drink. Left with little alternative, they ended up digging deep for water.

This is literally the story of Joel Mwale, a 20-year-old Kenyan who in 2009 launched SkyDrop, a technology to filter rainwater and make it drinkable. Since then, SkyDrop has turned into a 20-employee-strong enterprise, which now has the capacity to drill boreholes that will allow SkyDrop to produce clean water at a rate of 6000 litres per hour.

Leading and interacting with Gen Y's entrepreneurs requires a change paradigm. You can start by forgetting most of how you were taught to engage with people, especially those younger than yourself. Keep the respect; lose the stereotypes.

Every day of every week, I have conversations with business owners and corporate leaders who ask me, 'What's wrong with me just expecting my Gen Y employees to do the job I hired them to do? And why should I treat them any differently to the rest?'

Well, you shouldn't; you should probably start treating your *other* staff differently. The problem often comes during the interview process: most interviews focus on the *company's* goals, not the candidate's. Traditionally, the candidate is trying to impress upon the interviewer that she possesses all of the skills, education and training required to do the job.

Enter Gen Y, who doesn't just want to talk about what's important to the company – but also wants to discuss what *their* goals and abilities are. So what if the interview process first focused on the person's *personality*? What if it gave more attention to how well they would fit with the other employees and the company overall? Employees can acquire professional skills, and most of the skills on a CV have been exaggerated anyway. A person's *soft skills* can make or break the atmosphere within an office and an organisation. These are what determine the type and nature of the communications the employees will have.

Additionally – what if part of the interview process focused on the candidate's personal and professional aspirations? Not the often cursory questions about hobbies and 'what you want from your career' – but deeper and more meaningful questions that help you establish a true rapport, like 'How do you evaluate success' or 'What are your goals for the future?' Even if you don't end up hiring the person, why not build real rapport with a candidate? You might learn something valuable about the type of person sitting in front of you; and they might feel that there is something different about working for this company that inspires them.

Gen Ys were born into an era with a decaying leadership model that would all but crumble by the time they reached adulthood. They witnessed the destruction of trust in both business and public sectors on a scale not seen since the Great Depression. They experienced the fallout that this lost trust had on their lifestyle – and, as a result, they asked, 'Why?'

Gen Ys are demanding trust with their employers. They want meaningful relationships that require meaningful communication to establish and maintain. If Gen Ys trust you, they will go to great lengths to maintain a relationship with you. Understanding what makes people jump out of bed every morning with unbridled enthusiasm – and knowing your role in helping them achieve it – builds depth and longevity in the relationship. Give people what they want, and they'll give you what you want. Ignoring societal stereotypes or other prejudices and opening your mind to the potential of those you lead will also help them to improve.

The jury is still out on whether Gen Ys are any more entrepreneurial than their predecessors. Perhaps the media's fascination with generational 'change' has distorted our historical memory, facilitating the perception that Gen Ys are more entrepreneurial than their parents. Perhaps Gen Ys simply have an easier path to entrepreneurship, given the technology that's undoubtedly been a great enabler for all businesses.

Regardless of which 'gen' is more entrepreneurial than the others, Gen Ys are only just starting to get their foothold in what is guaranteed to be a white-hot space over the coming decade. Disruption and innovation are set to thrive due to the 'Y not' mindsets of Y.

CHAPTER 17

Y Redefine the Metrics of Success

Stephanie Holland

People are hungry for success — that's nothing new. What's changed is the definition of that success. Increasingly, the quest for success is not the same as the quest for status and money. The definition has broadened to include contributing something to the world and living and working on one's own terms.

Blake Mycoskie

It's 2013 and we're in transition, caught in the slipstream of a global financial crisis and broken promises. Late twenty- and thirty-somethings no longer dream of a lifelong career, financial security and owning our own home. Many of us are faced with job insecurity, credit card and student debt, and no chance in hell at getting on the housing ladder.

The system is broken, but this climate is a catalyst for an awakening of consciousness. We are actively opting out and taking control. We can't have — nor do we want — what our parents had. We don't want to work harder and longer; we want to work passionately and purposefully. We want to create, build and grow our lives, businesses, products and services in a world that we care about.

We care about people. Community. Environment. Sustainability. And we're taking it all on our personal quest for a greater meaning and purpose behind what we do. We're placing greater emphasis on the *why* and the *how*. And a new breed of consumer is 100 per cent behind us. The meaning behind the products and services we're offered is important to us.

Unlike the generations before us, our definition of success no longer pivots around an inward focus. We are motivated by more than money. We want to connect with each other and with the world around us. We let our beliefs and values guide our actions as consumers. We rally behind those who use their unique passions, talents and resources to do something that matters by joining their tribes, supporting their vision and spreading the word. And we want what *we* do to matter, too.

Some of us have rejected the status quo from the get-go. We've either been priced out of a higher education (whose models boast Wall Street ethics rather than the sharing of wisdom passed down through the centuries), graduated with bachelor degrees and MBAs only to discover we are unemployable, or have simply felt that something is missing. Entrepreneurship is no more a strategy than a response to broken promises and a desire to create a better world.

It's been predicted that by 2014, Millennials will comprise 36 per cent of the workforce (growing to 46 per cent by 2020). Sixty-five per cent of us already say that personal development is the most influential factor in our current job. And the desire to connect with others is the driving force behind many of the grassroots start-ups with Millennials at the helm. Srinivas Rao founded the podcast platform Unmistakable Creative, which shares the collective wisdom of mainstream and alternative voices in the creative and business communities. It encourages participants to follow their passion, purpose and vision, and speak with their distinctive voices. Rao brings these powerful voices together to inspire discovery and let people know they are not alone.

This sense of community is not only empowering; it's also inspiring and educational. Faced with an apparent lack of resources (like jobs and pay cheques), members of this generation inspire and educate as they themselves discover a *better way*. Like Rao, thousands of fresh-faced graduates have found themselves unemployable – something that's a driving force of our entrepreneurialism. Not content with signing up for benefits, we are instead solving the problems we face and using the solutions to rally others to help us create a world we want to live in.

Millennials don't deserve the 'selfish and entitled' label that's often slapped on us; most of us just want to make something better. 'I crave purpose, and I love being a teeny tiny part of a solution that makes a difference', says Kristin Glenn, 26, co-founder of the wildly successful {r}evolution apparel clothing line and Seamly.co, both of which have been living manifestos for revolutionising the wasteful and exploitative fashion industry.

As communities grow, they harness the power of the crowd to deliver sustainable change. What at first is a 'fun' engagement with other like-minded people becomes a way to be a better consumer, and a better human. As Glenn explains:

> With Seamly.co I get people involved through a voting process. The community votes on designs, and then we share with them the entire process of how their clothes are made. It's a fun way to learn about manufacturing, the environment and domestic production. I believe we should all know where our 'stuff' comes from.

But all these companies are really doing is tapping into the fundamental human desire *to do the right thing*. Shannon Whitehead, 26, co-founder of {r}evolution apparel and now a sustainability consultant for the fashion industry, agrees:

> None of us actually wants to support child labour, or pollute public drinking sources, or cause landfill overflow; the reasons for those things come down to a lack of consumer engagement and a general lack of awareness.

The desire to 'do the right thing' is what compels so many Gen Ys to help *others* achieve their goals and define their own metrics for success. Liz Forkin Bohannon graduated from college in 2008 with a plan to do PR and communications for a non-profit; but, after spending time in Uganda, what she thought she had to offer changed. She founded Sseko Designs, a global online marketplace for beautiful sandals with interchangeable fabric straps. These sandals create income for talented young Ugandan women so that they can continue on to university. Bohannon's mission is to end the cycle of poverty and encourage a more equitable society in East Africa. As she explains it:

> I think I have always had a bent towards social justice. When I was seven years old, my family was in downtown Chicago and I disappeared. My panicked parents finally found me, marching in a protest line carrying a giant sign that said, 'Free Tibet'. I thought I would become a lawyer and quite literally fight for justice in that capacity; but life has a funny way of taking you down unanticipated roads.

Fundamentally, Bohannon contends, it comes down to asking ourselves the right questions:

> Are we creating [an adventure] that allows every person who takes part in it to become more of who they were created to be? If I can answer yes to that question, I will be quite satisfied.

One of Millennials' most defining traits is the flexibility with which we approach our 'career path'. We're happy to change our vision, as Bohannon did, to match our passion and purpose. We're not seeking stability from a world in which this no longer exists, nor are we defined by a large pay cheque. Rather, Millennials feel free to explore and discover the many different ways our impact can be felt across our lifetime. As Kristin Glenn of {r}evolution apparel tells the story:

> After a crazy summer on the road, Shannon and I took some time away from the business to reflect. I really wanted to explore a different kind of model for sustainable fashion and customer involvement.

These women truly demonstrate the belief that we can see a business as more than a way to earn a living; we can see it as an experience and an adventure as well.

> We asked ourselves what we wanted our lives to look like, and came to envision something that was no longer aligned with our plans for {r}evolution apparel. We walked away from one adventure so we could walk into the next one.

The emphasis placed on experience and impact is defining a new model for business filtering up into Generation X and beyond. Millennials don't just believe but *know* that business can be a force for both economic and social good, and that you don't have to donate to charity or start a non-profit to 'do the right thing'. Simply acknowledging our available resources and learning how to use them without harming people or the planet is the key to good business. Says Whitehead:

> In reality, for-profit businesses have the power to create the most impactful change. If we all ran businesses that were inherently good, then everyone—owners, shareholders, employees, and consumers—would profit.

We know that this success relies on our story's authenticity and believability. Demonstrating who we are, what we do and how we do it replaces the old-school CV. Unmistakable Creative, Seamly.co and Sseko Designs are the CVs of Generation Y; the businesses are the stories. When we infuse products and services with meaning at each end of the spectrum—from source to consumer—more people support the vision and philosophy. As Sseko Designs' Holly Hulett explains:

> Our products are made in East Africa; the products themselves are globetrotters! From Uganda, Kenya and Ethiopia, to our warehouse in Kansas City, Missouri, and Headquarters in Portland, Oregon, to our customers in China, Japan, Australia and France. Our tagline, 'Every Sseko has a story' is so true when you think of the many cultures transcended, and hands that have played a part in making each individual product unique.

Millennials tell real stories to bring connection between, and meaning to, what we do and what we buy. They fuel our sense of connection to other people and the planet—rendering traditional advertising a relic of another, less meaningful age.

Traditionally, when people mention 'success', they are referring to a benchmark determined by the establishment, meaning: work-for-pay earning oodles of money, and the material possessions and lifestyle that accompany it. But success is a very individual experience and far less easy to quantify than it used to be. Self-care and balance are at the heart of entrepreneurial success, says Glenn:

Success will mean a financially stress-free life, full of meaningful work, and time to enjoy the moments in-between. Being able to read books, get outside and move my body, cook for friends, design; those are things that make me — and therefore, my business — better, stronger, healthier and more inspired.

According to Whitehead:

My version of success is waking up every morning excited to start the day ... feeling that 'zest for life' you feel when you know you are doing meaningful, purpose-driven work. Despite what society has told us about chasing after our dreams to eventually reach *success*, I think it's truly something we can measure daily.

With ideas spreading as quickly as they are conceived, we can create, lead, join and follow tribes of like-minded people. In doing so, we are rediscovering what it's like to be part of a community. We're connecting to others through our quest for purpose and meaning on a global scale. We no longer define success according to how wealthy we are; rather, we measure it based on sustainability, impact and service to others, the strength of our connections and contribution. Our ability to deliver on these measures is directly proportionate to our focus on our passions, the strength of our purpose, and the clarity of our vision.

It has become essential to design our life around our passions, our purpose, and our vision. It's now a foundational and vital ingredient for us to create impact, and to magnify our contribution and, ultimately, our success.

CHAPTER 18

Start-Up Y

Chris Piper

Few will have the greatness to bend history itself; but each of us can work to change a small portion of events, and in the total of all those acts will be written the history of this generation.

Robert Kennedy

I never did like the status quo.

In kindergarten I was convinced my teacher and I were in love and it was perfectly acceptable for me to give her foot massages while she was reading Berenstain Bears books to our class, as we sat eagerly listening on our classroom floor. Now I realise how creepy that was but, nonetheless, the twenty-something-year age gap between us wasn't my concern as a five year old. I like to think that I was attempting to assert my alpha male status early on.

After graduating college with a bachelor's degree in marketing and armed to the gills with a large ego and little experience, I was ready to take the world by storm. Little did I know I would be greeted only with unpaid internship offers that included benefits such as 'free pay' or which required 'three to five years of relevant experience' – the latter of which I didn't have and the former I couldn't accept.

I was terrified of becoming one of *those* people who had a master's degree in biology but somehow ended up working as a human resources coordinator for a clothing company – not because they lost their love for dolphins, but because it's what was available.

Concession after concession, their career (life) dream floats away, only to find themselves 20 years later, unhappy, in a stable yet unsatisfying job until they retire.

Sad panda.

I graduated from college around the same time the epic global financial meltdown of 2007–2008 occurred. People close to me had their retirement savings wiped out; pensions evaporated, or they were suddenly laid off from their 'secure' job. Friends and family that were close to retirement age now had to wonder if retirement was even *possible* for them.

I refused to let this happen to me, so I began researching alternate means to my goal. After reading Timothy Ferriss's best-selling book *The 4-Hour Workweek*, I quickly realised that if I wanted to work in the field in which I had earned my marketing degree, I'd have to do so by my own means – without depending on employers to give me the opportunity to do so. That is when I decided to start my first business.

My eyes opened to the fact that you don't have to follow any of the pre-established rules that society (or your parents) tell you to. In our generation, more than ever, you can create your own lifestyle and manifest your dreams; but only if you look for unconventional solutions and disregard the status quo.

We Gen Ys are idealists and have always been encouraged to follow our passions, which we hope will lead us to a fulfilling career. Conversely, our parents chased security within the confines of corporations that boasted a consistent pay cheque, benefits and a retirement plan. To truly understand why it was so important for them to work for a big business, you must first understand where our grandparents' views on careers came from.

Our grandparents are part of the 'G.I. Generation', aka 'the Greatest Generation'; they grew up during the Great Depression (in the US) and fought tooth and nail through World War II. The hardships that the entire generation faced compelled them to become obsessed with securing prosperous and stable careers.

This mentality trickled down to their own children – the parents of Gen Y – who experienced decades of prosperity and growth throughout the 1980s and 1990s. Their own successful careers led to a vast sense of optimism, which instilled a healthy dose of self-entitlement in Gen Y. They came to expect that their lives and careers would be as fulfilling as their parents'.

Unfortunately, this expectation has brought Gen Y a momumental load of disappointment. Paul Harvey, a University of New Hampshire professor and Gen Y expert, finds that:

> ...a great source of frustration for people with a strong sense of entitlement is *unmet expectations*. They often feel entitled to a level of respect and rewards that aren't in line with their actual ability and effort levels; and so they might not get [what they think is coming to them].

This disconnect between Gen Y and bureaucratic organisations with old-school policies is the root of why the traditional path of college, grad school, entry-level job, higher position with a corner office, retirement, is dead.

Enter start-ups.

Creating or just simply working for a start-up allows you to think big, have freedom from work for work's sake, and potentially make stacks of cash while chasing your dream. Traditional companies simply can't – and won't – offer these things. Plus, it's way more fun than filing TPS reports.

The landscape of start-up companies has drastically changed since the dotcom boom – and even more so with the exploding popularity of crowdfunding. Now, anyone can take their idea and, with the proper execution and strategy, become fully operational without ever writing out a formal business plan, taking out a loan or giving up equity to an angel investor or venture capitalist. The barrier to entry has simply vanished into thin air.

Dreams, behold!

The internet has allowed teens and twenty-somethings to write the title 'CEO' after their name; some are even rapidly gaining respect within their industries. These entrepreneurs are an emerging class that is reversing how we think businesses are created and how they should be operated.

Noah Kagan, employee number 30 at Facebook, employee number four at Mint and founder of AppSumo – is only 31 years old, ancient by today's standards. He recently challenged his blog readers at okdork.com to start a business and make a *profit* of $1000 within 24 hours. As proof that he wasn't delusional, Noah decided to prove this feat was possible by selling beef jerky online, and lo and behold – using only quant-based marketing and carafes of coffee – he generated $3030 in revenue and profited $1003.20 in less than 24 hours. Selling dehydrated beef – on the internet. Not exactly a hot commodity.

Noah's 24-hour experiment showed that you don't need to get business cards, file for a business license and create a professional website just to get started, like so many aspiring entrepreneurs believe. Get straight to hustling, and not only will you validate your business idea (which is a hugely important part of the process); you'll make some cash doing so.

The idea of just getting 'straight to selling' isn't new; plenty of people take this approach without even knowing they are doing it. It shows how incredibly simple it is for anyone who is the slightest bit tech-savvy and armed with an idea that solves a problem can launch a business and make money all in a day's work.

Everyone has heard the claims that Gen Y is the 'me' generation. If there is one thing that is all about you, it's your start-up. It's you doing what you want with your own idea, making money with it and providing yourself with your dream life within the next few years – not decades.

Gen Ys are born entrepreneurs. Luckily for us, it's significantly easier to venture out on your own than in prior generations. We have the good fortune of seeing on Facebook, Twitter and Pinterest what people want to buy. We own devices that make taking pictures and shooting videos incredibly simple. And should one of these go viral, we're suddenly monetising our popularity and selling T-shirts or advertising space on our blog (that we probably learned to create ourselves).

Our courage is relentless. We go for broke on every single thing we do. We know how to test our limits and push our boundaries. After all, it's likely we have nothing to lose. I mean it: nothing.

We delay moving out of our parents' house, don't care about taking public transportation or driving around our rust-bucket 1989 Honda hatchback. Renting a studio apartment 'makes more sense for us'. As for food, have you actually tried a ramen burger? It's amazing. Seriously.

We can take the risks prior generations couldn't, because it's not only in our nature; it's *expected* of us. We want to capture these moments of excitement and inspiration now, rather than delay it for our golden years.

Start-ups can offer all of this and more in a convenient, easy-to-digest package. In fact, it's almost out of the ordinary for a Millennial *not* to be involved in a start-up or some sort of side business. Several of my close friends make (great) money with personal ventures that they've undertaken in addition to their nine-to-five jobs. Others are working on their second or third start-up. Almost all are under the age of 30, myself included – and none of us has the desire to take the 'deferred life' plan.

While prior generations spent their extra time in a leisurely state, it seems as if Gen Y is the workaholic generation. Not that prior generations aren't just as hardworking – I don't want to start that argument! But Gen Y is obsessively connected 24/7, and we can work from anywhere in the world. It's convenient and it's always there.

It's also become *expected* of us – by our employers, by our own companies and by our friends. The funny thing is, we don't mind it.

The idea of working every waking, breathing moment now is fun for us, just as long as we don't have to do it until we are 65, and as long as we love what we are doing.

Never has the 'work hard, play hard' ethos been put to better use. By living abroad and taking mini-retirements, Gen Ys want to experience all they can, now. Waiting until the standard retirement age simply is not an option, and we are willing to put in the work now so we don't have to later.

The start-up culture rewards its top performers – not always with monetary benefits, but sometimes with unusual perks and even C-level celebrity status.

My own 'aspire to be like' list doesn't include many household names – just some influential bloggers, published authors and successful entrepreneurs, none of whom have a net worth of over a few million or so – not exactly uber rich by today's standards. Gen Y looks up to the people that have made their own success – not the ones with born with silver spoon in their mouth or a subscription to *Yachting Magazine.*

I've surrounded myself with the writings and musing of other Gen Y entrepreneurs – and I encourage you to do the same. If I can impart one piece of advice to you, it is to understand that *you are the average of the five people you are closest to.* This doesn't have to be people you are physically around, or even know personally. So choose wisely. My short list includes:

- **Timothy Ferriss:** Author of the '4-Hour' book series, entrepreneur, angel investor, Chinese kickboxing champion, world-record tango holder, and so on. You can learn more from his blog at fourhourblog.com than you can in college. I did.

- **Ramit Sethi:** Author of book with a fairly scam-y book title, *I Will Teach You To Be Rich* – but it is the most legit, no-B.S. piece of work on personal finance, starting a side business or finding your dream job that you will find anywhere. His blog and online courses also fit the bill.

- **Charlie Hoehn:** The man behind the curtain of over a dozen best-selling authors and world-class marketers. He's the author of *Recession-Proof Graduate* and *Play It Away:* two books I recommend to learn how to find meaningful work, then learn how to manage it to avoid burnout.

- The aforementioned **Noah Kagan:** Not an author, but someone who you should know for his brutally simple advice on how to build a business right this moment without messing around. His no-nonsense approach to marketing helped me rapidly grow my business, just by following his plans on okdork.com/blog.

- **Ryan Holiday:** Became director of marketing of international clothing brand American Apparel at age 23. If you want to know how to execute real PR and marketing, his books, *Trust Me, I'm Lying: Confessions of a Media Manipulator* and *Growth Hacker Marketing* are the Holy Grail.

Understanding Gen Y is fairly simple: we are a new generation, just like the ones before us and like the ones that will follow. Famous British rock band Queen said it best: 'I want it all and I want it now'. We want:

- our work to have real meaning in the world

- to be rewarded for our successes

- to learn from our failures, so we can kick ass later

- to live life outside of a cubicle, and not vicariously through YouTube videos.

If you are reading this book in an attempt to understand what makes Gen Y tick, I hope you understand by now it isn't money or a preferred health plan. It's unforgettable life experiences, finding true meaning in their work and having the flexibility for their personal lives to co-exist with their work. It's probably not too far off from what most people in every generation want.

If you are a Gen Y, my advice to you is to simply expand on your creative thinking and take your passion and courage and capitalise on this wonderful time we are living in – and always stay humble. If you're thinking of starting a company, remember to always think like a customer, move fast and completely forget about mediocrity.

We aren't the generation of 'I wish I coulda'; we are the generation of 'I'll have one more, please.'

CHAPTER 19

The Anti-Plan Masters

Jane Anderson

> And the *only* way to do great work is to love what you do... Don't settle
>
> *Steve Jobs*

Looking back 20 years, it was not uncommon to meet people who were in a 'job for life'—more than three decades. Nowadays, it's extremely rare to find employees who have been in their jobs for longer than ten years.

This is where the notion of the 'Anti-Plan' plays out. Baby Boomers and many Generation Xers grew up with a plan on how their careers would look. It was often as simple as finishing school, getting a degree or apprenticeship, finding a job, then working hard and climbing the corporate ladder—within one company.

Gen Ys, however, want much more than sitting in a chair pushing the same paperwork around for their entire career. In a recent study on Millennials' attitudes towards work, oDesk, the world's largest online workplace, found that 72 per cent of Gen Ys—although currently in 'regular jobs'—still want to quit and become self-employed (and 61 per cent want to do this within the next two years).

This means employers' major challenge is retaining key talent within their businesses in order to remain competitive.

Yet despite Millennials' desire to become entrepreneurs, not many are *actually doing it*. Statistics from the Royal Bank of Scotland's Youth Enterprise Tracker show that more than half of Generation Y stated that they would like to start their own business and be self-employed; yet only 8 per cent of these would-be entrepreneurs are actually in the process of starting a business. Nearly 70 per cent of them are put off by the fear of failure, compared to 56 per cent of the general population.

Portfolio careers

The 'portfolio career' is a term usually associated with and coined by management thinker Charles Handy, who first used it in 1984. It is defined as a situation where, instead of working a full-time job, jobseekers work multiple part-time jobs (including part-time employment, temporary jobs, freelancing and self-employment). When combined, these are the equivalent of a full-time position.

As a career coach, I often find my Gen Y clients aren't always familiar with this term, but do feel like they have two careers in them. They worry that they don't seem to be like everyone else – that there's something wrong with their approach to work.

However, there is an external force that has forced the 'part-time' pressure onto Gen Ys – and it hasn't come from them. It's come from the world economy that they soon will inherit.

Natasha Bita's article titled 'Gen Y in Grip of Unemployment Crisis as Jobless Rate Soars, Centrelink Data Reveals', highlights the director of employment and education for the Australian Chamber of Commerce and Industry, Jenny Lambert, warning that youth unemployment would only get worse in coming years. The number of 16-to-21 year olds living on unemployment benefits in Australia has hit 110 830 – up 63 per cent since June 2007 – as Gen Y graduates face the brunt of job losses post GFC. The jobless rate among school leavers and graduates in parts of Australia was four times higher than the national average of 5.7 per cent in June 2013, Australian Bureau of Statistics data reveals.

This is a reality for Generation Y professionals that's not isolated to Australia – in fact, Australian Millennials are far better placed than the vast majority of Gen Ys around the world. Currently, Millennials entering the workforce are finding careers that once were gateways to high pay and upwardly mobile lives to be nothing more than detours and dead ends. Elliot Blair Smith's article 'American Dream Fades for Generation Y Professionals' describes how the average incomes for individuals aged 25 to 34 have fallen 8 per cent – double the adult population's total drop – since the recession began in December 2007. Their unemployment rate in the US remains stuck one-half to 1 percentage point above the national figure.

Three and a half years after the worst recession since the Great Depression, the earnings and employment gap between those in the under-35 population and their parents and grandparents threatens to unravel the 'American dream' of each generation doing better than the last. The US's younger workers have benefited least from an economic recovery that has been the most uneven in recent history.

Earlier this year, Jordan Weissmann published '53% of Recent College Grads Are Jobless or Underemployed – How?' in *The Atlantic*, and pointed to data indicating that 53 per cent of recent college grads were either jobless or underemployed. While underemployment is of course preferable to unemployment, many of the jobs new grads are taking don't pay well enough to make much of a dent in their student loan debt.

As stated by Dan Schawbel in his 2012 article 'Just How Underemployed Is Gen Y?':

> ...the average college graduate in the US owes roughly $25 000 in debt, with the nation's total student loans now greater than a trillion dollars. Large numbers of Gen Y graduates are thus forced to take non-professional jobs, such as in retail or hospitality, until they can find ones tied to the career they'd been preparing for.

The outlook is even bleaker for Europe's Gen Y: sky-high youth joblessness in southern Europe poses a significant threat of Millennials becoming a 'lost generation' if the current situation is not addressed. The current state of the world economy in the fallout from the global financial crisis has shaped, and continues to shape, Gen Y's access to and attitudes towards careers. It might just happen that Gen Y is the best-placed generation to cope with the 'part-time only' jobs on offer.

Portfolio careers may well be part of the solution to this dire situation. They offer more flexibility, variety and freedom; however, they're not for everyone. Strong organisational and time management skills are required to juggle this newfound freedom. Many people became what management consultant Charles Handy describes in his book *The Empty Raincoat* as 'slashers': unintentionally forced to take on multiple roles due to redundancy, rises in living costs and other environmental factors outside of their control.

For example, I have a client who is a milliner (hat maker) two days per week and a nurse the other three days. She's creative and does very well in her business—but she finds her hat-making work a bit isolating, and likes working in a team. So a portfolio career is perfect for her. Some Gen Ys find it overwhelming to manage a portfolio career. It can occasionally hinder them moving forward at all. Portfolio careers are best for those who can multitask, who crave the chance to be creative and who need a flexible environment in which to work. It is said that most who become 'slashers' never return to a traditional nine-to-five single-employer role. They thrive so much in their newly self-constructed career that doing anything differently would be against what they believe in.

Stepping out—the rise of the entrepreneur

With so many Gen Ys seeking opportunities to start their own businesses (and many actually being *able* to do so), the trend of the entrepreneur has started to become mainstream. According to oDesk's 'Millennials and the Future of Work' report, 58 per cent of people surveyed identified themselves as an entrepreneur.

As discussed in greater detail in the previous chapter, Gen Ys have determined how to make fully-fledged businesses out of passions their parents may have considered hobbies. The ever-changing world of technology has given them the ability to work anywhere, at any time, for anyone. They've also used social media platforms, such as Facebook and Twitter, which have allowed a plethora of micro-businesses to flourish and grow at rapid speeds.

Volunteer work

Gen Ys also want to feel as though their endeavours are making a difference to the world. This most globally connected generation has found it much more difficult to ignore other global citizens' needs – and easier to make a difference, whether by donating time or financial contributions to causes close to their heart. Many are now undertaking gap years or schoolies trips as volunteer work overseas. Some are taking short breaks from work or study and getting involved in organisations like Australian Volunteers Abroad and building villages or teaching in schools. Others look at local opportunities to volunteer, such as working in food banks or supporting the integration of refugees.

A study conducted by Optus RockCorps found that two-thirds of Australians aged 18 to 34 have undertaken volunteer and community work, and almost all (96 per cent) consider it important to actively contribute to society. This makes Gen Y the nation's most charitable generational group.

There are countless reasons why jobseekers should provide the details of their volunteer work on their resume. Fifty per cent of recruiters and hiring managers who use social media as part of their recruitment process will extend the offer to a candidate if they get a good feel for the candidate's personality. Volunteer work shows a penchant for thinking of others – and discredits the myth that Gen Ys are 'all about me.'

Targeting employers who support the anti-plan

The job-search coaching arm of my business has increased by over 500 per cent in the last year due to the oversupply of candidates in the market versus available jobs. I've found that Gen Y's ability to manage their social media makes them better networked; other generation groups actually need more help, as they are finding the Gen Y candidates harder to compete with.

The following are what Gen Ys typically look for when dealing with a potential employer.

Growth and learning

Gen Ys seek more than just a job; they want *opportunities* that will help them build resumes and advance careers. Many organisations have identified that the typical Millennial will only stay for up to two years. However, they may stay longer if they feel that they are advancing their career and achieving their potential.

Gen Ys are also looking for *mentors* or *coaches* as a way to learn through previous generations' experiences. Such interaction enables them to apply past lessons to future decisions, while giving them the chance to quickly find solutions to current company issues.

Gen Ys want to work *with* you, not *for* you — making the alumni process vital. They require mentors who can help them understand corporate culture and business decision-making. Older members of businesses need to help the younger generation grow, as working successfully with this generation demands adaptation.

Many will feel like they're interviewing the organisation as much as the organisation is interviewing them at recruitment time. Their need for coaching and mentoring is high. They are more than happy to do the work; they want to learn to improve quickly *by getting feedback faster*. The notion that you need to be a certain age to learn something or undertake a given responsibility is completely foreign to Generation Y.

Google has taken the lead with this and realised that opportunities are thrown at their Gen Y staff every day through the likes of LinkedIn, recruiters and other job sites. To counteract this pressure and remind their staff that they can progress their careers at Google, they have created a unique internal talent management program, much like shopping on Amazon. This program allows team members to manage their own careers online. It identifies opportunities to collaborate with incoming new staff members that have certain skillsets who could be a potential match as a mentor for them – in the same way that Amazon.com suggests products you might like based on previous products purchased.

Companies should embrace what these employees can bring to the table by providing the chance for their staff to shadow and learn from mentors within the company – or even outside of those on the payroll. Learning can take place in so many ways – like secondments (relieving another person's role to gain experience) and job shadowing, to name two. Gen Y candidates will be looking for organisations that provide innovative ways to learn quickly. Sitting in a classroom for days on end is not the solution for this group.

Flexibility

Flexibility in the workplace is paramount to retaining Gen Y; as discussed previously, these employees appreciate and expect the flexibility to travel, study and choose their own work hours. This leads to a greater sense of fulfilment within their roles, as well as a better connection with their employers.

Gen Y employees will be loyal to the company, but will expect the same respect in return. This is why it's crucial for organisations to mention their support of work–life balance and flexibility on their careers pages to attract talented Gen Y candidates.

The 'Anti-Plan' for Gen Y is more about taking opportunities where they see them, having the chance to develop their skills fast with mentors and coaches around them who are the right fit at that time. It is not so much about a set-in-stone 'career trajectory', but rather about building a resume and portfolio that will look attractive to *any* employer – and launch them on their journey of starting their own businesses.

CHAPTER 20

Financial Matters (Not)

Charlie Caruso

> It is incumbent on every generation to pay its own debts
> as it goes. A principle which, if acted on, would save
> one-half the wars of the world.
>
> *Thomas Jefferson*

Why are so many Millennials still living at home?

Over 81 million young people are unemployed worldwide, with $1 trillion in collective debt. That's Y.

When it comes to managing their finances, Gen Ys are largely misunderstood to be debt-plagued, reckless spenders with a preference for travel over financial security. The global financial crisis (GFC), while significant, did not seem to pack the punch that previous recessions and market collapses have. Gen Y hasn't had to ration food and, despite the significant impact that the GFC has had, the majority of Gen Ys were able to keep their smart phones (even buy the latest releases), and most likely are still well clothed and well fed. As a cohort, Gen Y is well educated and has lived in a time of relative peace (no serious threat of atomic warfare) and stability. So how has all this affected their ideas and beliefs?

A lot!

As the most connected, media-savvy generation to date, members of Gen Y crave information. Yet, despite the drive to gather facts, figures and data through multiple channels, they are more motivated by their peers' influence than any other group. In many ways, attaining property had been the Australian/American/Western (or global) dream of generations gone by. The question is whether this will continue as Gen Y matures – or whether their 'dream' is significantly different. Do the dreams of Gen Y reject the existing paradigms of what is considered successful, attainable or desirable? Are they more focused on enjoyment and fulfilment, in ways that Gen Y has deemed acceptable? It's hard to know.

Y's spending habits

This generation's inclination for all things new and shiny, coupled with their free-spirited nature and love for travel, *and* the fact they are so far removed from a time of world war, rations and inflation, indicates that they don't seem to be in any hurry to toe the 'standard' adult line of mortgage, debt and a lifelong contract tied to repayments – at least not at the age previous generations would have been expected to.

Former CEO of leading security company Genworth Financial, Peter Hall, concedes that the majority of Gen Y is primarily focused on socialising and fast-moving consumer goods and leisure. The wealthy young of the world are largely choosing to spend their cash on *experiences* – food, wine, even intergalactic travel – rather than on possessions. Rich Hogan, private banking wealth advisor for Merrill Lynch, says more than a few of his clients have bought seats on the Virgin spaceship at a couple of hundred thousand dollars a pop: 'Those are the kind of cool things that they think about. It's discretionary income to somebody with millions.'

This might be true for the wealthy young, but this Gen Y segment is a *very* small one; and certainly does not account for the overwhelming majority of Gen Y in the Western world. Despite this, it seems that the bulk of Gen Y has been labelled as a generation with similar nonchalance when it comes to their financial security. Many fear that this generation of upstarts has coasted through today's tough economic times unscathed, and has failed to learn tough lessons. Many believe that Gen Y is focused on living large and carefree compared to more serious previous generations.

Yet, like the many misconceptions and quick-to-judge labels slapped all over Gen Ys, there are two – actually *more* than two – sides to the story.

Many believe that Gen Ys simply do not have money and have not had the opportunities to access the consistent cash that comes with a full-time job. There is no denying that not enough Baby Boomers have left the labour market to make room for them – so have Gen Ys even had the chance to take long-term savings and property ownership seriously?

'The idea that Gen Y has no money is a view that needs to be quashed', says Peter Hall. Genworth Financial's 2008 report, 'Generation Y – Profile of the New Generation' states that 20 per cent of its current portfolio is made up of Gen Y borrowers, compared with 44 per cent Gen X and 36 per cent Baby Boomers.

Gen Y salaries are no doubt increasing with experience gained in the workforce. However, the higher loan volumes that Gen Y requires – coupled with their tendency to spend rather than save – highlights the need for ongoing lender product innovation to facilitate home ownership. This is why tailored loans, shared equity and longer-term loans are ideal for Gen Ys looking to gain a foothold in the market. According to Hall:

> The flexibility these products offer should match the Y's saving habits well. Their penchant for spending and relatively high disposable income gives them the capacity to service a mortgage debt; all they need is the opportunity to get a foothold in the market.

This just might just happen as Baby Boomers age and their mortgage needs and position in the market decrease. We can expect that

Gen Y will become an increasingly important market segment for the world's lenders. There's little doubt that the Millennial generation's purchasing power and appetite for fast-moving consumer goods makes it an attractive target market.

The propertY market

As Gen Ys get closer to the age where they will dominate the property market, many have questioned just how prepared and competent they are when it comes to purchasing property and taking on debt. Considering that Gen Ys have only recently reached the age where they seek mortgages, they already represent a significant portion of Genworth's portfolio – one that looks set to grow. This has been supported by the recent findings of Mortgage Choice's 2013 'First Time Property Investors Survey': 'Forty per cent of the [Y] respondents [were] willing to forgo any available First Home Owner Grant on their first property purchase in favour of buying an *investment property* as opposed to a home.'

These findings are mirrored by the results of a study by Australian comparison site finder.com.au – with more than 50 per cent of Gen Y home buyers surveyed planning to make their first major purchase an investment property, preferring to build a real estate portfolio rather than take a traditional first-home owner's approach. Meanwhile, the other 60 per cent of the Gen Y respondents already own their first or subsequent home and are now branching out to make an investment property purchase.

But intention to enter the property market is one thing. Actually being able to achieve it is a whole other kettle of fish. As Hall explains, 'Gen Ys are currently finding it hard to invest. While they appear motivated to enter the investment market, the added strain of meeting extra repayments can be a burden'.

Such burden is apparent when one looks at the recent delinquency rates – a key indicator of the performance of loans and the impact of economic conditions on home owners. According to Genworth Financial's spotlight report, rates for Gen Y tend to be higher than for other groups, with Millennials typically performing between 1.0 and 1.5 times worse than Gen Xers and Baby Boomers.

Despite tough times, it seems that Gen Ys are pushing through and approaching their personal entry into the property market in a far more pragmatic manner than has been previously thought.

It seems that members of this generation *do* understand the financial pressures involved with entering the property market. Eighty per cent of Gen Ys surveyed by finder.com.au admitted to buying an investment property to set themselves up financially for the future, with 14 per cent admitting that they are investing because they can't afford their ideal home.

It is worth noting that a home buyer needed only 5.8 times their average annual salary to service a median home loan back in the 1970s. That figure has almost doubled to 8.9 times today! With figures like these, it's no wonder Gen Ys are choosing to live with their parents for longer.

Yet the situation is far more complex than a simple cost-of-living issue. Gen Ys in Europe and the US are facing circumstances that are much more challenging than those that Australia's comparatively sheltered Ys are experiencing.

Even young Americans who have jobs are struggling to make ends meet, given the problems that low wages, non-existent benefits and poor job security present. At the same time, costs for middle-class 'basics' such as education, health care and energy have skyrocketed. While a college education has long been viewed as the ticket to a well-paying job and a middle-class life, the price of a college education for Millennials is *more than 1000 times* what their parents paid.

Consequently, student-debt levels have ballooned, and many young Americans – crushed under the weight of these loans – are increasingly forced to move *back* home with their parents, forgoing buying cars and houses and even putting off marriage and children. Faced with these immediate economic challenges, young Americans are not saving for retirement – something that poses a serious threat to this generation's long-term financial security.

Despite this, American Gen Ys are well off compared to the Gen Ys attempting to enter the property market in the beleaguered economies on the periphery of the euro zone. According to a 2013 *Economist* article 'Home truths', housing prices have dropped by 9.3 per cent in Spain, with the overall European housing market trending down. Gen Y Europeans are fearful for their countries' futures, believing their best days have already gone and that the economic future looks bleak.

Spanish broadband and telecommunications provider Telefonica recently partnered with the *Financial Times* to commission the largest and most comprehensive study of adult Millennials to date. Their research found that only 41 per cent of Europeans agreed with the idea that their country's 'best days are ahead'.

Y the debt?

For many, the aspiration of home ownership is being hampered by the debt they have accrued, with 57 per cent of Gen Ys stating that paying off debt is their number one priority, compared to purchasing a home, buying a new car, going on holiday, investing in property or investing in the stock market. Genworth Financial reported that 56 per cent of Gen Ys have credit card debt – with *only 13 per cent* of Gen Ys stating that they do not have any form of debt.

In February 2013, financial management website and app SaveUp compiled its first US consumer savings and debt report, titled 'Gen X and Y Lead US Trend as a Nation of Debtors'. They found that Gen Ys have:

- an average mortgage debt of over $161 000 (7.5 per cent above the US average)

- an average student loan debt of $40 273 (65.7 per cent higher than US average)

- an average credit card debt of $4113 (42.8 per cent lower than US average).

The report revealed a shocking trend in the America's consumer debt, especially as it relates to Generation Y: for Americans under the age of 47, the average total debt load was about $37 000. But the breakdown of this number is what should make heads turn.

It seems that Millennials are losing the debt battle at an alarming pace. Not only are they in debt, but too much of that debt will never produce wealth – in fact, quite the opposite. It might be time for Generation Ys to re-evaluate their investment strategies.

The good news is that there appears to be light at the end of this incredibly dark tunnel, with asset management in a state of flux. According to the paper 'Why the $41 Trillion Wealth Transfer Estimate Is Still Valid: A Review of Challenges and Questions' by John J. Havens and Paul G. Schervish, Generation X and the Millennials will potentially inherit an estimated US$41 trillion from the Baby Boomers over the next 40 years.

And you don't even have to look to the future to find some hope for Gen Y. Despite the current economic, social, financial and generational conditions, a sizeable minority of Gen Ys are doing quite well.

WealthY

According to market research firm Ipsos MediaCT's 'Mendelsohn Affluent Survey', 12 million Gen Ys – many of whom work in technology fields – make more than $100 000. These Gen Ys live frugal, work-based lifestyles and are not saddled with the six-digit student debt that doctors and lawyers hold – and they view their quickly accumulating wealth differently. For one thing, they do not seem as interested in the trappings of wealth, nor are they concerned about stuffing traditional retirement accounts. They see money as a path to career freedom, where they can pick up and start again as soon as a more interesting offer comes along.

Wealthfront's chief operating officer, Adam Nash, estimates that Gen Y techies control about $100 billion in assets. 'This current generation isn't looking at money the way people did during the 1980s – that you'd make some money and use that money to make more money', says Nash:

> The typical software engineer isn't dreaming of the day he can quit the rat race. They use their money instead to gain a little bit of control over what they work on and what they do.

The money is for breeding new success, not tucking away until old age. This no-fuss attitude can present a challenge for the financial firms handling the core of Gen Y's wealth. Merrill Lynch private banking wealth adviser Rich Hogan says his clients have their own agenda when it comes to the investment choices they make: they're choosing to focus on green technologies and doing social good with their investing, and less strictly on high return.

The World Economic Forum published a report in September 2013 titled 'From the Margins to the Mainstream' that covered the rising potential of impact investing, an innovative and fresh approach to investing that seems to have grabbed the attention of many Millennial investors. According to the report, impact investing is the 'investment approach that intentionally seeks to create both financial return and measurable positive social or environmental impact'.

While $8 billion of capital was committed to this strategy in 2012, the number was expected to reach $400 billion to $1 trillion by 2010, according to a report titled 'Perspectives on Progress', released by J.P. Morgan and the Global Impact Investing Network. Furthermore, research carried out by Deloitte in 2012 found that 5000 Millennials across 18 countries ranked 'their number one priority in business 'to improve society'.

Data like this goes a long way towards explaining why new propositions such as 'values-based investing' (VBI) and 'impact philanthropy' have gained so much traction among Millennials – more any other generational segment of the population.

Even Gen Y's *consumer* behaviour patterns have been shaped by their need for social equality, with 89 per cent of Gen Y admitting that they would switch brands to one that they perceived supported good causes.

Gen Y's predisposition toward 'improving society' has significantly shaped their approach toward their financial wealth and security. It seems their innovative and socially responsible predisposition has the potential to limit the amount of risk they're willing to take on with their investments.

Investing in the information age

Social accountability isn't the only major influence on Gen Y's approach to building wealth. We must also account for the fact that Millennials are the first full generation to have grown up alongside the internet in the digital age. This increased global connectivity has facilitated a new generation of investors who are fully equipped to overcome the informational and logistical challenges that previously deterred investors from exploring opaque, non-traditional markets.

'This availability of information has been a game changer for investing', explains Nate Suppaiah of Alternative Emerging Investor:

> While quality investment information is still superficial, immediate access to emerging market professionals, contacts, and vehicles opens the door to these regions for many investors. As a result, the number of [Global limited partners] looking to invest in emerging markets is certainly growing.

The internet has made it easier than ever for Gen Ys to teach themselves how to make money — something that our predecessors could only learn on Wall Street or in certain university courses. Because of the efforts made by Baby Boomers and Xers, the internet (their creation) has reduced the many barriers that existed for them, which not longer exist for Gen Y; we have access to information via online platforms in exchange for basic membership fees. We also have an overwhelming amount of data at the tip of our fingers that we can use to research market trends and crucial investment data – information that previous generations could only have dreamt of. That beats an online library catalogue any day.

What emerges when we look beyond the stereotype is a new, more accurate picture of the Millennials. We discover a construct that is almost perfectly at odds with the pre-existing stereotype. By and large, the Millennials surveyed are not entitled youth disengaged from the real world, or individuals in thrall to instant gratification. Gen Ys are doing it their way. The research uncovers a group that is oriented towards the future, that has a strong sense of familial and social responsibility.

This is also a generation that has their work cut out for them: as a whole, they have accrued a lot of debt well before they are expected to inherit any Baby Boomer wealth.

CHAPTER 21

Leading Y

Stacey Ashley

Freedom is never more than one generation away from extinction. We didn't pass it to our children in the bloodstream. It must be fought for, protected, and handed on for them to do the same.

Ronald Reagan

As a leadership coach, I hear all too frequently complaints from my clients – mainly Baby Boomers and Gen Xers – that Generation Y just doesn't know what true *work ethic* is. They maintain that Millennials have little or no commitment and are simply too demanding or difficult to manage. However, my experience as a coach has been quite different. I have witnessed firsthand how Gen Y can represent the very best of human behaviour; many individuals I've encountered are determined to make this world a better place for all of us. When provided with the environment and opportunity to bring out their best, they are a huge asset to any organisation.

Many Baby Boomers and Gen Xers have worked hard to get where they are in their careers, and have been rewarded with status, responsibility and financial returns. It therefore makes perfect sense to them that other people need to do the same if they are to achieve the same kind of recognition and results.

Now, imagine how different these Boomers' and Xers' lives may have been if they had been told from an early age that they could be anything, do anything, achieve *anything* they desired. In addition, what if members of these generations were urged to follow their dreams and true calling—rather than just getting a job that pays the bills?

Now, for all you Boomers and Gen Xers, imagine that you had access to multiple modes of faster and more immediate communication throughout your life, thanks to countless technological advances. You also have more information at your fingertips than any other previous generation. You are among the first people that can be described as digital natives.

However, as it turns out, you discover that this wealth of information makes it a bit *more* difficult to discover your calling than you first thought. In fact, you end up feeling disappointed; nobody seems to be able to advise you on how to actually uncover your 'true north'. Then, as if you were not already confused enough, nobody thought to mention to you that you do need to make some sort of effort in order *to actually achieve* what you want—and that hard work and timing are all part of the process.

When you do finally find yourself in a workplace, you are dismayed to discover that many of your colleagues are not digital natives like you. You can't understand why the others in your team aren't just waiting around for you to communicate with them so they can instantly email, text or IM you back—just like your friends always do. Some of your colleagues—including your manager—actually prefer to speak to you *face-to-face*!

When you consider all this, it shouldn't come as a surprise that the different generations within organisations are prone to misunderstandings. However, with a little bit of effort and insight, it doesn't always have to be that way.

Let's examine some of the opportunities that bring out the best of Gen Y.

Building understanding

It is vital that today's workforce, and leaders in particular, develop their own understanding of the different generations in their workplace. This includes working out what the key differences are – and what they mean in the context of communicating, working with and leading people across a diverse workforce.

We've already discussed in prior chapters how Baby Boomers were, and still are, focused on having 'a job for life'. This generation's primary goal is to earn a crust in order to meet core financial and family responsibilities. They were brought up to fulfil this role from an early age.

Key workplace characteristics of Baby Boomers include:

- preferring being told what do – this creates a feeling of safety

- having high levels of respect for those in management positions, often calling their boss 'Sir' or 'Ma'am'

- experiencing fleeting moments of pleasure – fun and laughs – then getting back to work.

We also discussed earlier how Gen Xers prefer to seek a career rather than simply 'get a job'. This more ambitious generation has sought status, career progression, rewards and higher financial returns. As a result, far more effort, tenacity and enduring commitment goes into a Gen X career. Their workplace characteristics include:

- being self-reliant and preferring minimal supervision

- being sceptical of the absolutes of authority and tending not to respect hierarchy for the sake of it; putting far more weight on a person's credentials and experience

- having a high interest in rewards and perks

- having higher levels of education, for example an MBA

- being highly productive and preferring to complete tasks as quickly as possible, with the focus on achieving results

- enjoying the authority that comes with being a manager.

Gen Y represents the most diverse of all the generational groups. Now firmly established within our organisations, they are optimistic, confident and fully committed to moral and ethical principles. As long as their basic needs are met, making a difference is of huge importance. They have very high expectations about work and life in general and often become disappointed if these expectations are not met quickly – hence their tendency to move around from one job and organisation to another, as discussed in chapter 19.

Key workplace characteristics for Gen Ys include:

- high levels of social responsibility, contribution to community, and connection

- a sense of disdain for being told what to do; they are more likely to contribute if tasks align to their values and sense of purpose, and they feel they are making a difference

- not hesitating to leave an organisation if it is not right for them

- a preference for constant email communications and multitasking across communication channels

- thriving on small goals with short deadlines, as their attention span seems to be shorter.

Adapting your leadership approach

Leaders can avoid misunderstandings by adapting their approach based on each generation's differences – and remembering to keep in mind that what works for one person won't necessarily work for another.

Baby Boomers prefer a more task-orientated 'command and control' leadership style. They're more concerned about getting results than 'the way we get results'. They respect a leader's position of authority.

When a Baby Boomer leader says to another Boomer, 'We need to finish this project' – the employee will generally interpret this as a clear order that they must complete immediately.

Leadership for Gen Xers focused more on ensuring that people felt *rewarded*. Staff gained promotions earlier but also worked longer hours, which often led to more stress and anxiety. Gen X managers tend to take more of a mentoring approach. It may seem that they understand their staff needs, but their main priority is ensuring a task is completed to meet their results-oriented goals.

If a Baby Boomer manager was to say to a Gen Xer, 'We need to finish this project', the Gen Xer is more likely to just hear this as a general statement. They will not perceive this as a direct command.

Leaders working with Gen Ys find a coaching approach to be more effective. Millennials value being invited into conversations, and appreciate leaders who connect with them on a deeper level.

Considering this, if a Baby Boomer manager says to a Gen Y 'We need to finish this project', the Gen Y is more likely to question why they need to do whatever it is in the first place!

We've already discussed in prior chapters how leading Gen Y effectively requires managers to discover what motivates them to do their best work – and then ask them to contribute. The environment needs to cultivate advocacy, continuous improvement and innovation in order for Gen Ys to thrive.

Managers can actively seek to understand what's important to the Gen Ys in their teams. How? Just *ask them*. Once they're equipped with this information, managers can gain a greater understanding of what motivates Gen Y team members. Additionally, taking the time to explain what makes a project or activity important before inviting your Gen Y team members to participate creates a shared understanding of what's crucial and why.

Another opportunity for managers to bring out the best in their Gen Y team members is through asking them thought-provoking questions. This creates the feeling of connection and the potential to contribute. For example, check with a team member how they feel they can best contribute or participate in a task, or gauge their level of interest on a project. Just ask.

Social intercourse

Gen Y will use the variety of communication channels they have available – often, all at the same time. They demand immediate responses; and when this doesn't happen, they will resort to using a different channel to get your attention. For example, if you don't reply to an email, they might IM or call you – something older generations can find confusing and rather irritating.

Less technology-savvy Baby Boomers prefer clear and direct communication through a smaller number of channels. Gen Xers, however, want to ensure that they have covered any risks to themselves – and therefore prefer to follow verbal communication with written communication. They will also question and challenge so they understand the implications before they begin.

It is crucial when working in a diverse generational group to create understanding of these differences – and set clear expectations of who will communicate what to whom, how, and how often.

Communicating effectively with Gen Y requires managers to set expectations around agreed-upon channels, frequency and reasonable turnaround times. For example, make sure they receive clear direction on turnaround times to respond to queries, and that they know to only expect email responses during working hours. Also consider that introducing some of Gen Y's preferred communication channels might benefit everyone – for example, an organisation-wide IM channel. Again, you want to agree upon parameters around preferred use.

On the other end of the spectrum – it can also be advantageous to introduce Gen Y to the power of face-to-face and voice communication. Try inviting them into the conversation in order to develop their understanding of the importance of these types of interactions and approaches. In turn, this will also create opportunities for Gen Y to work well alongside the other generations and provide benefits such as relationship building, collaboration, continuous improvement and transfer of knowledge. However, you may need to explain to them the benefits of actually having a face-to-face meeting!

As Gen Y move up the corporate ladder, '*How* things are done' becomes more important than just '*What* gets done'. Fortunately, many organisations now recognise that people are essential to their success, and consequently are aiming to create environments and opportunities in which people can thrive. One of the most widely accepted methods for leaders working with Gen Ys is coaching as a leadership approach. This approach enables leaders to invite Gen Ys into conversations and connect on a deeper level. Not surprisingly, coaching is one of the most effective ways to both transfer knowledge and develop talent while creating clear accountability in individuals and promoting continuous improvement – and is being recognised as such.

Explaining the 'Y'

Managers who take the time to explain the 'Why' of doing things to Gen Y will reap the benefit of their full engagement, enthusiasm and energy. Forget to tell them 'why', and don't be surprised if they continue to fire endless questions at you rather than doing the actual work. Do this continually and perhaps they'll just go and do something else that means more to them at another company.

Gen Ys have the potential to make a fantastic contribution – but it needs to be in an environment that cultivates *advocacy, continuous improvement* and *innovation*. Likewise, Gen Y managers need to feel that any tasks they ask their staff to complete have meaning and are aligned with the team's values. The coaching approach they're likely to use can be quite confusing for the two earlier generations – so be clear about explaining the 'why' to them as well.

Professional leaders have a huge opportunity to create understanding between the different generations in the workplace. You simply need to take some clear steps to create the environment and opportunity for workers to thrive in order to bring out the very best in your Gen Y colleagues – really, in all your employees. This generation has the ability to challenge and teach us all. Their lessons and insights may very well provide the competitive edge you need in today's ever-changing professional landscape.

CHAPTER 22

Social Consciousness

Charlie Caruso

> The ultimate test of man's conscience may be his willingness
> to sacrifice something today for future generations
> whose words of thanks will not be heard.
>
> *Gaylord Nelson*

Gen Ys are accustomed to having choices – and are acutely aware of their influence and power as consumers. They've come to expect customisation and instantaneous feedback. They've also gotten used to hearing how negatively the world views them. It's likely that most, raised with the encouragement and support of Boomers who told them they were special, might not be fazed by the criticism. And we certainly have admirable qualities as a cohort. Countless research cites Gen Y as the most tolerant of diversity, open-minded and least judgemental generation to date; perhaps the need to ridicule and point fingers at younger generations might just stop with us.

We have been raised in an environment that has encouraged us to ask questions and seek answers in a non-linear fashion. We think outside the box and like to challenge the norm. Not necessarily because we think we can do things better, but because that's the way we're wired. We take nothing on face value, and question everything.

In our lifetime, nothing has lasted forever. We have witnessed the continual increase of marital separation and divorce, and have come to accept that, for the vast majority of individuals, marriage is unlikely to last forever. Even our planet – our environment, the seasons and weather patterns, things that our predecessors could rely upon – has not been as stable for Gen Y. With weather patterns breaking new records each day, not even our physical environment is a sure, dependable thing. But are we freaking out?

No.

The vast majority of us are lucky; we have been raised to handle, even embrace change. It's something we strive for, and something that we feel we have the ability to create ourselves. We might not always succeed in creating the change we seek; but we're committed to continue trying. As US President Barack Obama so eloquently said:

> Change will not come if we wait for some other person or some other time. We are the ones we've been waiting for. We are the change that we seek.

Innovative campaigns

It turns out there are a *lot* of things Gen Y wants and needs to change. We are transforming communities, relieving suffering and pursuing social change in our ways. Members of this generation don't do things traditionally. Gen Ys work best in groups, collaboratively, transparently, interactively and entrepreneurially – and have already created positive change in many local communities and around the world.

In collaboration with AMP Agency, PR and marketing firm Cone Inc. published a Millennial case study titled 'The Millennial Generation: Pro-Social and Empowered to Change the World' in 2006. The study presented Gen Y as a generation of individuals who are extremely ambitious and not only have high expectations for themselves, but also for those around them – including their friends, families, communities and brands. It is also a generation that has been shaped by tragic world events such as 9/11, and natural disasters such as the multiple tsunamis in Asia, Hurricane Katrina and Typhoon Haiyan.

The result is a group that has developed a strong social conscience amplified by technology.

Today's activism looks nothing like the strikes and sit-ins of years past. Business investigations and intelligence firm The Intelligence Group sought to uncover some answers about this generation in a survey of young Americans titled 'Generation Y: Slacktivists or Socially Conscious?'. They discovered that Gen Ys do indeed display signs of strong social awareness and activism, and are uniquely positioned to have a meaningful impact on today's technology-driven global society. The 'echo boomer' generation is harnessing their creativity, digital skills and 'we-volution' mindset to create entirely new forms of activism, complete with hack-a-thons and boycotts to bring issues to light and effect change.

According to the survey, Gen Ys:

> ...are a generation that believes knowledge is power and they define themselves by the information they share. They show their social consciousness through the products they choose, the entertainment they consume, and the activities they pursue.

Despite the commonly held negative perception that Gen Ys are more concerned about the latest action on reality TV than the fallout in Syria, it seems the numbers are starting to set the record straight about Gen Y's social awareness and activism.

Gen-erositY

The 2013 'Millennial Impact Report' produced by Achieve and Johnson, Grossnickle and Associates, underscores the philanthropic generosity of Gen Y: three out of four young adults donated money to a charity or cause last year.

The report found that Gen Ys are highly selective about what organisations they follow in a crowded and noisy media landscape; and they're connecting actively to between one and five organisations on social media. The report noted the rise of supportive activism, such as sharing and signing petitions – indicating the opportunity social media presents to showcase organisations' work.

The 2013 SfunCube Solar Hackathon, held in California, is an example of such a campaign. This event brought innovative programmers, designers and businesspeople together for one weekend to develop ways to accelerate solar energy adoption. Participants were instructed to build web-based solutions to make it easier, more efficient and more enjoyable for people to power their lives with sunshine. Raices de Esperanza, a non-profit organisation focused on empowering Cuban youth, launched the first ever 'Hackathon for Cuba' in February 2014 in hopes of using innovative software technologies to help Cuba's Gen Ys connect with the outside world and each other.

Millennials might not give a lot of money to charities compared to other generations – but they give what they have. Figure 22.1 provides a thorough representation of Gen Y's contributions compared to that of other generations.

Figure 22.1: generous generation

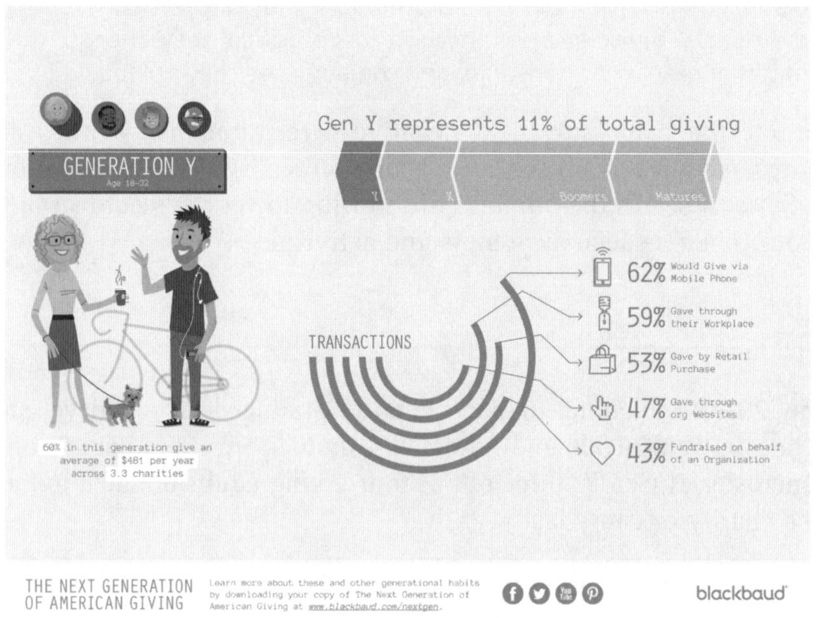

Source: Generation Y segment of Blackbaud graphic *The Next Generation of American Giving*. A copy of the graphic appears at www.blackbaud.com/nextgen

The majority of studies identify Boomers as the leading cohort for charitable donations in the US and around the world. But with the Baby Boomers also accounting for the most wealth, this is hardly surprising. 'The Next Generation of American Giving', published by Blackbaud, found that 72 per cent of Boomers gave to charity last year, well above the 59 per cent of Gen Xers and 60 per cent of Gen Ys.

Similarly, figure 22.2 highlights Gen Y's giving history – as well as the fact that 83 per cent of Millennial respondents made a financial gift to a not-for-profit organisation in 2012.

Figure 22.2: the Millennial Impact GIVE 2013 research

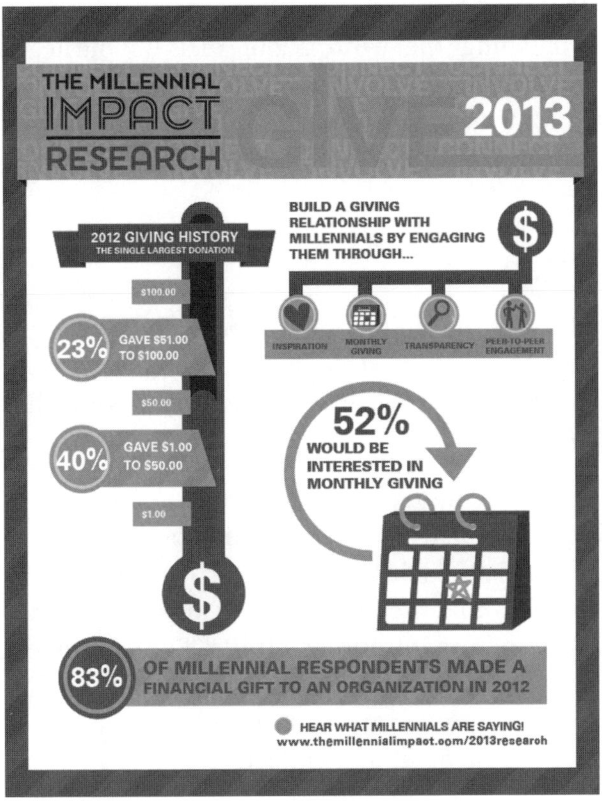

Source: Reproduced with permission from Achieve Guidance, from 'The 2013 Millennial Impact Report'.

Younger Americans are really starting to give, which is both a welcome trend and a surprise, given Gen Y's high unemployment rate. And research shows that Gen Ys are demanding accountability from the charities to which they donate, with 60 per cent of Gen Y donors expressing a desire to 'see the impact of their donation' directly – a figure that is well beyond other demographics, according to Blackbaud, a leading supplier of software and services specifically designed for nonprofit organisations, and creator of 'The Next Generation of American Giving' report.

Gen Ys see philanthropic strategy as the major distinguishing factor between themselves and the generations before them. They expect to change the way charitable decisions are made – and they're not shy about spreading the word about their favourite non-profits. According to the '2012 Millennial Impact Report' by Achieve and Johnson, Grossnickle and Associates, 70 per cent of Gen Ys admit they encouraged donations from friends and colleagues.

Slacktivism

This is a generation of digital activists who consider posting, liking, tweeting, hashtagging, and re-blogging to be just as valid as taking to the streets. Interestingly, though, there is a word that describes this Gen Y phenomenon: 'slacktivism'.

The term – which combines 'slacker' and 'activism' – is used to describe Gen Y's propensity to sign online petitions, repost statuses or alter profile pictures in the name of 'social change' – thereby, some maintain, joining a community organisation without actually contributing to the organisation's efforts. Research is beginning to explore the connection between the concept and modern activism and advocacy, as groups are increasingly using social media to facilitate civic engagement and collective action.

According to The Intelligence Group, when given a list of 18 activities related to displaying their social consciousness – ranging from donating clothes to purchasing or wearing a cause-related bracelet – the top answer from Millennials was 'liked a cause on Facebook'.

The Joint United Nations Programme on HIV/AIDS describes the term 'slacktivist', saying it 'posits that people who support a cause by performing simple measures are not truly engaged or devoted to making a change'. Yet, according to The Intelligence Group's report, two out of three Gen Ys feel that 'a person on a computer, being aware and spreading the word' can create more change than 'a person on the street, rallying and protesting'.

An iconic example of this so-called 'slacktivism' was discussed in Debbie Haski-Leventhal's article for the *Financial Review* in 2012 titled 'Rampant Clicktivism: Lessons from 'Kony 2012''. The article – which discussed the Kony case and video originally discussed in chapter 10 – pointed out the true power of social media and the internet, noting that over 8 million people worldwide had viewed this video within four days.

On 4 March 2012, most of us had never heard of Joseph Kony and the unimaginable crimes of the LRA. By the 8th – because of one simple video campaign – millions were viewing, sharing, tweeting, talking, blogging and donating money to the cause that vowed to stop him.

The article poignantly highlights that the 'Kony 2012' campaign was highly attractive for Gen Y because it not only evoked high levels of social awareness; it offered Gen Ys an idea that fed their propensity and desire to fix social problems very quickly. 'Kony 2012' provided Gen Ys with their coveted 'quick fix'; and Gen Y felt proud of their efforts. They were left feeling as though they had achieved something for the good of the world without having to sacrifice too much of their time and attention. Haski-Leventhal explains:

> Through the power of this generation, we are moving from social activism to social clicktivism. While only a few will actually go to Uganda to help Invisible Children, many more—millions in fact—will share the clip and donate money—in just a click of a mouse. It is not hard to share videos and donate money, and in return the individual feels they have done something meaningful.

So, is this kind of effort meaningful – or a complete waste of time?

The Kony example shows just how powerful 'slacktivism' can be, and demonstrates that, with enough worldwide awareness and social pressure, movements like this one have the power to make politicians *move*. It also makes the ignorant less so. No-one knew who Kony was before the campaign. The atrocities were happening, and it wasn't even a blip on the social consciousness radar. It's encouraging that there's a way to spread information like this so quickly.

However, that's not reason enough for the Y cohort – or any other generation – to become complacent. 'Social clicktivism' is a knee-jerk response to problems most of the slacktivists do not understand, or even strive to understand. Because it is quick, effortless and requires little commitment, it has little of the depth and emotional involvement that has characterised the many social movements of the past – like those of the suffragettes, the worldwide protests against the Vietnam War, or the Tiananmen Square protests of 1989. Clicktivism turns social causes into yesterday's news far too quickly.

What's also discouraging is that research from the University of British Columbia's Sauder School of Business titled 'The Nature of Slacktivism: How the Social Observability of an Initial Act of Token Support Affects Subsequent Prosocial Action' has identified that when people declare support for a charity publicly via social media, they are then far less likely to donate to the cause later on. They have already felt a sense of 'dues paid' without actually *financially supporting* the cause.

Social media is a powerful tool to raise awareness and create change. But we must take care not to rely upon it as a reflection of our charitable efforts.

Working for a better world

There are other ways Gen Ys feel they are able to contribute socially and for the good of the planet – and that's through their careers. Per The Intelligence Group, 56 per cent of Gen Ys would take a pay cut to work somewhere that is positively changing the world.

It's not just who they work for, but the application of their work paradigm. Gen Ys are passionate social entrepreneurs who think they can do well both financially and for the world around them. According to The Intelligence Group report, more than two-thirds believe that they could make more of a difference in the world by running their own business than they could by running for political office.

Jason Aramburu, the 27-year-old founder of re:char, is an example of such a Gen Y. Jason is a Millennial making a significant difference in East Africa, where he is using biochar – a solid material obtained from the carbonisation of biomass – to help farmers fight climate change and increase crop yields by 26 per cent, as well as reduce fertiliser consumption by a whopping 80 per cent.

Or take the co-founders of Vera Solutions as another of the many examples of Gen Ys taking social change into their own hands. Taylor Downs was working at a non-profit combating HIV/AIDS in South Africa when he came across a mountain of paperwork that contained life-saving information that simply wasn't being used. He and his co-founders – Zak Kaufman and Karti Subramanian – decided to tackle this issue head on, and did so by successfully launching their social enterprise, Vera Solutions, an organisation that manages and organises critical data to help nonprofits get to key information that was once buried in paper and spreadsheets. Vera has worked with more than 50 social-impact organisations across more than 30 countries.

I could spend an entire day proudly chanting about the change-making Gen Ys – there are literally thousands of them, all of whom make me incredibly proud. And they make such transformations because they *believe they can*. According to The Intelligence Group, when asked who is most capable of making a difference in the world, Gen Ys ranked only the president ahead of themselves.

Consider Malala Yousafzai, who was shot in the head by a member of the Taliban in 2012 for campaigning in Pakistan for girls' education rights. Malala survived, and spent her sixteenth birthday addressing the UN with a demand for universal access to education.

Gen Ys aren't known for their patience. And they are tackling the world's social and environmental problems head-on in droves. Rather than waiting until the sunset of their lives to decide who they are as philanthropists and what legacies they want to leave, these next-gen social activists are already crafting their identities and actively thinking about their own legacies *now*.

As a group, Gen Y embodies a spirit of optimism and cooperation. Experts believe that this group is better educated as well as more disciplined and achievement-oriented than the generations that have preceded them.

Admittedly, technology has made participation easier for Millennials than for past generations. Growing up with the internet has exposed them to an entire global community and increased their awareness of news and world events. Although they've been labelled 'slacktivists', Gen Ys believe it is their responsibility to incite positive change in the world. Many have high expectations for this generation — and Millennials are happy to take on this challenge. We are only beginning to feel the impact of these 80 million Gen Ys.

CHAPTER 23

Current and Future Challenges

Charlie Caruso

Figuring out young people...is an industry.

Eric Hoover

Many Millennials (61 per cent) say their generation has a unique and distinctive identity. Although this is not a specifically 'Y thing', as validated by Pew Social Trends publication 'Millennials: A Portrait of Generation Next', which indicates that roughly two-thirds of Silents, nearly six in ten Boomers and about half of Gen Xers feel the same way about their generation.

Are Gen Ys different? Are their collective behaviors more than a product of 'their' time? Is Gen Y simply emblematic of a much broader cultural shift – one that is more accepting of sexual orientation and race, one far more connected, yet engulfed by a new level of challenges? It's hard to know for sure.

But let me throw this out there. Is Y a cohort – or a mindset?

I work with countless Baby Boomers and Gen Xers who 'act' Y. They are entrepreneurial, young at heart, think outside the square, are digitally connected and tech savvy – but they weren't born in the 1980s (or surrounding years). Like Bernard mentioned in chapter 1, I also disagree with the sentiment that generational theory is like demographic astrology – because I know there are certain unique characteristics that generational cohorts exhibit, which are important to understand in a world where multiple generations are working side by side.

Yet, I have been troubled by the labels branded on the Y cohort, which actually apply to Gen–everyone else too!

Learning how young people work is imperative – because getting the most out of employees can be the difference between success and failure for many companies.

It has been said already, but bears repeating: no blanket statement can sum up an entire group of people. No book, no chapter, no study, no research report can attempt to do that either. Instead, this book attempts to start a conversation – one that we hope will delve a little deeper and dispel some commonly held assumptions about Generation Y, a conversation that we hope is the first of many.

The human compulsion to group people and objects together has always been ingrained in our being. We need to group things, distinguish the dangerous and unknown from the 'safe to eat' or the 'it won't eat you' categories. Without the ability to categorise threats, our ancestors wouldn't have survived. Forget Gen Y – we wouldn't have had humankind.

To quote from Dreamworks film *The Croods*:

> Tonight, we'll hear the story of Crispy Bear. A long time ago, this little bear was alive. She was alive, because she listened to her father, so she was happy. But Crispy had one terrible problem, she was filled with...curiosity! Yes! And one day, she saw something new and died!

Through experience, our ancient ancestors taught the younger generations what to put in the dangerous group and what to categorise as safe.

Once we began the journey of *Understanding Y*, it became clear that we were not simply discussing Gen Y; we were discussing the Western world as we know it today. We Gen Ys are a product of our time, and the embodiment of future hope.

We attempted to discuss how current affairs influence, and are influenced by, this particular cohort of people. Gen Ys are coming of age; we will be the ones fixing our predecessors' mistakes, guiding the 'Facebook Generation' (or Gen Z) through whatever issues their digitally connected lives might leave them dealing with as emerging adults.

Gen Y will have to come up with better ways to slow down the heating of the planet, reduce our dependence on natural resources and replace them with renewable energy with enough scale to dampen the effects of global warming.

Whether or not it has fully dawned on society, the reality is that Gen Y will soon have to assume the responsibility for a world crafted by previous generations. According to the US Bureau of Labor Statistics, Baby Boomers' rapid retirement will mean that Millennials represent 50 per cent of the workforce by 2030.

Gen Y will have to determine how to support Baby Boomers when they retire and need care in their old age. This older generation – who have so affectionately and lovingly cared for us – deserve the same in kind. Because we were the first to be offered such 'special' treatment from our parents, it only seems right that Gen Ys offer their retiring parents the kindness they deserve. We must work hard to solve the retirement housing and care needs that will steadily increase over the coming years – with seemingly little in the way of infrastructure planning or strategic development for such an enormous transition.

Gen Y won't only be charged with the duty of caring for their ageing parents and addressing the world issues created by their predecessors. The rise of the internet, something that has been so fondly associated with the Y clan, is causing serious, perhaps irreparable damage to the mental welfare of the Facebook Generation.

Carolyn Ross, M.D, M.P.H., is an expert in eating disorders, addictions and integrative medicine and author of *The Binge Eating and Compulsive Overeating Workbook*. She published an article that discusses one of the most concerning social issues of our time – something we briefly discussed in chapter 6 – the exposure of children under 12 to pornography, and the impact this is having on how Millennials will have to demonstrate what is considered normal sexual behaviour and gender roles:

> Children today are being sexualised earlier…in part because they are exposed to sexual material in movies, television, music and other media earlier than ever. [Their] widespread access to the internet [allows] curious teens access to millions of pages of uncensored, sexually explicit, often inaccurate and potentially harmful…material.

Young boys and girls are getting so much visual information that was previously *never* available on such a diverse and often scale to previous generations. Because these videos are available so cheaply, so freely, Generation Z is consuming it as if it was a form of sexual education – and there is a concerning disconnect between this and the boundaries young boys and young girls are able to set between each other with respect to their sexual relationships.

Almost 93 per cent of kids age 12 to 17 are online, and most exhibit a level of digital proficiency bewildering to those of us who want to protect them. The data, courtesy of internetsafety101.org's article 'The Perfect Storm', also highlights the pressure young people are feeling to post provocative pictures and videos, and blog about their deepest personal experiences in a very public forum. Few think through the implications of their online actions – and many of the legal measures we need to protect kids on our virtual streets are unenforced or outdated, with law enforcement and prosecutorial efforts often underfunded.

There are significant gaps between the internet's dangers to children and the level of action dedicated to protecting them. Parents – the 'digital immigrants' in this situation – must therefore stand as the 'first line of defence' in internet victimisation against children – the 'digital natives'. Though they're often left feeling overwhelmed and ill equipped to protect their kids online, it's up to Gen Y and Gen X to offer up useful, practical and speedy solutions to curtail this concerning phenomenon and its impact on our youth.

Unfortunately, the challenge doesn't end here. Gen Y must contend with other issues – including child pornography and the impact social media addiction has on Y and Z's psychological development. And there's the obesity epidemic, which poses one of the most serious public health challenges of the twenty-first century, with an estimated 42 million overweight children worldwide.

The lack of drinking water for impoverished nations, the overpopulation of the earth, the increasing prevalence of erratic weather patterns and natural disasters due to the damage created by our predecessors – these are just some of the problems Gen Y will inherit and must figure out a way to overcome to some degree.

Gen Y has all this responsibility, and is making all this headway – yet has to contend with individuals like Mark Bauerlein, who authored a book titled, *The Dumbest Generation: How the Digital Age Stupefies Young Americans and Jeopardizes Our Future.* I won't give the book any more discussion beyond this, and I don't think it's warranted. But it's a great case to point out the kind of slander Gen Ys face on an ongoing basis.

It's clear that there is a serious injustice being perpetrated by those who condemn Gen Y for behaviour that has been conditioned into them by previous generations. Yet despite the overwhelming enormity of the destruction, chaos and blatant lack of accountability or respect for our fellow man and environment that we have inherited – we remain one of the most *optimistic generations* in recorded history. Just as each generation has found its own unique way to approach the crises of its day, the Millennials will use the lessons of our youth to shape the world. We will not and cannot end all the conflicts that plague the planet; however, our efforts will likely include a greater focus on the environment, greater tolerance of diverse practices and values and an even greater reliance on technology. In addition to progress, it is certain that new problems will arise. But we will contribute to the steady development of our world with perseverance.

As products of an environment composed of ever-changing values, Millennials have grown extremely open and tolerant. The Pew results in the report 'Forty Years after Woodstock, a Gentler Generation Gap' indicate that many members of this generation believe that they have better attitudes toward different races and groups than the generations who have preceded them. The report shows that an overwhelming proportion of the public says the young and old are different in many aspects of their lives, including attitudes toward different races and groups (70 per cent), and their religious beliefs (68 per cent).

Gen Ys *are* more tolerant. The vast majority of Gen Ys reject the bigots of the world, and fight against racism and homophobia (as the quote that is often associated with Morgan Freeman, despite no one actually knowing who said it, 'I hate the word homophobia. It's not a phobia. You are not scared; you are an asshole.'). Equality is something Gen Y expects, demands even, and they find opposition to gay marriage utterly absurd.

LA-based comedian Ahmed Bharoocha brilliantly summed up the sentiment of Gen Y (and a vast majority of the world's population) in his analogy between gay marriage and ordering cake, titled 'Have Your Gay and Eat It Too':

> It's crazy to outlaw marriage – marriage is a happy thing. There shouldn't be a vote on someone else's happiness. These people don't know these gay people, they're not going to know them, they're not going to be their friends. [Yet] they have control over their lives—that's not fair.
>
> That's like if you went to a restaurant, and you were like 'Uh, waiter? I'll have the cake.'
>
> And then the guy at the table next to you was like, 'Uh waiter? Cancel that cake.'
>
> 'But—I was going to have the cake?'
>
> 'Oh—I don't like cake … No.'
>
> 'Yeah—but I was going to have the cake over here, by myself …'

'I don't want anyone to have cake.'

'Why—what's wrong with cake?'

'God hates cake.'

'You just made that up?'

'My kids are here. If they see you eating cake, they're gonna want to have cake too. You can go home and eat cake in private, and we'd prefer it if you didn't call it cake. Maybe a civil muffin?'

It's actually irrelevant whether Gen Ys are the drivers or simply passengers in the global cultural shift towards equality and away from intolerance. Y? Because the only thing worth knowing is that Gen Y expect it, demand it – and will fight for it. Bigots beware!

Perhaps the most amazing response from the many surveys I have encountered in the course of writing this book was the beauty of the Y sense of hope. In response to the simple statement, 'I believe I can do something great', about 60 per cent of Gen Ys agreed strongly with this statement, and another 36 per cent agreed somewhat. That was almost every respondent: 96 per cent in total.

Some say entitled. I say empowered.

Every day I encounter a new ray of light – some person, event or some act that inspires and assures me that Gen Ys have the potential to turn the world in the right direction. When I first watched Ashton Kutcher's 2013 Teen Choice Awards acceptance speech, I fell silent. I was beaming with pride and a sense of excitement that the young kids of today are exposed to the inspirational words he spoke in that speech.

When Ashton took the stage he immediately clarified that his real name is Chris, and that Ashton is his middle name. He spoke of the amazing life lessons he had learned as Chris, the guy who acts, as opposed to Ashton the 'celebrity'.

He talked of opportunity. That opportunity looks a lot like hard work. He detailed the many jobs he had growing up, then said something that truly resonated with me 'I've never had a job in my life that I was better than.'

He also spoke about being 'sexy':

> The sexiest thing in the entire world is being really smart. And being thoughtful, and being generous. Everything else is crap, I promise you. It's just crap that people try to sell to you to make you feel like less, so don't buy it. Be smart, be thoughtful, be generous.

His words still take my breath away. They take my breath away because I think of the potential impact this message might have on our youth, and on the world.

Gen Y has responded creatively and with integrity when faced with challenges. We've used our unique talents and natural capacities to surge forward. Our openness, tolerance, and application of the technological foundations we have inherited have indicated our preparedness to bring about change. Real change. Sustainable, endurable, and radical change. We are ready to excel further and continue to contribute to the world. We will continue to prove that the paradigm that is used to frame us, to blame us, has shifted. It will continue to shift because we are not restricted by the same perception of limitations that our parents were, nor are we trapped by the definitions of what we should be or could be. We are Y. Nice to meet you

If nothing else, I hope this book made you stop and think. I hope it prompted you to question any previously held notions about the Millennial cohort, and in some way better aided you in *Understanding Y*.

ABOUT THE EDITOR

Charlie Caruso

Charlie Caruso is on a mission to change the world! Disenchanted with the current state of media, Charlie is committed to shaking up the media industry and re-introducing quality content – minus the sleaze and spin.

A writer, producer, NFP executive, and a start-up(erer), Charlie embraces entrepreneurship in all facets, and has done so since the ripe old age of 16.

Her first NFP start-up, PuggleFM (disruptive radio model for parents) was listed in Shoe String Australia's Top 10 Start-ups for 2013. PuggleFM was developed as an online radio and podcasting station created especially for parents and children. Since its inception, PuggleFM has found audiences in the US, Europe, across Australia and Asia, that are looking for an alternative to commercial radio. Charlie was listed in Anthill Australia's 30under30 (Young Entrepreneur Awards) and received the Special Inspiration Recognition Award at the 2013 WAITTA Awards Gala night for her contribution to ICT.

Charlie has become a sought-after speaker, and in 2014 has already agreed to speak at various events in London, New York and throughout Australia, speaking on Gen Y, female leadership and the media revolution.

Visit www.charliecaruso.com to find out more about Charlie.

ABOUT THE CONTRIBUTORS

Bernard Salt

Bernard Salt is a best-selling author, a twice-weekly columnist with *The Australian* newspaper, a regular on the Australian speaking circuit, and a business adviser. He heads a group of consultants within KPMG providing demographic advice to business and government.

His first best-selling book *The Big Shift* (Hardie Grant 2001) predicted a surge in the demand for lifestyle and residential property underpinned by the imminent retirement of the Baby Boom generation.

His second book, also a bestseller, *The Big Picture* (Hardie Grant 2006) looked at how work, life and relationships are changing in the first decade of the 21st century.

Bernard has directed and authored a number of global studies for KPMG International, including 'Beyond the Baby Boomers' (2007) and 'The Global Skills Convergence' (2008), both of which attracted global media coverage.

Also in 2008, Bernard produced his third book, the quirky and immensely popular *Man Drought* (Hardie Grant), which not only attracted global media attention but catapulted new terminology (man drought) into the Australian lexicon.

In 2010 Bernard produced KPMG's 'Future Focus' report aimed at business and government, which looked at development options for Australia in the 2010s.

Bernard's views are regularly sought by the business community and by the general media. He appears regularly on radio and television programs including *7.30 Report, Sunrise, Today Tonight, A Current Affair* and *60 Minutes*.

Leanne Hall

Leanne is an experienced clinical psychologist, health and nutrition coach and personal trainer. For 15 years she has worked with young people (Gen Y), assessing and treating a range of psychological issues, from eating disorders, self-harm, depression and anxiety to relationship problems and sexuality issues.

She has been involved in the implementation and management of both state- and federally funded early intervention services for young people aged 12 to 25 years, and has worked in private practice for over ten years. During her career Leanne has been involved in teaching university students, supervising young psychologists, delivering seminars to local high schools and developing research programs, all with the aim of improving the mental health of young Australians.

Leanne is often consulted by the media as an expert on mental health, body image and teenage development, having been featured in a number of national publications. More recently, part of Leanne's drive to deliver positive messages about mental and physical health to the general public has seen her branch out as a TV presenter, as the Mind and Body expert on Network 10's *The Living Room*, where she will be tackling a number of health-related issues.

Rob Kaldor

Rob Kaldor is an experienced senior management professional with broad-based experience across various industries, including books, online retail, toys and children's furniture, health and wellness biotechnology, medical devices, pharmaceuticals, education, IT and international trade. Rob is currently running his own consultancy, eTales, and has most recently been responsible for the digital strategy for the Dymocks chain of bookstores. Rob is an experienced interviewer, having interviewed some of the world's most popular authors. He has interviewed Jackie Collins, Ruby Wax, Pamela Stephenson, Rod Laver and Ricky Ponting, to name a few. Rob is an early adopter and enthusiastic user of technology to facilitate positive and efficient change. He is available to speak at conferences and seminars. Additionally Rob is an Australian correspondent for South Africa radio station 702/Cape Talk. Rob is married to a psychotherapist and is the father of three feisty kids. He is stuck in the middle of Generation X.

David Burstein

David is the CEO and co-founder of Run for America, a disruptive post-partisan initiative to bring a new generation of talent into our political system and catalyse political leaders to start solving our biggest problems. He is the author of *Fast Future: How the Millennial Generation is Shaping Our World*. He is also the founder of Generation18, a nonpartisan young voter engagement organisation. The organisation grew out of the documentary film, *18 in '08*, which David directed and produced, about young voters in the 2008 election. From 2007 to 2008, Generation18 registered over 25000 new voters, and held over 1000 events in 35 states. David is a frequent speaker and commentator on Millennials, social innovation and politics. He has appeared on CNN, FOX News, MSNBC, NPR, ABC Evening News, and C-SPAN, and in *The New York Times*, *USA Today*, *The Boston Globe*, *Politico*, *Salon*, *The Huffington Post*, and many others. David is a contributor to *Fast Company*, where he writes about disruptive innovation, social entrepreneurship, entertainment, and creativity. He has served as a consultant to many not-for-profits and companies on how to understand and engage Millennials. More at www.davidburstein.com.

Scott Broome

Coffee, tattoos and pug dogs — these are just a few of Scott's favourite things!

After graduating from Monash University, Scott quickly began his career in marketing, climbing the corporate ladder until he secured a brand management role for one of Australia's most iconic youth brands. Following his sweet success, Scott opted for a change in pace and migrated over to the world of PR, where he managed a number of large accounts in consumer brands.

With his newly found entrepreneurial spirit, Scott teamed up with long-standing friend and university alumnus Stacey Taylor to create BlackSixteen — a communications agency with a distinctive Gen Y edge. Scott and Stacey sought to redefine society's perception of Generation Y and demonstrate the value of young blood in an old industry.

When Scott isn't working, he is busy caring for his pug, Charlie, or taking a shameless selfie (or two!).

Stacey Taylor

For Melbourne gal Stacey Taylor, corporate life sucks!

After graduating university, Stacey volunteered at a handful of not-for-profit organisations. Following her reputable charity work, Stacey proceeded to represent a number of Australian brands within the beauty industry.

Her passion for local brands inspired Stacey to explore Melbourne's underground music scene and freelance as a publicist. Her exposure to new genres strengthened her love for music and led to a number of promotional affiliations.

With her love for unconventional working styles recognised, Stacey collaborated with former university colleague Scott Broome to create BlackSixteen.

As a twenty-something professional, Stacey sought to redefine society's perception of Generation Y and establish a modern working environment with a contemporary youthful culture and flat hierarchal structure.

When not taking the PR world by storm, Stacey can be found enjoying a cheeky glass of red with friends and family on the Mornington Peninsula.

Professor Mary Quigley

Source: © Yvonne Catty

Professor Mary W. Quigley created the genyu.net blog, for her New York University (NYU) undergraduate journalism course, 'Beat Reporting: Covering Gen Y'. In this course, NYU undergrads research, report and write on Gen Y topics ranging from 'emerging adulthood' to social networking, relationships, technology, work, friends, family, and anything else that seems uniquely Millennial.

Ms Quigley writes a weekly blog on parenting adult children at www.mothering21.com. The author of two books, *Going Back to Work* and *What Do You Do?*, she is a journalism professor at New York University's Arthur Carter Institute.

Dr Samantha Smith

Source: © Laura Manariti Photographs

Dr Samantha Smith, director of communications agency Pinnacle, is an experienced communications, marketing and social researcher – having spent nearly two decades in campaign development and delivery.

Samantha has a doctorate from Monash University, which she obtained for her communications- and behaviour change-related social research into Generation Y.

She is regularly invited to present her research findings to marketing practitioners and academics in Australia and overseas, and spoke at the 41st European Marketing Academy Conference (EMAC) in Lisbon and the International Conference on Climate Change at the University of Washington.

Samantha is a Foundation Member of the Australian Association of Social Marketing, a member of the Australian & New Zealand Marketing Academy and the European Marketing Academy.

Ryan Heath

Ryan is an Australian author, speechwriter and social commentator living in Europe. Since 2008 Ryan has worked as speechwriter to President of the European Commission Jose Manuel Barroso, and is now spokesperson for European Commission Vice President Neelie Kroes. He has worked for Peter Garrett, and Tony Blair's government, and is a contributor to the *Griffith Review*. His writing has been published in 25 languages.

One of the fundamental questions of today's world is undoubtedly the question of equitable globalisation.

Ryan Gibson

Ryan Gibson is a 28-year-old digital marketing guy residing in Leeds, England. His skill is in search marketing and he has gathered over six years' experience of working on large multilingual campaigns for a number of FTSE 250 organisations. His specialities cover all distinctions of online marketing, including blogger engagement, outreach, affiliate marketing and strengthening relationships with key online influencers.

After accepting a role with a business based in Singapore, Ryan began questioning traditional business practice and employee retention. His blog GenerationY.com was therefore born with focus on Y in the workplace. A Millennial child at heart, Ryan provides a voice for the 'misunderstood' generation and his goal is simply to change perception and corporate mindset on work–life attitudes, inspiring companies and individuals to seek change.

Paul Lange

Paul is chairman and co-founder of CleverX Business Incubators, a serial entrepreneur, performance leadership expert and international speaker.

Paul is originally from Australia and has travelled most of his life, living on every continent except the polar caps. He's an online veteran predating the commercial internet, and has founded or co-founded more than a dozen successful businesses in the last 25 years, across various industries and countries.

Paul's purpose is to be the catalyst for other great people to realise the purpose they are meant to achieve and to bring it to the world. He does this by sharing with others the experiences and skills he has collected, by continuing to learn and put into action the learnings he gains from those that inspire him.

What drives and inspires Paul is working with people who can visualise what they want, are passionate about achieving it, and take action toward it.

Stephanie Holland

Source: © Dori Kaba

Stephanie Holland is a startup strategist and passion + purpose + vision coach, the author of *Absolutely on Purpose* and creator of The Startup Sessions. She is a writer, aromatherapist and foodie, passionate about life, wellbeing and maximising human potential. A dot connector at heart, she has shared her strategic thinking with cool cats like yahoo!, MSN and AOL, but now her energy is directed towards inspiring heart-centred entrepreneurs to make their imprint, and writing about all the amazing ways we can fire up our body, heart, mind and spirit. She drinks a lot of Earl Grey tea, thinks a lot about coconut macaroons, and loves roses. A London girl at heart, she follows a location-independent lifestyle and thrives next to the ocean.

Visit http://StephanieTHolland.com

Source: © Cameron Bunch

Chris Piper

Chris Piper, age 28, is a serial entrepreneur and is the founder and president of CPMarketing, a digital marketing agency that specialises in creating internet marketing strategies for micro-businesses and start-ups.

He is the co-founder of zoomStand, a Phoenix, Arizona–based start-up creating the first ever modular, mobile standing desk and laptop stand. ZoomStand debuted in January 2013 in Las Vegas at the International Consumer Electronics Show and is gearing up for a Kickstarter launch this fall.

He also spends his time working on The Kassi Project, an educational resource for Gen-Y non-custodial parents to successfully navigate the family courts, happily co-parent and raise their kids.

Jane Anderson

Source: © Personal Branding Expert Zahrina Robertson

Jane is one of Australia's leading elite career experts, with more than ten years of experience as a speaker, facilitator, mentor and coach. Jane has worked with thousands of people to take control of their careers using the Science of Happiness at Work, personal branding and career counselling. She is essentially a people marketer and spends much of her time speaking, training, writing and coaching to help people love their work.

Jane is one of two accredited master career directors in Australia, a certified employment interview consultant, accredited career counsellor, certified personal brand strategist and is a professional executive coach. She has been featured in *The Age*, *The Sydney Morning Herald*, *Management Today*, *Marie Claire* and as the 'Job Whisperer' on *Today Tonight*. She also is one of the top 1 per cent of viewed LinkedIn profiles globally.

Stacey Ashley

Nominated for the Telstra Business Women's Awards 2013, Stacey Ashley is managing director of Ashley Coaching and Consulting. Stacey is a master coach and leader within the Australian coaching community and holds an impressive array of national and international accreditations. Stacey's passion lies in the personal and professional development field, where she utilises the latest thinking in neuroscience and positive psychology combined with ancient wisdom to support the development of authentic leadership and happiness at work. She works with executives, senior management and teams from many of Australia's leading corporations.

INDEX

Learn more with practical advice from our experts

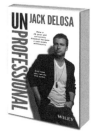

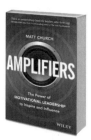